Lokāyata/Cārvāka

Lokāyata/Cārvāka

A Philosophical Inquiry

PRADEEP P. GOKHALE

OXFORD
UNIVERSITY PRESS

OXFORD
UNIVERSITY PRESS

Oxford University Press is a department of the University of Oxford. It furthers the University's objective of excellence in research, scholarship, and education by publishing worldwide. Oxford is a registered trademark of Oxford University Press in the UK and in certain other countries

Published in India by
Oxford University Press
YMCA Library Building, 1 Jai Singh Road, New Delhi 110 001, India

First Edition published in 2015

ISBN-13: 978-0-19-946063-2
ISBN-10: 0-19-946063-9

Typeset in Scala Pro 10/13
by Tranistics Data Technologies, New Delhi 110 044
Printed and bound in India at Repro India Ltd., Mumbai

Contents

Preface

In my college days, when I was studying selected chapters of the *Sarvadarśanasaṅgraha* (*SDS*) of Sāyaṇa-Mādhava as a part of the course curriculum for the 'Entrance to Śāstra' examination of Tilak Maharashtra University, I was fascinated by Cārvāka-darśana due to its critical and down-to-earth approach. My heretic temperament was boosted by the reading of Cārvāka-darśana from *SDS* and from a short but exhaustive discussion in Marathi written by Sadashiv Athavale on the history and philosophy of Cārvākas.[1] In the days of my post-graduate studies, I presented a paper on Cārvāka-darśana in a regional seminar which was presided over by the late Pandit Laxman Shastri Joshi, who in his presidential speech drew the attention of the audience to an important text, the *Tattvopaplavasiṁha* of Jayarāśibhaṭṭa. Though the text was very difficult for me at that time, stimulated by Pandit Joshi's speech, I read a few parts of it, tried to make sense of them, and wrote an article on the text. Though eventually I worked on many other issues in classical Indian philosophy, my personal philosophical affiliation remained Lokāyata/Cārvāka for many years. The only addition that took place in the course of time was because of Vipassana meditation and the interest developed in Ambedkar studies due to which I started calling myself a secular Buddhist and also an Ambedkarite Buddhist. However, this did not amount to a deviation from Cārvāka affiliation, rather an extension of it.

1. Athavale (1997). I read at that time the first edition of the book published in 1958.

The traditional pandits are generally satisfied with a singularist understanding of the Cārvāka position as found in *SDS*. Among the historians of Lokāyata, however, both the singularist and pluralist tendencies are seen. Debiprasad Chattopadhyaya, through his *Lokāyata: A Study in Ancient Materialism* and many other writings, developed a singularist account of Lokāyata-darśana (which differed from the traditional singularist account in some important respects). Ramkrishna Bhattacharya follows the same tradition as that of Chattopadhyaya with a shift of emphasis from Lokāyata to Cārvāka. He finds discontinuity and disintegrated-ness between earlier and later Lokāyata, but greater unity and integrity in Cārvāka as the materialist philosophy. I was brought up in the Cārvāka tradition through Sadashiv Athavale's book mentioned previously, which was based on his independent research, not falling in Chattopadhyaya's line. His approach on Cārvāka was pluralist. He looked at Cārvāka mainly as a representative of 'freedom of thought and expression' and materialism was just one of its offshoots, where the possibility of scepticism as another offshoot was not ruled out. Basically I am following this line of thought.

For me, the Cārvāka or Lokāyata perspective was largely a rebellion against otherworldly and ritualistic tendencies in Indian tradition and it was quite natural that this perspective could have assumed various philosophical forms.

As a free thinker I could easily imagine that a rebellion need not stick to a specific ideology, ontology, or epistemology. So I did not feel like adhering to a specific narrow interpretation of Cārvāka-darśana. At the same time, although I had my own intellectual choice of epistemology, ontology, and axiology from the different versions available in Cārvāka literature, I did not want to colour my interpretation of historical Cārvāka by my choices. Hence my understanding of the historical Cārvāka remained pluralist as against singularist. Instead of attributing a single philosophical position to Cārvākas, I thought it appropriate to study different philosophical positions in their own right which might have been presented by different rebel philosophers who either took pride in associating themselves with the Lokāyata or Cārvāka or Bārhaspatya tradition or to whom such an association was attributed by their opponents. The result is a book where I have tried to present separately the major philosophical positions that have been attributed to Cārvākas as a whole or to specific schools of Cārvākas.

A focused study of the philosophical elements in the Lokāyata/Cārvāka school is relevant today not just because it is one of the schools of Indian philosophy, or even because it is a comparatively neglected and disrespected school, but rather because it is a school which carries the true philosophical spirit to its greatest extent. All other schools accept certain authentic texts as their own, not to be questioned, but to be dogmatically adhered to. They believe in life after death and also the goal of life, termed differently as *mokṣa* (emancipation), *apavarga* (the goal beyond the three goals[2]), *nirvāṇa* (extinction or cessation of cravings), *kaivalya* (isolatedness), and *svarga* (heaven), explained in otherworldly and/or trans-empirical terms. All these schools in this sense carried a religious dogma with them that could not be challenged by reason, however influential it may be in the respective school. But if the true philosophical spirit lies in a tendency to question and examine all types of dogmas and religious beliefs, then the Lokāyata/Cārvāka school carried it. It is for this reason that the study of the philosophical avenues the school opens becomes important.

Of course I do not want to belittle the importance of tracing Lokāyata and Cārvāka thought historically. Lokāyata scholarship for the last one and a half centuries has concentrated on this single project of collecting references pertaining to Lokāyata and Cārvāka and arranging them historically and consistently. J. Muir, Rhys Davids, G. Tucci, Stcherbatsky, D. R. Shastri, Gopinath Kaviraj, Eric Frauwallner, Walter Ruben, Debiprasad Chattopadhyaya, Eli Franco, and Ramkrishna Bhattacharya, among others, have contributed to this activity. Some scholars read the references without any particular bias whereas some read them with an interpretative bias. But in spite of such idiosyncratic differences, Lokāyata scholarship remains largely historical in nature. One can say that with the works of the last three scholars mentioned, the historical studies in Cārvāka have almost reached a point of saturation.

Though the historical researches have helped the students of Indian philosophy in enriching their understanding of the philosophical position/positions of Cārvākas, the philosophical study

2. The term *apavarga* literally means 'out of class'. The term refers to the theory of *puruṣārthas* (human goals). Historically, the theory of three goals (*artha*, *kāma*, and *dharma*) was presented earlier. The three goals together were called *trivarga* ('the class of three'). *Mokṣa* as a goal was outside this class. Hence it was called *apavarga*.

of Lokāyata/Cārvāka is still in an immature stage. For example, Lokāyata scholars with a materialist bias have generally kept Jayarāśi, a sceptic, aside. The scholars like Eli Franco have taken Jayarāśi seriously. But there is scope for more work in this area. Jayarāśi's scepticism needs to be looked at in the context of Lokāyata as well as other forms of Indian scepticism. The Lokāyata scholars with materialist bias are insensitive even to the diversity within materialist epistemology. They regard the extreme-empiricist epistemology (according to which perception is the only authoritative source of knowledge) as not genuinely Lokāyata/Cārvāka epistemology at all. In doing so, they not only make textually inconsistent claims, but also bypass the philosophical insights involved in the extreme-empiricist position. They attribute a kind of moderate empiricism to Cārvākas, but by and large they seem to be insensitive to the diversity possible within moderate empiricism and also to the philosophical issues such diversity is likely to give rise to. In general, there is a need to handle the philosophical issues which arise in relation to diverse philosophical thoughts attributed to Lokāyata/Cārvāka, to analyse them, reconstruct them, and examine them sympathetically as well as critically. The present work is a humble attempt in that direction.

As indicated above, my focus in this book has been on philosophical doctrines, arguments, and issues, not on the history. However, I have a broad historical framework at the background, which has the following features:

1. I have accepted the view of many scholars that the philosophy in the name of Cārvāka-darśana might have emerged after 6th century A.D., that the term 'lokāyata' was used before this period.
2. Sometimes it is held that there was discontinuity between Lokāyata (of pre-classical phase) and Cārvāka. Accordingly 'lokāyata' only meant the science of disputation whereas Cārvāka-darśana emerged as a materialist philosophy. I do not agree with this. Lokāyata was a rational (anti-dogmatic, anti-religious) intellectual movement in which materialism (being anti-otherworldly, anti-dogmatic, and so on) could be easily accommodated. But although materialism might have been a dominating trend within Lokāyata, other trends, such as scepticism, could also be accommodated in it. Similarly,

Cārvāka-darśana too had diversity by way of accommodating materialism and different epistemological trends including scepticism. In this sense there was continuity between Lokāyata and Cārvāka.

3. Sometimes diverse trends under the head Lokāyata/Cārvāka are accepted, but they are divided into different periods. Dakshina Ranjan Shastri,[3] for example, divides the history of Indian materialism and sensationalism into four stages: (*a*) a negative and destructive stage where Lokāyata was identified as *vitaṇḍā* (negative debate); (*b*) *svabhāvavāda* (naturalism), which accepts perception as the only authority, this empirical domain as the only world, and sensual pleasure as the only value; (*c*) a phase in which hedonism degenerated into licentiousness, extreme empiricism—according to which perception is the only authority—was withdrawn, and inferences useful in daily life were accepted as additional means to knowledge; and (*d*) the period when Lokāyata was pushed down as the lowest philosophical system due to a reaction against *nāstika* (non-believer) schools in general and Lokāyata in particular. D. R. Shastri seems to be reconstructing the history of Lokāyata on the model of origination, growth, degeneration, and death. The model does not seem to fit with Lokāyata thought. When Lokāyata was identified as vitaṇḍā, it indicated the emphasis on negative argumentation, but that Lokāyata was only concerned with negative argumentation was the perception of its opponents. Kauṭilya's description of Lokāyata indicates that it involved constructive use of reasoning as well. So I am assuming that Lokāyata must have stood for diverse (but anti-otherworldly) trends even in the first stage. These different trends might have gradually developed and assumed a more systematic form due to their interaction with the religious philosophies of other schools. Hence, a similar but more systematic diversity is seen in the Cārvāka philosophy of the later period, as it is recorded in Jayanta's *Nyāyamañjarī* and Cakradhara's *Granthibhaṅga*. But after this (possibly by 10th century A.D.), further systematization and diversification of

3. Shastri (1990: 396–431).

> the Lokāyata/Cārvāka system seem to have stopped. Hence, the later work *SDS* of Mādhava refers to the popular version of Cārvāka without referring to its diversity.

I suggest that Lokāyata as a 'rationalist', anti-otherworldly movement may not have been an organized movement. It is possible that the unity and identity as a single *darśana* was conferred on the diverse trends by their 'religious' opponents rather than being accepted by the thinkers belonging to those trends themselves. It is possible that Lokāyata, as an unorthodox intellectual movement, contained and entertained diverse trends simultaneously. One need not consider the diverse trends as evolving in succession. Hence I am discussing the major trends here a-historically, almost as existing side by side.

Lokāyata/Cārvāka-darśana is studied in the departments of philosophy, religious studies, cultural studies, Sanskrit, and also social sciences like sociology and history. I hope that the students, research scholars, and teachers in these departments will find the book interesting. Even outside the university systems, there are many secularist intellectuals and materialist activists interested in the school. I hope the book will give them food for thought. I will be happy if the book and its critical estimate by the scholars in the field help to bring about more clarity and richness in this area of studies.

The discussion of the subject matter involves the use of many Sanskrit (and some Pali) terms that do not have exact English parallels. So, in the text, I had to use many such terms as they are. However, in order to reach a wider range of English readership, I have used approximate English translations wherever possible. This policy may cause inconvenience to the Sanskritist readers who prefer the use of original Sanskrit words for the sake of precision. To minimize their inconvenience, I have explained the translated terms wherever possible in the text. To minimize the inconvenience of both the types of readers I have included two glossaries (Sanskrit to English and English to Sanskrit) at the end.

Sarnath
2 April 2014

Pradeep P. Gokhale

Acknowledgements

I am grateful to the Sanskrit pandits who taught me Sanskrit philosophical texts. Noteworthy among them were the late Pandit Vaman Shastri Bhagavat and the late Pandit Shrinivas Shastri. I am grateful to the senior scholar-friend Dr Ganesh Thite, the late Pandit Laxman Shastri Joshi, my late philosophy teacher and doctoral guide Professor S. S. Barlingay, the late Debiprasad Chattopadhyaya (who visited the Department of Philosophy, University of Pune, in the late eighties, as a visiting fellow), and Ramkrishna Bhattacharya, who encouraged my interests in Cārvāka. Ramkrishna Bhattacharya has benefitted me through his encouragement and also through his work which provides the latest material on the theme. The late Professor Shriniwas Dixit and Professor S. S. Antarkar benefitted me as academic critics of my writings. Professor V. N. Jha invited me to two ICPR workshops (held in 2008 and 2013) to present my views on Lokāyata. My friend Professor Dilip Kumar Mohanta invited me to a seminar dedicated to Debiprasad's Lokāyata in 2010, where I could reshape my understanding of Cārvāka materialism. Professor Kanchana Mahadevan and my other colleagues from Mumbai University took keen interest in my views on Lokāyata and invited me from time to time to share my views with them.

Among other friends and well-wishers were Shrikant Bahulkar, Vilas Wagh, Tej Nivalikar, Sanjay Pawar, Joseph Pinto, Aniket Jaware, and Kanchana Mahadevan, to mention a few, with whom I could freely disclose my

Cārvāka affiliation; rather, in whose company, the Cārvāka in me felt at home. The encouragement and help I got from Dr Mangesh Kulkarni also cannot go without mention. Kanchana Mahadevan devoted a lot of time and energy to go through my draft chapters and made suggestions towards the improvement of content and style. Particularly, some comparable Western philosophical ideas could be incorporated in the book because of her. It must be asserted, however, that the responsibility for the errors or the debatable elements in the book is entirely mine.

The libraries of Tilak Maharashtra Vidyapeeth, Pune; Bhandarkar Oriental Research Institute, Pune; University of Pune (Central Library as well as the library of the Department of Philosophy); and Central University of Tibetan Studies, Sarnath, have been very helpful to me by providing reading and reference material. I am grateful to the staff of all these libraries.

The late Pandit Bhagavat took the initiative to publish my first Marathi book on Cārvāka through Tilak Maharashtra Vidyapeeth and my second Marathi book was recently published by Mr Aravind Patkar of Mano-Vikas Publication. The present work is in fact a modified, enlarged, and refined English version of my recent Marathi book. I am grateful to Mr Aravind Patkar for permitting and encouraging me to bring out the English version. I am also grateful to Bloomsbury Publishing Plc, London, and IPQ Publication, Pune, for allowing me to publish revised versions of my articles published in their anthologies as Chapters 5 and 6 respectively of this book.

My late parents, though practising Hindus, loved me and tolerated my affiliation to the *nāstika* thought and way of life. My wife, Nandini, follows the practice of tolerance and continues to love me in spite of my heresies. My children, Mudita and Satyakam, though not interested in philosophy, love me as a person and perhaps also like the non-believer in me. These complex domestic conditions have always stimulated and encouraged me to think and rethink my identity as a modern Cārvāka.

Pradeep P. Gokhale

1

Unity and Diversity in the Lokāyata/Cārvāka Perspective

Cārvāka-darśana, also called Lokāyata and Bārhaspatya-darśana, is popularly recognized as a materialistic philosophical system of ancient India which upholds that (*a*) perception is the only means to knowledge; (*b*) consciousness is the product of matter; (*c*) pleasure—rather, sensuous pleasure—is the only goal of life, which could be achieved even by immoral means; and (*d*) there is no God, no other world, and no life after death. This understanding of Cārvāka-darśana has been propagated by the doxographical works like *Ṣaḍdarśanasamuccaya* (*SDSam*) and *Sarvadarśanasaṅgraha* (*SDS*) and many polemical works written by authors of other schools such as Buddhism, Jainism, Nyāya, and Vedānta, who in their works presented this picture of Cārvāka-darśana in their attempt to refute it. Modern scholars of Indian philosophy generally took this picture as the authentic one, drew implications from it, and appreciated or criticized Cārvāka on that basis.[1]

In the last century, Debiprasad Chattopadhyaya, an advocate of secularism and materialism (of the Marxist variety), who was aware of the rich and complex philosophical heritage of India, was naturally sympathetic

1. This is seen, for instance, in Radhakrishnan (1996), Hiriyanna (1973), Sharma (1973), and Sinha (1999).

to Lokāyata. But he was unhappy about the popular image of Lokāyata as described. He attempted to defend Lokāyata by presenting it as a materialist system which accepted experience as well as reasoning (perception and inference) as the two sources of knowledge, and which was against other-worldly religions but not against morality.[2] Chattopadhyaya reconstructed this image of Cārvāka-darśana from sources such as *Arthaśāstra of Kauṭilya* (*AK*)[3] and *Tattvasaṅgrahapañjikā* (*TSP*).[4] In *AK*, Kauṭilya regards Lokāyata as a part of reason-oriented inquiry (*ānvīkṣikī*), and describes the latter as a philosophical discipline which investigates the strengths and weaknesses of different sciences by applying reason. Hence, Lokāyata in Kauṭilya's view must accept reasoning (that is, application of *hetus*, or reasons) as a means to knowledge. Similarly, Purandara, a Cārvāka thinker, as quoted in *TSP*, claimed that Cārvākas do accept a kind of inference as a means to knowledge. According to Chattopadhyaya, this description of Cārvāka/Lokāyata-darśana as a materialist school, which accepts a kind of inference in addition to perception as a means to knowledge, is the authentic description. That Cārvākas accepted only perception as the means to knowledge and accepted sensualist hedonism is the distortion of Cārvāka-darśana made by opponents of Cārvāka in order to present it in a weaker form. Many progressive-minded scholars of Indian philosophy were influenced by this reconstruction of Cārvāka-darśana.[5] Chattopadhyaya's estimate of Cārvāka-darśana as discussed earlier was further strengthened by another original scholar, Ramkrishna Bhattacharya. He collected and rearranged the scattered references to Lokāyata, Cārvāka, and Indian materialism, tried to restore Lokāyata aphorisms, and reinterpreted this literature and

2. Debiprasad Chattopadhyaya (1978: 34–5) claims that Cārvāka of the *Mahābhārata* advocated the ethics of *ahiṁsā*. According to Chattopadhyaya, the ethics of pleasure were advocated not by Cārvākas but by their opponents.

3. Chattopadhyaya (1976: 240–5).

4. Chattopadhyaya (1978: 28–30), by using Purandara's statement quoted by Kamalaśīla in *Tattvasaṅgrahapañjikā* (*TSP*) and by other evidences, concludes that 'there are sufficiently strong grounds in favour of it that Lokāyatikas were the first logicians of this country'.

5. In Maharashtra, A. H. Salunke and S. R. Gadgil wrote books on Cārvāka/Lokāyata, and S. G. Sardesai wrote a book on Indian philosophy, largely following the line of Debiprasad Chattopadhyaya. Some scholars wrote independently or even in opposition to him, notably Sadashiv Athavale, Shubhada Joshi, Pradeep Gokhale, and Uday Kumthekar.

strengthened, apart from some points of disagreement,[6] the basic framework of Chattopadhyaya's version.

In addition to the two versions of Cārvāka-darśana as stated earlier, namely its crude and popular version on the one hand, and a materialist version based on a sophisticated epistemology on the other, there must have existed other varieties of Cārvāka philosophy as well. For example, the version of epistemic indeterminism (a mild variety of scepticism) attributed to knave Cārvākas (Cārvāka-dhūrta) by Jayantabhaṭṭa and the sceptical strand of Jayarāśibhaṭṭa found in his *Tattvopaplavasiṁha* (*TUS*).[7]

The *TUS* needs a special mention because it is the only available independent treatise which develops a cognitive scepticism, but is claimed by its author to be following the line of Bṛhaspati, the latter being an alleged founder of the Lokāyata school. It gives a sceptical interpretation of Bṛhaspati's aphorisms, which are generally taken to be materialistic.

The previously discussed images of Cārvāka as the popular-materialist, the sophisticated-materialist, and the sceptical are unitary in nature. Each image claims to be the only correct and complete description of Cārvāka-darśana and discards other descriptions as inauthentic. But is it necessary that only one of the descriptions of Cārvāka-darśana must be correct and the others incorrect? Is it again necessary that all those who claimed to be Lokāyatikas or Cārvākas must have been unanimous on all important philosophical issues? It is quite possible that Lokāyatikas held different epistemological, ontological, and axiological positions and formed in this way, at least potentially, different sub-schools. The popular version of Lokāyata need not be discarded simply on the ground that it appears to be weak. The version has its weaknesses, but it has strong points as well. Even the extreme position that perception is the only means to knowledge is not easy to refute. At the same time, the popular version is not the only and the complete version of Lokāyata. And this is acknowledged even by the opponents of Cārvākas. Jayanta, for example, refers to different categories of Cārvākas

6. One of the points of disagreement could be the interpretation of the term 'lokāyata'. Chattopadhyaya (1978: 1) interprets it as 'the philosophy of the people' as well as 'the philosophy of this-worldliness or materialism'. On the other hand, Ramkrishna Bhattacharya (2012: 135) interprets it as 'science of disputation'.

7. For the discussion of this version of Lokāyata, see Chapter 2.

such as knave (*dhūrta*), learned (*suśikṣita*), and more learned (*suśikṣitatara*). As against this, modern scholars like Chattopadhyaya and Bhattacharya claim their version, which they broadly identify with Purandara's version and the version attributed by Jayanta[8] to the more learned Cārvākas, to be the authentic Cārvāka view. But I want to suggest that though sophisticated materialism might be a dominant and a philosophically strong trend in Cārvāka thought, it need not be regarded as the representative view of all Cārvākas. Though Purandara in his statement asserting commonsensically acceptable inference is speaking on behalf of all Cārvākas,[9] this by itself cannot be an evidence to show that his view represents all Cārvākas. Third, though the sceptical version of Cārvāka is neither popular nor materialistic, it need not be regarded as inauthentic only on that ground. The situation is similar to that of Vedānta, where the founder of a particular school of Vedānta claims that his interpretation of *Brahmasūtras* and *Upaniṣads* is *the* authentic one, and that it is the true Vedānta. As impartial students of Vedānta, we would say that these different Vedāntins represent different schools of Vedānta. (This line of argument applies to any school following the *sūtra-bhāṣya* tradition—an intellectual tradition which starts with an aphorismic work and develops through its commentaries and sub-commentaries.) Similarly we should say in the case of Cārvāka-darśana that though Jayarāśi (the author of *TUS*), more learned Cārvākas (as described by Jayanta), Purandara, and the popular Cārvākas (as depicted in the works like *Sarva-darśana-saṅgraha*)—all claimed explicitly or implicitly that their view was the authentic Cārvāka view (or 'Bṛhaspati's view'), we, as impartial students of Cārvāka-darśana, can understand the situation better by regarding them as representing different schools of, or trends in the Cārvāka-darśana. To claim rigidly that only one trend out of them is the genuine Cārvāka-darśana and that others are deviations or distortions would be a kind of dogmatism.

8. Chattopadhyaya and Bhattacharya do not distinguish between the version of *suśikṣita–cārvāka* and that of Purandara. But logically speaking, the two versions must be distinguished as I have argued in Chapter 4.

9. '*purandarastu āha, lokaprasiddhamanumānaṁ cārvākairapi iṣyata eva. yattu kaiścit laukikaṁ mārgamatikramya anumānamucyate tanniṣidhyate*' (*TSP*, v. 1481 of *Tattvasaṅgraha* [*TS*]). [But Purandara says: Cārvākas do admit *lokaprasiddha-anumāna*, but the kind of *anumāna* (inference) which is made by transcending the worldly way (*laukika-mārga*) is denied by them.] (The translations given in square brackets are my own translations unless otherwise stated.)

I want to suggest that the views of Chattopadhyaya and Bhattacharya are dogmatic in this sense. Chattopadhyaya, who reads Indian history from a Marxist perspective, refuses to accept both the popular and sceptical versions as authentic versions of Lokāyata.[10] Bhattacharya joins Chattopadhyaya on this issue.[11] A problem with their arguments is that they move in a circle. They have simply assumed that the essence of Cārvāka/Lokāyata is materialism. Hence according to them, other interpretations must be wrong because they are not materialistic. Similarly, acceptance of perception as well as a kind of inference as the means to knowledge must be the authentic Cārvāka view and hence, according to them, other epistemological views must be discarded as fake. In this way of thinking, pluralism as a genuine possibility is simply ruled out.

In this book I am trying to develop a pluralistic approach to Cārvāka-darśana as against the monistic trend in the Cārvāka scholarship mentioned earlier. Fortunately, there are scholars who acknowledge plurality in Lokāyata. D. R. Shastri[12] in his writings, Sarvananda Pathak[13] in his Hindi work, and Sadashiv Athavle[14] in his Marathi work, to cite a few, have acknowledged plurality in the Lokāyata School. D. R. Shastri, in particular, has rearranged different trends in Lokāyata/Cārvāka philosophy historically. Though the way he has done it is debatable; I will not enter into the historical debate because that is not my purpose here. More recently, Eli Franco in his study of Jayarāśi's scepticism has held that 'there were at least two trends in the Lokāyata School or tradition, the one materialistic, the other skeptic'.[15] I will take up Franco's view here as a point of departure.

Franco's view, I feel, is in need of some qualification, because to regard materialism and scepticism as the only major trends in the

10. Chattopadhyaya (1989: 36ff.).

11. Bhattacharya (2012: 51 fn. 32) points out that this view is shared by Walter Ruben, K. K. Dixit, and D. Chattopadhyaya. Bhattacharya argues something like this: 'One cannot be a materialist if one denies even perception as the source of knowledge. And Cārvāka was a materialist. Jayarāśi does not accept perception. Hence he is not a Cārvāka.' The argument moves in a circle. Whether Cārvāka should be identified with materialism is precisely the question.

12. Shastri, D. R., as included in Chattopadhyaya (1990).

13. As in Pathak (1965).

14. As in Athavale (1997).

15. Franco (1987: IX).

Lokāyata tradition would be inadequate in some respects. Scepticism is primarily known as an epistemological position whereas materialism is primarily a metaphysical position. It will be conceptually more elegant to classify philosophical schools in epistemological, ontological, and axiological terms distinctly, and then correlate these classifications with each other wherever possible. Accordingly if we consider the epistemological positions held by Cārvākas, one can notice a great diversity in them starting from scepticism to common-sense empiricism. Similar diversity, though not the parallel one, can be noticed in ontological and axiological positions held by Cārvākas. On account of this diversity, Lokāyata or Cārvāka-darśana can be conceived of as a family (having affinity to Wittgenstein's 'family' in his notion of family resemblance)[16] of schools which were trying to criticize the otherworldly view of life by using different policies or strategies.

Take, for instance, the Cārvāka view/s concerning *pramāṇas* (the means to knowledge):

1. Lokāyatikas were often called *vaitaṇḍika*[17] (that is, captious debaters—who took pleasure in refuting others' positions

16. The term 'family' I am using here has affinity to Wittgenstein's notion of family resemblance. We can say, for instance, that members of a family have mutual similarities, but it is hard to find out a common characteristic among all the members. Sometimes the common identity of the family members is negative; we may be able to indicate what all the members commonly lack, rather than what they commonly possess. (In the case of different trends in Cārvāka philosophy, we can say that all of them are opposed to otherworldly, religious metaphysics; but what they commonly possess may be difficult to bring out.) Hence the common character will be exclusive (like *apoha* of the Buddhists), rather than inclusive. Or, what is regarded as common to all may be functional rather than structural. So, in the case of Cārvākas, the different 'schools' may have different epistemologies and ontologies, but they share a common pragmatic aim. Sometimes what is common to all the members would be just verbal (like a common surname possessed by all the members). In the case of Cārvāka, one may say that what is common to different schools of Cārvāka-darśana is that they are simply called Cārvāka or Lokāyata or Bārhaspatya schools and there is nothing more common to them than that. This would be a nominalistic conception of family resemblance. I feel that while treating Cārvāka as a family, the apoha model will be more appropriate than the nominalistic model. I have, however, held that more positive commonness can also be traced, when, for example, I say that all Cārvākas are applying reasoning (constructively or destructively) without resorting to any religious text.

17. Lokāyata was called *vaitaṇḍika-kathā* by Jayanta (*Nyāyamañjarī* [*NM*], part I, p. 247). Even in Buddhist and Jaina texts, it was called *vitaṇḍā-śāstra* (*Sumaṅgalavilāsinī* [*SMV*] 1.90.1).

without upholding any position as their own) by their opponents. Though all Cārvākas cannot be called vaitaṇḍika in the strict sense of the term, the possibility of some of them being so could be allowed. Such a possibility is seen to be materialized by Jayarāśi, who denies even perception as an authoritative means to knowledge, and still declares his legacy to Bṛhaspati, the so-called founder of the Lokāyata system.[18]

2. There must have been some Lokāyatikas/Cārvākas who held that perception is the only means to knowledge. This naïve position which can be called a narrow or an extreme form of empiricism is attributed to Cārvākas in the works like *Sarvadarśanasaṅgraha*.[19]
3. There must have been some Cārvākas who held a broader form of empiricism according to which not only perception, but a kind of inference, which is testable by perception (*utpanna-pratīti anumāna*), is also a means to knowledge. Such Cārvākas were called more learned (suśikṣitatara) in the works like *Nyayāmañjari* (*NM*).[20]
4. There must have been some Cārvākas who accepted the still wider epistemological framework which may be called the framework of common-sense empiricism. In this framework, commonsensical inference (*lokaprasiddha-anumāna*) is accepted in addition to perception. The inferences which make our individual and social life in this world intelligible are acceptable in this framework. But those which transcend the limits of worldly life are not acceptable. This view is attributed to a Cārvāka thinker, Purandara, by Kamalaśīla in his *Tattvasaṁgrahapañjikā*.[21]

It is possible in this way to present the epistemological views of Cārvākas as possessing diversity rather than unity. Now, since means to knowledge (pramāṇas) are the grounds for establishing ontological categories (*prameyas*) and also for justifying values, the diversity in

18. For details, see Chapter 2.
19. For the discussion of the extreme empiricism of Cārvākas, see Chapter 3.
20. For the discussion of the mitigated empiricism of this type, see Chapter 4.
21. For the discussion of the common-sense empiricism of this type, see Chapter 4.

Cārvāka epistemology is likely to lead to diversity in their ontology and axiology.

The diversity in Cārvāka ontology could be traced along the following lines:

1. A sceptic Cārvāka like Jayarāśi not only denies all means to knowledge, but also the doctrine of four ontological principles (*tattvas*), namely earth, water, fire, and air, which is popularly attributed to Cārvākas.[22]
2. The objects of direct experience could be accepted by the narrow-empiricist Cārvāka. Cārvākas who accept perception as well as inference (of a certain kind) can also legitimately accept the existence of material elements and consciousness which is inseparable from them.[23] At the same time since these Cārvākas do not accept inference of the alleged transcendent entities, they naturally deny the existence of God, soul, and other worlds.
3. Depending upon a narrow or broad empiricist framework, the Cārvāka thesis that 'body is the self' (*dehātmavāda*) assumes two different versions. A version which can be accepted by a narrow empiricist is that the body itself is the self. The version which a common-sense-empiricist Cārvāka can accept is that the body qualified by consciousness is the self.[24]

Similarly, it is possible to trace diversity in the Cārvākas' value-perspectives along the following lines:

1. Jayarāsi, who denies all means to knowledge and objects of knowledge in *TUS*, does not discuss the problem of values. But his last remark is sufficiently suggestive about his general approach. He says, 'When in this way all doctrines are refuted, all the practices are all right, as they are beautiful insofar as they are not reflected upon.' He seems to allow a kind of anarchism in the realm of values.[25]

22. See Chapter 2.

23. I have called this the cosmological materialism of Cārvākas. See Chapter 5.

24. I have called the two versions the reductive and non-reductive versions of the psychological materialism of Cārvākas. See Chapter 5.

25. See the Chapters 2 and 6.

2. When we pass from scepticism of Jayarāsi to the 'narrow empiricism' of some Cārvākas, we find that one is now in a position to recognize at least one's own sensuous pleasure as a value.[26]
3. A broad-empiricist Cārvāka can go further. He can appreciate wealth (*artha*) as a value, along with pleasure (*kāma*). Similarly he can consistently uphold a universalistic form of hedonism.[27]

Thus, the narrow empiricism seems to make a narrow axiological approach possible whereas a broad empiricism seems to make a broad axiological approach possible.

Although there are traces of a variety of views attributed to Cārvākas, generally these views, as they are extant, were presented as 'refutable views' (*pūrvapakṣa*, literally, prior view, that is, opponent's view to be presented and refuted before establishing one's own view) by the opponents of Cārvāka and were often presented in a weaker form. Naturally, sometimes diverse views attributed to Cārvākas are presented in a mixed or confused form without distinguishing them sharply from each other. It is also possible that different versions of Cārvāka-darśana were presented by different Cārvāka thinkers at different periods of time, but the opponents of Cārvāka presented them as simultaneous and overlapping views. Hence, we do not have any record of the views of different sub-systems of Cārvākas as consistent wholes, with the possible exception of Jayarāśi's sceptical position. However, in order to have a better philosophical understanding of Cārvāka, it is necessary to distinguish between or amongst various views which pass under the name of Cārvāka-darśana or Lokāyata. They should be rearranged as belonging to different members of the Cārvāka family rather than to a single system called Cārvāka-darśana.

A question can be asked here: how did the diversity in Cārvāka-darśana come about? Franco traces the root of the dichotomy of Lokāyata scepticism and materialism to the deficiencies of the original Lokāyatika epistemological position that perception is the only means of valid knowledge. When these deficiencies were realized by

26. See Chapter 6.

27. I have held that a broad-empiricist Cārvāka can accept even dharma and liberation as the goals of life (*puruṣārthas*) if they are accepted as modal and not substantial goals and are interpreted in secular terms. See Chapter 6.

Lokāyatikas, they, according to Franco, reacted in two ways. Some philosophers like Purandara accepted a kind of inference along with perception; some philosophers like Jayarāśi opted for scepticism by forgoing both perception and inference.[28]

Franco's explanation can be doubted. Even before the popular Cārvāka epistemology (which grants only perception as the authentic form of knowledge) appears on the scene, Lokāyata was sometimes identified with *vaitaṇḍika-kathā* whereby it was implied that Lokāyatikas did not have any position of their own; they only refuted positions of others. It is quite possible that Lokāyatikas created this impression through their way of argumentation whereas some of them were actually engaged in advancing sceptical arguments. Hence there could have been 'sceptic Lokāyatikas' even in the early stage of the Lokāyata movement. On the other hand, Kauṭilya describes Lokāyata as a school of philosophy (ānvīkṣikī) which examines with reasons, strengths and weaknesses of other disciplines, namely religion, commerce, and jurisprudence. This suggests that there must have been Lokāyatikas using reasoning power in a more constructive way, giving empirical and practical reasons for making individual and social life happier. Hence neither the sceptical form of Lokāyata nor the sophisticated-empiricist Lokāyata (which accepts inference along with perception) appears as a reaction to extreme empiricism. Both of them could be as old as, if not older than, extreme empiricism. It would be more appropriate therefore to regard diversity in Lokāyata-darśana not as a later development (though specific manifestations of this diversity are found in the later period), but as inherent in the nature of Lokāyata itself.

This leads us to the question about the nature of Lokāyata. Chattopadhyaya explains Lokāyata as proto-materialism spread among common people, and also identifies it as the materialist school of Indian philosophy.[29] Bhattacharya delinks early usage of the term

28. Franco (1987: 8).

29. Chattopadhyaya (1978: 36–75) seems to hold that Lokāyata was both simultaneously. While understanding Lokāyata as proto-materialism, Chattopadhyaya includes in it the *asura* view, early Tantra, and Sāṅkhya. He also opines that though early Lokāyatikas were opposed to Brahmanical otherworldly ritualism, they had their own rituals and *mantras*. Insofar as the nature of Lokāyata as a philosophical school is concerned, Chattopadhyaya (1978: 1–36) critically examines the Lokāyata of *Sarvadarśanasaṅgraha* and reconstructs it as a materialist school which accepts perception as well as inference and advocates the ethics of ahiṁsā.

'lokāyata' from its later use in the sense of materialist school of Indian philosophy.[30] The term in its early usage, according to him, meant the science of disputation. Both these explanations are unsatisfactory to me. Here I am not concerned with the non-philosophical usage of the term 'lokāyata (as a proto-materialist way of life including magico-ritualistic superstitions and practices, spread among people). I am, however, concerned with the philosophical sense of the word, which Chattopadhyaya identifies with a materialist philosophical school and Bhattacharya with the science of disputation. I would like to concentrate on three points here:

1. Derivation of the term 'lokāyata'.
2. Description of Lokāyata as vaitaṇḍika-kathā or *vitaṇḍā-śāstram* (a discipline which conducts debates of vitaṇḍā type).
3. Inclusion of Lokāyata by Kauṭilya in ānvīkṣikī.

Let us consider the three points separately and see whether something emerges by considering the three points together.

The Term 'Lokāyata'

The term 'lokāyata' is generally derived from *lokeṣu āyatam* and is interpreted as 'spread (āyatam) among people (lokeṣu)' or 'prevalent among people'.[31] This interpretation of the term raises some problems. Lokāyata, as understood in its philosophical sense, is not spread among people. Common people are generally guided by religious superstitions and are involved in ritualistic practices as prescribed by the priestly class. In fact it was the opponents of Cārvākas who described Lokāyata as the philosophy of the common people. While doing so, they either reduced Lokāyata to the pleasure-seeking approach of the common people, which is not the essence of

30. Of course it should be granted that Bhattacharya also tries to see the link between the two ideas when he says: 'What was common to the older Lokāyatikas and the new Cārvāka materialists was perhaps disputatiousness: nothing was sacred to them' (Bhattacharya 2012: 195). The question before me is: Why does he not see this itself—arguing freely and disregarding anything as sacred—as the core of the methodological approach of Cārvākas/Lokāyatikas?

31. The etymology given by Dasgupta following *Divyāvadāna*, as quoted in Bhattacharya (2012: 194).

Lokāyata philosophy, or, they meant to ridicule Lokāyata by implying that it is the philosophy of the ordinary, that is, unwise people.[32] But the word 'lokāyata' is also found to be used respectfully to refer to a philosophical approach. The word 'lokāyata' interpreted as 'the view spread among people' does not do justice to the respectful usage of the word. It rather gives a derogatory sense of the word.

Here I would like to suggest an alternative derivation of the word, which I think is more objective and neutral. The word 'loka' is used many times to mean 'world', rather, 'this world', and is contrasted with *alaukika* or *lokottara*. Similarly the word 'laukika' derived from the word 'loka' means worldly as against otherworldly. The word 'āyata' means 'spread'. But it also has another meaning, namely, 'restrained'[33] or 'controlled'. The word 'lokāyata' now can be derived as *lokena āyatam* (literally, restrained by the world), which can be interpreted as 'limited by the belief that this is the only world', or 'limited by this-worldly approach', or 'limited by the approach which disregards other worlds'. I think it is more or less obvious that Lokāyata philosophy in all its versions denies the existence of other worlds. Hence the interpretation suggested by me brings out this unique feature of the Lokāyata approach, that it is this-worldly.

Lokāyata and Vitaṇḍā

Scholars have pointed out that in Pali Buddhist literature, Lokāyata has been described as *vitaṇḍasatthaṁ* or *vitaṇḍavādasattham* (Sanskrit: *vitaṇḍāśāstram* or *vitaṇḍāvādaśāstram*).[34] In English it has been translated as 'science of disputation' or 'a text-book of disputation'.[35] Two

32. The attitude of ridiculing Lokāyata through such etymology is clear in Buddhaghoṣa's explanation of the term as '*bālaputhujjanalokassa āyataṁ mahantaṁ gambhīraṁ ti upadiṭṭhaṁ parittaṁ chavaṁ diṭṭhigataṁ*' (quoted in Bhattacharya (2012: 200) from *Śāratthapakāsinī* edited by Woodward; Woodward's version accepts *āyataṁ* as the reading in place of *āyatanaṁ*, in which case it will mean 'extended' and not 'basis'). [Lokāyata is a dogma extended among the people (loka) who are ignorant and ordinary; it is low and wretched, but is put forth as great and deep.]

33. The word 'āyata' is the past participle of the verb *ā*+ √*yam*, which according to Monier Williams' dictionary has both the meanings, (*a*) to stretch, extend, and (*b*) to keep, stop, restrain.

34. Athavale (1997: 11); Bhattacharya (2012: 187–91).

35. Bhattacharya (2012: 195).

points need to be noted in this context. One, though the words 'śāstra' (science, a systematic study of a subject) and 'darśana' (philosophical system presenting a comprehensive view on world, knowledge, and values) need to be distinguished as we shall see in the last chapter, this does not imply that Lokāyata was not such a comprehensive view, simply because it was called 'śāstra'. That is because the word 'śāstra' was used sometimes in a loose way. For example, Nyāya was sometimes called Nyāyaśāstra, but it was not only a science of inference, it had its ontological and axiological stand as well. Similar could have been the case with Lokāyata. Second, vitaṇḍā does not mean simply disputation. Rather, it referred to that kind of dispute where one of the parties was engaged only with refuting the opponent's position without presenting a position of its own. Performing vitaṇḍā type of disputation meant engaging in destructive argumentation without any constructive commitment.[36] So when Buddhists described Lokāyata as vitaṇḍāśāstram, they did not give it a neutral description, but, rather accused it of being engaged with destructive argumentation without constructive commitment. (When Jayanta calls Lokāyata as vaitaṇḍika-kathā, he makes a similar accusation.[37]) Why were Buddhists and others accusing Lokāyatikas of engaging in vitaṇḍā? The kind of debate a sceptic engages in can be called vitaṇḍā. But then, were all Lokāyatikas sceptics? The possibility need not be ruled out that some of them were ready to go to that extreme (and this gives scope for plurality even in ancient Lokāyata thought). But most of them might have had a positive commitment to the existence of the material world and to leading a happy life based on secular values. Even then, they were blamed as vaitaṇḍika. In order to understand the significance of this accusation, we have to slightly extend the notion of vitaṇḍā. In the extended sense, vitaṇḍā means arguing without any restrictions. The opponents of Lokāyatikas had accepted at least two types of restrictions in their thought:

1. They believed in rebirth and other worlds. They thought that moral and religious life is not possible without such beliefs.

36. *'sa eva svapakṣasthāpanāhīno vitaṇḍā. sā ca parapakṣadūṣaṇamātraparyavasānā. nāsya vaitaṇḍikasya sthāpyaḥ pakṣo'sti'* (*Tarkabhāṣā* [*TB*], p. 270). [*Jalpa* (= the debate between the persons desiring to win) itself is vitaṇḍā, when it lacks presentation of one's own position (by one of the parties). It results only in refutation of the other party. One who debates by vitaṇḍā has no position to establish.]

37. See opening pages and note 2 in Chapter 6.

2. In order to support such transcendental beliefs, they accepted some scriptures/sacred texts to control the scope of reasoning.

A constructive approach to a good life was possible only through such beliefs, according to them. So, one who does not entertain such beliefs and argues against them was naturally called 'nāstika' (heretic, non-believer) or 'vaitaṇḍika' (engaged in negative argumentation) by them. It is clear from the ancient references like Vātsyāyana's description of the Lokāyatikas' views on dharma (religious morality based on scriptures) that Lokāyatikas did not accept either of the two types of restrictions mentioned.[38] This must have been the reason why they were called vaitaṇḍikas. This point is relevant when we appreciate Lokāyata as ānvīkṣikī.[39]

Lokāyata as *Ānvīkṣikī*

Kauṭilya, in his *AK*, enumerates in the beginning four faculties of knowledge (*vidyās*) which a king should have expertise in. They are religion, economy, polity, and philosophy.[40] Under philosophy, he

38. '*na dharmāṁścaret. eṣyatphalatvāt. sāṁśayikatvācca. ko hyabāliśo hastagataṁ paragataṁ kuryāt? varamadyakapotaḥ śvomayūrāt. varaṁ sāṁśayikānniṣkādasāṁśayikaḥ kārṣāpaṇaḥ. iti laukāyatikāḥ.*' [The Lokāyatikas say that one should not observe dharma, because its results are to be gained in future and they are doubtful too. Who but a fool will hand over what is in his hand to some other? A pigeon today is better than a peacock tomorrow. A guaranteed copper coin is better than a doubtful golden coin (*Kāmasūtra* [*KS*] 1.2.21–4); here I have slightly modified Tripathi's translation.] It is important to note here that Vātsyāyana's statement of the Lokāyata view on dharma presupposes the definition of dharma which is scripture-oriented and otherworldly. For details, see Chapter 6.

39. That Lokāyatikas were arguing with reasons without paying any respect to religious texts is clear from the following verse from *Rāmāyaṇa* (Ayodhyākāṇḍa, adhyāya no. 100; quoted in Athavale [1997: fn. 13]):

dharmaśāstreṣu mukhyeṣu vidyamāeṣu durbudhāḥ/
buddhimānvīkṣikīṁ prāpya, nirarthaṁ pravadanti te//

[Those muddle-headed ones (namely Lokāyatikas) talk meaningless things by applying ratiocinating intellect, in spite of the presence of major religious texts.]

40. To be precise, they are *trayi* (the three Vedas including *dharmaśāstra*), *vārtā* (agriculture and commerce), *daṇḍanīti* (administration and jurisprudence), and *ānvikṣikī* (rational philosophy).

mentioned three philosophical schools: Sāṅkhya, Yoga, and Lokāyata.[41] Why Kauṭilya has grouped these three disciplines in this way under the title 'Philosophy' (Ānvīkṣikī) is a question that has provoked many scholars. According to Chattopadhyaya, Kauṭilya, by the term 'yoga', refers to Nyāya-Vaiśeṣika system and not to Patañjali's Yoga system.[42] Chattopadhyaya also claims that all the three systems referred to by Kauṭilya are materialistic in nature. Though the former view of Chattopadhyaya is insightful, the latter view can be doubted. Kauṭilya is grouping the three systems under the common title Ānvīkṣikī not on the basis of any common metaphysical view, but on the basis of their common methodological approach. Ānvīkṣikī is described as a faculty of knowledge (vidyā) which examines strengths and weaknesses of other faculties (namely religion, polity, and economy) by applying reasons.[43] Insofar as Ānvīkṣikī emphasizes reason rather than faith, one can say that the common point between the three philosophical systems which come under Ānvīkṣikī must be that they are rational systems. Here we can compare the group of three systems: Sāṅkhya, Yoga (that is, Nyāya-Vaiśeṣika), and Lokāyata with another group consisting of two systems, namely Pūrvamīmāṁsā and Vedānta. The latter group not only emphasizes verbal testimony against inference, but it claims itself to be rooted in verbal testimony, that is, Vedic scriptures. The former group, on the other hand, emphasizes inference along with perception and gives a somewhat subordinate status to scriptural authority. At least the systems in this group do not claim themselves to be solely dependent on scriptures. The word 'philosophy' in the West

41. 'Logic-based philosophy (*Ānvīkṣikī*) is represented by the following three: Sāṅkhya, Yoga, and Lokāyata,' *AK* as quoted (in translation) in Chattopadhyaya (1990: 74).

42. Chattopadhyay (1976: 245–51). Bhattacharya (2012: 132) points out that Phanibhushan Tarkavagish and others had a similar view. Chattopadhyaya (1990: 74) refers to M. M. Kuppuswami Shatri as well.

43. 'Logic-based philosophy, by critically examining the relative strength and weakness of all these (branches of knowledge) with the means of proper arguments (hetu), benefits the people, keeps the thinking steady in both the calamities and prosperities, and also brings about expertness in knowledge, speech and actions' (*AK* 1.2.11, quoted [in translation] in Chattopadhyaya [1990: 74–5; translation slightly revised by me]). Chattopadhyaya translates the term 'ānvīkṣikī' sometimes as logic, sometimes as logic-based philosophy. I have argued (Gokhale 2012) that it can be taken to mean philosophy as a rational inquiry.

is sometimes reserved for rational or argumentative inquiry and is distinguished from a religious inquiry which is based on dogma or faith. By applying this distinction, one may be inclined to call Pūrva-Mīmāṁsā and Vedānta as religious inquiries and the systems such as Sāṅkhya, Yoga, and Lokāyata as philosophical inquiries or philosophies in the true sense of the term. Kauṭilya's inclusion of them under Ānvīkṣikī justifies the meaning of the word 'ānvīkṣikī' as philosophy in this sense. In the modern studies of 'Indian philosophy', however, we find the word philosophy used for all these systems, whether they emphasize reasoning or scriptural authority. The word 'ānvīkṣikī' as used by Kauṭilya, in that case should be translated as 'reason-based philosophy' or 'rational philosophy' rather than 'philosophy'.

Although the three schools falling under Ānvīkṣikī can be called rational in a broad sense, they vary in the degree of rationality. For example, Vaiśeṣikas and Sāṅkhyas both use scientific and speculative reasoning. They use the latter for establishing transcendental metaphysics. In *Nyāyabhāṣya,* Vātsyāyana identifies ānvīkṣikī with *nyāyavidyā* (the science of reasoning). But there the term 'anvīkṣā', from which the term 'ānvīkṣikī' is derived, is defined as inference which is based on perception and verbal testimony.[44] Hence reasoning should not contradict with the Vedas. In *Sāṅkhyakārikā,* Īśvarakṛṣṇa maintains that subtle objects should be known by metaphysical reasoning (*sāmānyatodṛṣṭa-anumāna*), but the subtler objects which cannot be known by that should be known by verbal testimony.[45] Hence Sāṅkhya accepted verbal testimony (probably the testimony of the sage Kapila) as the last resort.

Lokāyata, as a school of philosophy, also must have been developing a rational approach. But unlike the other two rational philosophies, it must have been doing so without any regard for the scriptural

44. '*pratyakṣāgamāśritamanumānaṁ, sā'nvīkṣā. pratyakṣāgamābhyām īkṣitasya anvīkṣaṇam anvīkṣā. Tayā pravartata ityānvīkṣikī nyāyavidyā nyāyaśāstram*' (*Nyāyabhāṣya* [*NBh*] 1.1.1, p. 38–9). ['Posterior seeing' (anvīkṣā) means an inference based on perception and verbal testimony. Posterior seeing (anvīkṣā) means subsequent seeing of what has been seen through perception and verbal testimony. Ānvīkṣikī is that which proceeds through it (= posterior seeing). It is the same as the faculty of reasoning, the science of reasoning.]

45. (*Sāṁkhyakārikā* [*SK*] 6); an explanation of *sāmāyatodṛṣṭa* inference is given in Chapter 4.

authority, either Vedic or non-Vedic. It applied reasoning not in accordance with scriptures or in the service of scriptures, but by challenging scriptures. Disregarding scriptures and disregarding otherworldly beliefs such as soul, God, rebirth, and other worlds go hand in hand. Lokāyata in this sense could be understood as a rationalist philosophical movement which attempted to solve individual and social issues merely on empirical, rational, and practical grounds without taking recourse to religion. Kauṭilya seems to have respect for such a rationalist philosophy, as a result of which he included it in Ānvīkṣikī.

The consolidated picture of Lokāyata that emerges from our discussion is not that of a rigid philosophical doctrine (such as, say, materialism), nor that of just a science of logic or disputation, but a 'rationalist' philosophical movement.[46] As a movement rather than a rigid system, it could accommodate various trends from scepticism to common sense.[47]

Cārvāka-darśana and Bārhaspatya-darśana: New Identity

If Lokāyata was the earliest nomenclature of this rationalist school of thought (which was more like a movement than a rigid system), it assumed an additional identity in a later period, from the 6th century onwards, as historians record, as Cārvāka-darśana and Bārhaspatya-darśana. During this period, when philosophical systems were getting crystallized as epistemic-ontological systems (*pramāṇa-prameya*-systems) on the model of Nyāya-Vaiśeṣika and Sāṅkya or as

46. Here the word 'rationalist' is not to be contrasted with 'empiricist', but with 'religious and dogmatic'.

47. Dakshinaranjan Bhattacharya's estimate of the contribution of Cārvākas to the development of Indian philosophy comes close, I think, to my understanding of Lokāyata:

> The voice of the Cārvākas was the voice of revolt, of protest against the age-old superstitions and prejudices that had denied freedom of thought. It was an invitation for enjoying the beauties of life unperturbed by the ideas of heaven, hell, God. In the domain of philosophy the questions and doubts raised by the Cārvākas set problems for all the other schools, made them think more carefully and saved them from much of dogmatism. Every philosophy in India had to satisfy the Cārvākas before establishing its own view. Thus the contribution of this school to the development of Indian philosophy is really very great. Radhakrishnan (1952: 138)

reactions to them, each developing a sūtra-bhāṣya tradition of its own, Lokāyata-darśana also seems to have taken a crystallized shape in the form of Bṛhaspati's sūtras. The names Bṛhaspati and Cārvāka associated with the school remain mysterious. In a story in *Chāndogya Upaniṣad*, Prajāpati teaches the theory that the body is the self to Virocana and Indra, kings of *asuras* (demons) and gods respectively,[48] and Virocana, satisfied with the theory, carries it to asuras. The same model is carried forward in *Padmapurāṇa* where Prajāpati is replaced by Bṛhaspati, who teaches anti-Vedic, anti-sacrificial philosophy to asuras in order to mislead them.[49] Hence Bṛhaspati could be a mythical character attributed to the so-called founder of the Lokāyata philosophy by the opponents of Lokāyata, which seems to have been appropriated by the Lokāyatikas. Similarly, one does not know whether there was a Lokāyata philosopher called Cārvāka or whether Cārvāka of the *Mahābhārata* was depicted as a Lokāyata philosopher in the later period. Purandara, a Lokāyata philosopher, used the word 'cārvāka' in plural, implying thereby that it was not a proper name, but a common noun referring to 'a follower of the Lokāyata view'. In the later period, the titles Bṛhaspati and Cārvāka fortuitously became central to Lokāyata philosophy.

Bṛhaspati's sūtras, as Bhattacharya has restored them, seem to have asserted a materialistic ontology and an extreme-empiricist epistemology by accepting perception as the only means to knowledge. As will be pointed out in Chapter 3, Bṛhaspati's aphorisms have a clear implication of extreme empiricism; they do not intend to accept inference as a subordinate (*gauṇa*) means to knowledge (although Bhattacharya tries to interpret the aphorisms that way). However, the diversity in Lokāyata view, which seems to have been suppressed by the aphorismic crystallization, appears to have branched out through the emergence of a variety of Cārvākas giving diverse interpretations of the aphorisms. Here, of course, I am not concerned with the question of how all this must have happened historically. But I want simply to point out that there was such diversity. Bhattacharya's

48. *Chāndogya Upaniṣad* (*CU*, viii.7–9) as included in Chattopadhyaya (1990: 3–6).

49. *Padmapurāṇa*, *Sṛṣṭikhaṇḍa* (319–34, 36–8), as included in Pathak (1965: 157–60). In *Viṣṇupurāṇa* this role is assigned to Māyāmoha, a deluding character created by the lord Viṣṇu. See *Viṣṇupurāṇ* (3–18), as quoted in Jha (1969: 430–2).

researches[50] reveal that there were commentators who commented upon *Bṛhaspatisūtras* and that they did not interpret the sūtras uniformly. He notes, on the basis of Cakradhara's work *Nyāyamañjarīgranthibhaṅga*, that a commentator called Bhāvivikta was called traditional Cārvāka master (Cirantanacārvākācārya), and another commentator, Udbhaṭa, on account of his atypical interpretation of the aphorisms can be called 'revisionist'. Although Bhattacharya claims that Udbhaṭa's views on inference are the same as those of Purandara, this is dubitable.[51] Moreover, if Udbhaṭa was the same person whom Jayanta calls knave Cārvāka (Cārvāka-dhūrta) and learned Cārvāka (Suśikṣita-Cārvāka), then Udbhaṭa must have held indeterminism on the definition and number of means to knowledge and objects of knowledge as will be shown in the following chapter. Moreover, as we shall see in the following chapter, Jayarāśi tried to derive his scepticism from Bṛhaspati's aphorisms by interpreting them differently. In this way, the popular Cārvāka view (which is perhaps the view of Bhāvivikta, 'the traditional Cārvāka master'), the sophisticated view (of Purandara), and the sceptical view (mild scepticism of Udbhaṭa and absolute scepticism of Jayarāśi) all emerge around the *Bṛhaspatisūtras*, sometimes by adhering to them, sometimes by deviating from them.[52] Similarly, the varieties of Cārvākas come to be named as traditional Cārvāka, knave Cārvāka (also known as learned Cārvāka), and more learned Cārvāka. Though some of these titles are given by the opponents of Lokāyata and were not upheld by the Lokāyatikas themselves, these titles at least indicate the diversity among Lokāyata thinkers noticed even by their opponents. Hence I am suggesting that the titles such as Lokāyata-darśana, Cārvāka-darśana, and Bārhaspatya-darśana should not be treated as the names of a uniform single system, but of a family of systems or a family of philosophical trends.

50. See Bhattacharya (2012: 65–8).

51. Bhattacharya (2012: 61–2). In the passage quoted by Bhattacharya from Udbhaṭa's commentary, Udbhaṭa makes a distinction between *lokaprasiddha-anumāna* and *tantrasiddha-anumāna*, but he does not say clearly that the former is acceptable and the latter is not. On the contrary he says that anumāna is secondary (gauṇa), precisely because the invariable relation is reached in the same way in both, though we want to say that one gives knowledge but the other does not.

52. It should be noted here that we cannot expect orthodox adherence to sūtras from the Cārvākas as we can expect from the followers of other schools who took authenticity of the source text seriously.

This brings one to the question of unity of this Lokāyata/Cārvāka/Bārhaspatya family. How can these different members—one member, for instance, accepting two means to knowledge whereas another accepting one means and the third accepting no means—be said to belong to a single family of philosophical systems or trends? What is common among the so-called members of the Cārvāka family apart from the fact that the names like Cārvāka, Lokāyata, and Bṛhaspati are historically associated with them? Does it consist simply in the use of a common word (like a common family name)? The answer seems to be two-fold. One, there was a methodological similarity among Cārvākas, that they were using arguments constructively or destructively without accepting any restrictions based on verbal testimony. Second, there was a 'metaphysical element' common to the different members of the Cārvāka family, though this element was largely negative. All Cārvākas accepted worldly practices (*loka-vyavahāra*) in a strong or weak way; and this was the common positive element, though it was too general and vague. But the negative common element was stronger and clearer. It can be stated briefly as follows:

1. There is no soul or self apart from body; consciousness cannot exist independently of body.
2. There is no God, no other world; the doctrine of karma is not acceptable.
3. Inference cannot be established as a means to knowledge in the strict sense.
4. No religious scriptures (Vedas, Āgamas, and so on) are to be accepted as the source of knowledge.
5. Religious obligations (dharma) and disembodied liberation (*mokṣa*) are not acceptable as values.[53]

53. Here Franco (1987: IX) seems to be right in his claim that the hard core of this school was not the doctrine of four or five material elements, and such like, but its anti-religious or anti-clerical ethics. He rightly claims (Franco 1987: 8) that the purpose behind Bṛhaspati's rejection of all other means of cognition was pragmatic: '... to exclude any divine or supernatural factor from the foundation of social and ethical theories, and this meant fierce opposition to the religious weltanschauung which had sacrifices at its center'. I am claiming that the purpose which, according to Franco, was behind Bṛhaspati's aphorisms, was also behind different other schools of Lokāyata/Cārvāka.

The different epistemological theories that various Cārvāka schools adopted served as different ways of supporting this negative element. Hence the sceptic Cārvākas must have thought that otherworldly metaphysics can be denied if we deny metaphysics altogether. They did it by denying all ways of knowing. The narrow-empiricist Cārvākas must have thought that, after all, transcendental metaphysics is justified on the basis of the means to knowledge such as inference and verbal testimony; hence it can be denied by accepting perception as the only means to knowledge. The broad-empiricist Cārvākas must have followed a wiser policy of denying the specific types of inferences which are used for proving the transcendent entities but admitting ordinary and scientific inferences used for establishing worldly matters. Hence non-acceptance of otherworldly beliefs was achieved by different Cārvāka sub-schools at different costs. The various sub-schools are at different distances from the common-sense view of the world, but each one of them is making a different interesting and illuminating philosophical contribution.

***

The next three chapters will deal with the following three sub-schools or subsystems of Cārvākas with special emphasis on their *epistemological* theories and their implications for ontology and axiology:

1. Sceptic Cārvāka-darśana, which denies all ways of knowing.
2. Extreme- or narrow-empiricist Cārvāka-darśana, which accepts perception as the only means to knowledge.
3. Sophisticated-empiricist or broad-empiricist Cārvāka-darśana, which accepts perception and also a special kind of inference as means to knowledge.

Though it may not be possible to verify, due to non-availability of sufficient historical data, that there were such schools of Cārvākas or individual Cārvākas who held a narrow or broad approach consistently in epistemology, ontology, and axiology, the possibility of such consistent integrated sub-systems of Cārvākas can, I urge, at least be appreciated as a logical plausibility if not as a historical fact. A philosophical inquiry into Cārvāka-darśana would be different from a historical inquiry mainly in this way. The former would be an inquiry into different possible conceptual constructions and reconstructions of the subsystems of Cārvāka-darśana without any commitment to the history of Cārvāka-darśana, or with a relaxation of such a commitment.

A philosophical reconstruction could be made in the guise of reconstruction of history. But that is not my aim here. The philosophical contribution of Cārvākas that I am highlighting here draws on the materials attributed to 'historical' Cārvāka thinkers and again it is projected as a historical possibility, but not as a historical thesis. My main aim here is to present Cārvāka thought as a cluster of strong philosophical approaches.

2

Scepticism in Cārvāka-darśana

I have suggested in the first chapter that the unitary understanding of Cārvāka-darśana is not correct, neither the one which identifies it with materialism nor the one which regards that perception is the only means to knowledge. I also argued that there could have been some Cārvākas who did not accept any means to knowledge. In fact no ancient or classical Cārvāka monographs are available today with only one exception, namely *Tattvopaplavasiṁha* (hereafter *TUS*), a treatise written by Jayarāśi, which denies all the means to knowledge. Jayarāśi was an 8th-century philosopher who denied all the means to knowledge and objects of knowledge, but at the same time attributed this view to Bṛhaspati, the founder of the Lokāyata tradition himself, and interpreted the aphorisms of Bṛhaspati so as to suit his own sceptical position. It was observed in the last chapter that Chattopadhyaya denies the status of a Lokāyata thinker to Jayarāśi,[1] whereas Eli Franco claims that there were at least two trends in the Lokāyata school or tradition—one materialistic and the other sceptic.[2] Franco draws on a famous Lokāyata fragment, 'Everywhere (that is, throughout the text)

1. Chattopadhyaya (1989: 36ff.).
2. Franco (1987: IX).

the *sūtras* of Bṛhaspati have the sole purpose of questioning (the opinions or doctrines of) others.'[3] It was also noted that Lokāyata was described as *vitaṇḍasattha* (the discipline based on negative disputation) in some Buddhist texts and as *vaitaṇḍika-kathā* (negative debate) by Jayanta.[4] Jayantabhaṭṭa in *Nyāyamañjarī* (*NM*) refers to the view of the knave Cārvākas according to which the number and the definition of the means to knowledge cannot be determined. (This view can be seen as a form of scepticism about knowledge though not as a radical one like that of Jayarāśi.) Similarly Śrīharṣa in his *Khaṇḍanakhaṇḍa-khādya* (*KKK*) treats the three views—those of Lokāyata, Mādhyamika Buddhism, and Advaita Vedānta—as on par with each other in their application of the method of negative debate (*vitaṇḍā*) and denial of all the means to knowledge.[5] The complexity of these sources indicate that there must have been a philosophical position accepted by some Cārvāka thinkers which was a form of scepticism.

Before taking up Jayarāśi's scepticism—which is the major form of Lokāyatic scepticism—for discussion, it may be apt to first deal in brief with the view of the so-called knave Cārvākas (Cārvāka-dhūrta). The latter view can be described as a milder form of Cārvāka scepticism. This is because it does not question the possibility of knowledge itself; it only questions the possibility of classifying the means to knowledge and sharply distinguishing one means from

3. '*sarvatra paraparyanuyogaparāṇyeva bṛhaspateḥ sūtrāṇi*', Franco (1987: 6).
4. See the section 'Lokāyata and Vitaṇḍā' in Chapter 1.
5. *so'yamapūrvaḥ pramāṇādisattānabhyupagamātmā vākstambhanamantro bhavatā'bhyūhito nūnaṁ yasya prabhāvād bhagavatā suraguruṇā lokāyatikāni sūtrāṇi na praṇītāni, tathāgatena vā madhyamāgamā nopadiṣṭāḥ, bhagavatpādena vā bādarāyaṇīyeṣu sūtreṣu bhāṣyaṁ nābhāṣi* (*Khaṇḍanakhaṇḍakhādya* [*KKK* 1970], Pariccheda I, pp. 7–8)

[(Śrīharṣa here is criticizing the Naiyāyika's position that if a philosopher wants to refute the existence of all the means to knowledge, then he cannot express his position in a language.) You have really stated this novel magical spell of making one speechless, namely, non-acceptance of the existence of the means to knowledge, due to the influence of which, the lord Bṛhaspati (the teacher of gods) did not create the Lokāyata aphorisms, the Tathāgata Buddha did not preach Middle Way scriptures and the Lord Śaṁkarācārya did not state the commentary on Bādarāyaṇa's aphorisms.] This implies that Śrīharṣa was aware of the interpretation of Lokāyata-sūtras which denied all the means to knowledge. Śaṁkaramiśra, the commentator, was puzzled while explaining the statement with reference to Lokāyata. As a possible interpretation, he acknowledges the possibility that there might be a sect of Cārvākas which does not accept any means to knowledge ('*cārvākaikadeśī vā cārvākaḥ*' [*KKK* 1970, p. 7]).

another. This was probably the position held by a Cārvāka thinker called Udbhaṭa or Bhaṭṭodbhaṭa as suggested by Cakradhara.[6] The picture that emerges from *NM* (chapter I, part I), the commentary *Granthibhaṅga* on it, and some passages from *Syādvādaratnākara*, a Jaina text by Vādidevasūri, is as follows. Bhaṭṭodbhaṭa/Udbhaṭa, who wrote a commentary called *Tattvavṛtti* on *Lokāyatasūtras* of Bṛhaspati, explained the first two aphorisms of Bṛhaspati in an unconventional way. Perhaps this is the reason why he was called a knave Cārvāka (Cārvāka-dhūrta) and also a learned Cārvāka (Suśikṣita-Cārvāka) by Jayantabhaṭṭa.[7] The first two aphorisms of Bṛhaspati were:

1. *athātastattvaṁ vyākhyāsyāmaḥ/*
   [Now we explain the ultimate truth.]
2. *pṛthivyāpastejo vāyuriti tattvāni/*
   [Earth, water, fire, and air are the ultimate truths.]

Udbhaṭa does not explain these aphorisms in a literal way. He interprets the word *tattvam* (ultimate truth) in the first aphorism as indeterminability of number and essential characteristics of the sources of knowledge and the objects of knowledge (*'pramāṇa–prameya–saṅkhyā–lakṣaṇa–niyama–aśakya–karaṇīyatvam eva tattvam'*).[8] The second aphorism too according to him is not simply about the four elements—earth, water, fire, and air. He interprets the word *'iti'* in this aphorism not as indicating the end of the list but as other objects (such as consciousness, sound, pleasure, pain, and kinds of absences). Hence the import of the second aphorism according to Udbhaṭa is again indeterminacy of number and nature of the ontological categories. It seems that Udbhaṭa, who in this way applied the 'indeterminacy principle' to the knowables (prameyas) must have applied it to the means to knowledge (pramāṇas) as well. This is what Jayanta's report of the approach of the knave Cārvākas to the means to knowledge suggests.

6. *'suśikṣitacārvākā udbhaṭādayaḥ'* (*Nyāyamañjarīgranthibhaṅga* [*NMGB*], p. 19).

7. One may note here that Jayanta seems to identify Cārvāka-dhūrta (knave Cārvāka) with Suśikṣita-Cārvāka (learned Cārvāka) and further distinguishes him from Suśikṣitatara-Cārvāka (more learned Cārvāka). Both these varieties seem to be distinguished from Cirantana-Cārvākas (traditional Cārvākas), the upholders of the popular Cārvāka view to whose group a thinker called Bhāvivikta belonged (Bhattacharya 2012: 68).

8. *NM*, part I, p. 59. Cakradhara comments here that the Cārvāka-dhūrta mentioned here is the same as Udbhaṭa (*NMGB*, p. 43).

Jayanta reports that while explaining this position of indeterminacy, the knave Cārvākas cite as examples some knowledge situations which cannot be clearly brought under any one specific means to knowledge. Three such examples are given by Jayanta.[9]

1. One knows whether the fingers of one's hand are bent or expanded, even in darkness or even when one's eyes are shut. This cognition cannot be a tactual perception because a sense organ cannot cause the cognition of itself.[10]
2. When we see the flame of a lamp from a distance, we also see its light spread in remote places.[11]
3. A cluster of lotuses swinging due to wind makes its fragrance known even from a distance in the blowing wind.[12]

Jayanta tries to explain away these counter-examples cited by the 'knave Cārvāka'. He claims that the first case is that of perception and the last two cases are those of inference. Here Jayanta's explanation of the last two cases is not satisfactory. They seem to be clear cases of visual and olfactory perceptions respectively. But the main point of the 'knave Cārvāka', namely that there are many cases of cognition which cannot be accommodated under any specific means to knowledge and that the regimentation of pramāṇas into a closed system is not possible is well taken. One can see the followers of the Nyāya school confused while trying to include recognition (*pratyabhijñā*) under perception (*pratyakṣa*) and some unusual cases of cognition under extraordinary perception based on 'cognition itself as contact' (*jñānalakṣaṇā pratyāsatti*) and 'universal itself as contact' (*sāmānyalakṣaṇā pratyāsatti*). Two more remarks can be added with regard to the view of the 'knave Cārvākas' as mentioned by Jayanta:

9. *NMGB*, p. 60.

10. The knave Cārvāka here means that the fingers themselves constitute the sense organ of touch as well as the object of the tactual sense. The same thing cannot be the sense organ as well as its object.

11. The knave Cārvāka here means that the visual sense organ can have contact with the flame but not with the light spread by the flame. Hence, following the contact theory of perceptual cognition, only the flame can be perceived and not its light.

12. Here the knave Cārvāka seems to mean that since the fragrance seems to be known directly, its experience cannot be called an inference. And since the fragrance of a flower should be known directly only in a proximate place, the fragrance cannot be known in a remote place by perception.

1. The position of the knave Cārvākas does not amount to absolute scepticism—which questions the very possibility of knowledge—but is rather a statement of anarchism or a disorder in the realm of means and objects of knowledge.
2. The tendency to interpret Bṛhaspati's aphorisms in an unconventional way and to deviate from empiricist–materialist understanding of Lokāyata which we find here is not unique in Lokāyata tradition. We find another manifestation, perhaps a stronger one, of this tendency in Jayarāśibhaṭṭa's *TUS* as well. The latter interprets Bṛhaspati's aphorisms in an unconventional way in order to support his absolute scepticism. This will be the subject-matter of the sections to follow.

In the following sections of this chapter an attempt will be made, first and foremost, to understand the identity of Jayarāśi as a Lokāyata thinker. It will then proceed to comprehend the sceptical argument offered by Jayarāśi, after which Jayarāśi's position will be compared with other two sceptical positions—namely that of Nāgārjuna and Śrīharṣa. This chapter will conclude by locating Jayarāśi and the other two 'sceptics' on a global map of scepticism.

Jayarāśi's Identity as a Lokāyata Thinker

Jayarāśi, in *TUS*, quotes many aphorisms of Bṛhaspati and a few other popular Cārvāka sayings approvingly. Yet his interpretation of those aphorisms and sayings is neither empiricist nor materialist, but rather leading towards scepticism, in both epistemological and ontological senses. It becomes necessary, therefore, to see in what sense and in what way Jayarāśi can be called a Lokāyata thinker.

I have tried to show in the first chapter how there was diversity in the epistemological, ontological, and axiological approaches of different Lokāyatikas and how the common elements among the different sects or trends of Lokāyata were largely negative. About Jayarāśi, one can say that he would share these common negative elements with the other sects of Lokāyatikas, but not with the positive elements accepted by them (except one, namely the superficial acceptance of worldly practices or *loka-vyavahāra*). This becomes clear from the way he mentions and uses different aphorisms of Bṛhaspati and other popular Cārvāka sayings.

How Jayarāśi accepts the negative claims of Cārvāka becomes clear from the following considerations:

1. He cites and also accepts the Cārvāka aphorism which means that there is no other world because there is no soul which belongs to the other world.[13]
2. Similarly, he rejects the view that inference is an authentic source of knowledge and while doing so he argues in terms of the dilemma of inference which we find in different formulations of Cārvāka arguments against inference.[14]
3. With respect to the value-perspective of Jayarāśi, we can say that his denial of other worlds implies that he is opposed to values like religious obligations (dharma) and liberation (*mokṣa*) which presuppose the existence of other worlds and the disembodied self.

But Jayarāśi does not accept the positive views which are popularly attributed to Cārvāka. This becomes clear from the following considerations:

1. Jayarāśi not only denies other worlds, but claims that even the constituents of this world namely earth, water, fire, and air cannot be proved. He does this by interpreting Bṛhaspati's aphorism (that earth, water, fire, and air are the ultimate truths)[15] in an unconventional way. He says that Bṛhaspati in this aphorism is not saying that these are the ultimate categories (*tattva*), but he is only indicating (reflecting: *pratibimbana*) what is accepted as ultimate categories by the people. Bṛhaspati intends to say in this aphorism that if even these (so-called) ultimate categories cannot be established, what about others?[16]
2. Similarly it is clear from Jayarāśi's discussion of 'causal inference' (*kāryānumāna*) accepted by Buddhists that although he

13. '*paralokino'bhāvāt paralokābhāvaḥ*' (*TUS*, p. 45).
14. For discussion on the dilemma of inference, see Chapter 3.
15. '*pṛthivyāpastejo vāyuriti tattvāni*' (*TUS*, p. 1).
16. '*ityādi? na, anyārthatvāt. kimartham? pratibimbanārtham. kim punaratra pratibimbyate? pṛthivyādīni tattvāni loke prasiddhāni, tānyapi vicāryamāṇāni na vyavatiṣṭhante kiṁ punaranyāni?*' (*TUS*, p. 1). I accept Eli Franco's (1987: 5–6) interpretation.

acknowledges Bṛhaspati's view that life is only the product of the body[17] and treats it as a possibly acceptable view, he does not accept it wholeheartedly. Jayarāśi's argument runs as follows. If we agree that a causal inference—for instance the inference of fire from smoke—is a proper instance of inference as an authoritative means to knowledge, then we will have to agree that the material cause need not be of the same type of object (*sajātīya*) as the effect, as fire is utterly of different nature from smoke. By utilizing this liberty we may be in a position to say that body could be the material cause of the life in it, even though body and life or body and consciousness are utterly different in nature. If, on the contrary, we affirm that material cause must be of the same nature as the effect, then we could deny the causal relation between body and consciousness, but in that case we cannot establish the causal connection between smoke and fire either. Consequently the so called causal inference itself comes to an end. This argument of Jayarāśi suggests that he is using Bṛhaspati's thesis regarding the causal relation between mind and body for refuting causal inference, but he is not approving of the materialist explanation of consciousness categorically.[18]

It is worth noting here that accepting consciousness or life as the product of four elements is contingent upon accepting a causal connection between the two and the latter on the authenticity of inference as the means to knowledge. Naturally, denying inference as an authoritative means to knowledge and accepting consciousness as the product of four elements do not go together. Hence, Jayarāśi is self-consistent in non-acceptance of both.

3. But Jayarāśi does not stop at non-acceptance of inference. He does not accept the authenticity of perception either.
4. Jayarāśi is holding a parallel position regarding the objects of knowledge. He questions the existence of the perceptible/tangible objects like the four gross elements. It goes without saying that he denies the imperceptible, subtle, and

17. '*śarīrādeva*' (*TUS*, p. 88) [(Consciousness arises) only from the body.]
18. For more details, see Chapter 5, note 26.

transcendent elements accepted by other systems of philosophy.[19]

5. Similarly, in the realm of values he does not prescribe any specific normative approach (such as sensualist hedonism) but just allows all unsophisticated or un-reflected-over value-policies without discrimination.[20]

In this way Jayarāśi approves of those popular Cārvāka doctrines which are negative in nature, but he does not accept at all or does not accept wholeheartedly those popular Cārvāka doctrines which are positive in nature. Still, Jayarāśi can be identified as a Cārvāka philosopher mainly on two grounds:

1. After all, Cārvākas are isolated from all other systems mainly because of their negative doctrines; that is, because of the denial of what others have accepted, namely the doctrines like karma, rebirth, soul, and God. Hence, the core of Cārvāka-darśana can be said to lie in its negative doctrines, whereas the positive doctrines of Cārvākas could be regarded as peripheral, supplementary, or optional parts of Cārvāka-darśana as such. Jayarāśi does not deviate from the negative core, though he deviates from the supplementary or peripheral doctrines accepted by all other Cārvākas. Hence there is no serious difficulty in identifying Jayarāśi as a Cārvāka thinker.
2. Another significant point which brings Jayarāśi closer to other Cārvākas is his acceptance of what he calls worldly practices (loka-vyavahāra). Jayarāśi quotes the (so-called) 'knowers of ultimate reality' (*paramārthavid*), who say that both the ignorant and the learned are alike with respect to the worldly practices.[21] This statement implies that the worldly practices

19. '*kiṁ punaranyāni?*' (*TUS*, p. 1). [(When even earth and such like do not remain as the realities, when reflected upon) what to say of others?]

20. '*tadevam upaplutesveva tattveṣu avicāritaramaṇīyāḥ sarve vyavahārāḥ ghaṭante*' (*TUS*, p. 125). [When in this way all the (ontological and epistemological) categories are refuted, all the practices, worth entertaining insofar as they are not reflected upon, get accepted.]

21. '*taduktaṁ paramārthavidbhirapi, lokavyavahāraṁ prati sadṛśau bālapaṇḍitau*' (*TUS*, p. 1). [The (so-called) knowers of the ultimate truth also say: the ignorant and the learned are similar with respect to the worldly practices.]

have to be accepted by Cārvākas as well as Vedāntins. The difference is that Vedāntins would accept practices referring to other-worldly existence along with this-worldly practices and they would also accept ultimate reality beyond this world and another world. Cārvākas, on the other hand, accept worldly practices (meaning thereby, this-worldly practices), but they deny the practices referring to other-worldly existences and also the so-called ultimate reality beyond this world. Now Jayarāśi too accepts worldly practices and denies other worlds. The difference between Jayarāśi and other Cārvākas in this respect, as I have indicated before, is that for Jayarāśi, worldly practices are to be accepted without being reflected upon (*avicārita–ramaṇīya*), whereas other Cārvākas try to reflect upon the worldly practices and justify them philosophically.

Further, we will deal with Jayarāśi's development of his sceptical arguments.

The Sceptical Argument of Jayarāśi

Jayarāśi's scepticism is not mitigated, but absolute, not local, but global. He not only denies metaphysical beliefs and other-worldly beliefs accepted by other systems, but also common-sense beliefs, and even the popular Cārvāka belief, that there are four gross elements. Similarly, he not only denies the means like inference and verbal testimony causing indirect knowledge, but also perception, the means to direct knowledge; in fact, he denies the means to knowledge in general.

Jayarāśi starts his sceptical argument with two basic formal principles which, according to him, any philosopher has to accept. If these basic principles are not accepted by a philosopher then the refutation of all principles is pre-established. They are: (*a*) true cognition can be established only by defining it properly,[22] and (*b*) the reality of an object of cognition is dependent upon (the establishment of) the authentic means of its cognition.[23]

22. '*sallakṣaṇanibandhanam mānavyavasthānam*/' (*TUS*, p. 1).
23. '*mānanibandhanā ca meyasthitiḥ*/' (*TUS*, p. 1).

Traditionally, Cārvākas are said to accept four basic elements namely, earth, water, fire, and air as categories/types of things (tattvas). Similarly, there are other philosophical systems which accept other categories differing in nature, number, ontological, and epistemological status. The reality of different categories becomes dependent ultimately on the correctness of the definition of 'means to knowledge' in general given by the concerned system and also the definitions of the specific means to knowledge accepted by the respective system. With the two principles examined earlier as the background, Jayarāśi considers different definitions of pramāṇa (knowledge or means to knowledge) in general and also those of specific pramāṇas (types of knowledge or means to knowledge)[24] and examines them critically. Jayarāśi's critical argumentation reveals an important thesis that no definition of pramāṇa is free from all defects. One of the major fallacies committed by all the proposed definitions of pramāṇa is the fallacy of *petitio principii* (begging the question; *itaretarāśraya*).

Traditionally, Indian logic delineates three fallacies of definition: too narrow a definition (*avyāpti*), too wide a definition (*ativyāpti*) and inapplicable definition (*asambhava*). Accordingly, a good definition indicates a distinctive feature of the definiendum (the concept or object that is to be defined) by avoiding all the three fallacies. In other words, if p is the definiendum and q is the definiens (the term or conjunction of terms which define the definiendum) then q must be a distinctive feature of p and there must be logical equivalence between p and q. The three fallacies of definition indicate the three ways of violating the equivalence condition.[25]

Petitio principii (*itaretarāśraya*) is not included in the previously mentioned list of the fallacies of definition. But Jayarāśi holds petitio

24. Nyāya philosophers are particular about the distinction between 'pramā' and 'pramāṇa'. They understand pramā as knowledge and pramāṇa as means to knowledge, though they sometimes use the word pramāṇa to mean knowledge as well. Other systems generally use the word pramāṇa in the sense of knowledge and then extend the scope of the concept to cover means to knowledge. Hence, the different pramāṇas such as pratyakṣa, *anumāna*, *upamāna*, and *śabda*, according to Nyāya philosophers, are different means to knowledge whereas they are different forms of knowledge or types of knowledge for other systems.

25. Hence the definition of p as q would be too narrow when q implies p, but p does not imply q; the definition would be too wide when p implies q but q does not imply p, and it would be inapplicable when p and q imply the negations of each other.

principii to be a fallacy of a definition, and from a pragmatic point of view,[26] he seems to be right. This is because of the following reason: the intention while defining a term is making the term known clearly and distinctly. Now, if any definition is to be pragmatically significant, its definiens must be known clearly and distinctly, when it is presented. The function of the definition then will be to lead one in one's cognitive journey from the (clearly and distinctly) known definiens to the definiendum not known clearly and distinctly. As a result, this makes the definiendum known through the definitional equivalence between definiendum and definiens. But if the definiens themselves are not known clearly and distinctly and we need the knowledge of the definiendum for the knowledge of the definiens themselves, then the fallacy of petitio principii would occur. In the present case, the definiendum under consideration is the knowledge itself. So when any definition of knowledge is given, if it is to be pragmatically significant, one must already have the knowledge of its definiens. But whether one has the knowledge of the definiens is dubitable because there one does not know clearly and distinctly, what the knowledge is (which is the definiendum). Thus it is a case of petitio.

Jayarāśi begins his critical exercise with the Nyāya definition of perception.[27] The Nyāya definition of perception contains terms indicating some defining features of knowledge in general. These terms are *avyabhicāri* (non-deviant), *vyavasāyātmaka* (determinate) and *jñāna* (cognition).[28] Out of these three terms, Jayarāśi's main attack is on the term avyabhicāri. Jayarāśi considers different possible meanings of the term and criticizes the definition under the corresponding interpretation.

26. Generally two objectives are attributed to the act of 'defining something': (*a*) through the definition one excludes the given term or concept from other terms or concepts (*vyāvṛtti*) and (*b*) it makes linguistic usage of the term possible (*vyavahāra*). The fallacy of *petitio principii* affects the second objective.

27. Jayarāśi does not discuss the Nyāya concept of pramāṇa directly because there is no definition of pramāṇa in *Nyāyasūtra* (*NS*) of Gautama; there is only classification of pramāṇas and definitions of the four pramāṇas, namely, pratyakṣa, anumāna, upamāna, and śabda.

28. The *Nyāyasūtra* definition of pratyakṣa goes: '*indriyārthasannikarṣotpannaṁ jñānam avyapadeśyam avyabhicāri vyavasāyāmakaṁ pratyakṣam*' (*NS* 1.1.4, as in *Nyāyadarśanaṁ* [*ND*], p. 93). [Pratyakṣa is the cognition, which is produced by the contact between a sense-organ and an object, which is non-verbal, which does not deviate (from the object), and which is determinate in nature.]

If 'avyabhicārī' means 'that which is given by non-defective sense organs', then according to Jayarāśi, the question arises: 'How is the non-defectiveness of sense organs known?' It is of course not known by perception. If it is inferred from the true perception of the object itself, then it is a clear case of petitio.[29]

If, on the other hand, the term avyabhicāri is taken to mean that which gives the 'volitional success' (*pravṛtti-samarthana*), then apart from other objections, Jayarāśi raises a question whether this meaning of the term is known or not. He asks—'Is this [meaning] known or unknown? If it is unknown how do you say that it is [the meaning]? And if it is known, then how do you know that this knowledge satisfies the condition of being avyabhicāri?'[30]

The definition of 'pramāṇa' prescribed by the Bhāṭṭa school of Pūrvamīmāṁsā has two major elements: (*a*) pramāṇa is a cognition not falsified/sublated (*abādhita*) by other cognitions, and (*b*) it is the cognition of an object which is not already cognized (*agṛhītagrāhi*). The first element may be called 'non-falsification element' and the second as 'novelty element'. Jayarāśi questions the 'non-falsification element' in the course of the discussion of the term 'avyabhicārī'. He points out that given a cognition it can be regarded as 'not-falsified' simply because the falsifying cognition does not arise due to some conditions. This does not mean that the original cognition must be true.[31] He

29. *TUS*, p. 2, lines 6–12; free and abridged translation mine. Jayarāśī's attitude of bringing out the fallacy of petitio principii in the conception of knowledge is comparable with a similar tendency in the writings of Sextus Empiricus, an ancient Greek philosopher, who raised a similar question in the following words:

> By what means, then, can we establish that the apparent thing is really such as it appears? Either, certainly, by means of a non-evident fact or by means of an apparent one. But to do by means of a non-evident fact is absurd. For the non-evident is so far from being able to reveal anything; on the contrary, it is itself in need of something to establish it. And to do so by means of an apparent fact is as much more absurd, for it is itself the things in question and nothing that is in question is capable of confirming itself.' (*Against All Logicians*, Sextus Empiricus, referred to in Hamblin 1970: 95)

30. *'tatkimavagatam anavgataṁ vā? Yadi nāvagataṁ, tad astīti kathaṁ vetsi?, ath āvagataṁ,tadavagateravyabhicāritā kathamavagamyate iti pūrvoktam anusartavyam'* (*TUS*, p. 3).

31. *'dṛśyate hi bādhakajñānotpādakakārakavaikalyād bādhānutpādaḥ, yathā dūre marīcinicaye jalajñāne jāte bādhā na sampadyate, abhyāsadeśāvasthitasya kārakopanipāte satyutpadyate. Sā copajāyamānā saṁvatsarādikālavikalpena sañjāyate, kadācicca*

challenges the novelty element by pointing out that there is no reason why out of two cognitions of a single object arising in sequence, the first should be regarded as authentic and the second as inauthentic simply because the first occurs first and the second afterwards.[32]

The novelty element of Mīmāṁsakas' definition is also an element in the Buddhist definition of pramāṇa. But Buddhists, as Jayarāśi shows, have to face additional difficulty because of their doctrines of momentariness and that of the radical difference between the objects of perception and inference. Due to these reasons, no two cognitions can have the same object. Hence, the defining feature of pramāṇa, namely that it should cognize a new object, becomes redundant.[33] Jayarāśi also refutes the Buddhist definition of pramāṇa that 'pramāṇa is a non-discordant cognition'.[34]

---

kārakavaikalyānnaiva sampadyate. Na caitāvatā tasya yathārthatā upapadyate' (*TUS*, p. 2, lines 17–22). [For it is seen in some cases that the sublation is not produced because of the deficiency of the causal factor which (could have) produced the sublating cognition. For instance when a cognition of water is produced with reference to a faraway mass of sun-rays, the sublation is not produced, (but) when a causal factor is produced additionally for (a person) who stands nearby, (the sublation) is produced. And being produced additionally it is produced with a difference in time, after a year etc., and sometimes, due to the deficiency of the causal factor, it is not produced at all; but the non-erroneousness of a (cognition) is not established by that much (translation by Franco 1987: 75)]

32. *'vibhinnakārakotpāditaikārthavijñānānāṁ yathāvyavasthitaikārthagṛhītirūpat vāviśeṣe'pi pūrvotpannavijñānasya prāmāṇyaṁ nottarasya ityatra niyāmakaṁ vaktavyam'* (*TUS*, p. 22, lines 20–3). [You should state the determining condition (criterion) on the basis of which you say that among the cognitions of a single object, which are produced by different causes, the first cognition is to be regarded as authentic and not the later one, although, they have a common feature that they are the cognitions of a single object as it is.] Jayarāśi then proceeds to show how there is no satisfactory criterion.

33. *tathā, tāthāgatānāmapi anadhigatārthagantṛ-viśeṣaṇam apārthakam, apohyajñānāsambhavāt. na hi pūrvāparakālabhāvinī vijñāne ekaviṣaye staḥ* ... (*TUS*, p. 27, lines 8–10)

[Similarly, the qualification given by the Buddhists (in the definition of pramāṇa) namely 'that which cognizes what is not cognized', is meaningless (that is, redundant), as there is no possibility of cognition to be excluded (by another cognition). That is because the cognition which arises earlier and that which arises later is not about the same object...]

34. *'avisaṁvādi jñānaṁ pramāṇam'* (for Jayarāśi's discussion of the definition, see *TUS* [p. 28 {line 10 onwards}, p. 29]. For Franco's translation, see Franco [1987: 167–73]).

In this way, by criticizing the conceptions of pramāṇa given by all the major epistemology schools, Jayarāśi doubts the possibility of knowledge in general. He raises a basic question about the concept of knowledge as 'true cognition' and shows by his critical apparatus that no cognition can be determined to be true. Here, it is to be clearly noted that by saying that no cognition can be determined to be true, Jayarāśi does not mean that every cognition is necessarily false in the sense of being illusory. As he denies the so-called knowledge (that is, true cognition), he also denies illusion. What Jayarāśi asserts along with this is that no distinction can be made between true and false cognitions.[35] For him, every cognition has some object (which, according to him, is the content of that cognition), but from this it does not necessarily follow that the object of cognition also exists objectively.[36] Here, one has to take note of the distinction between illusion and appearance (*bhrama* and *avabhāsa*). While one has an illusion, one cognizes something, in place of another thing. That is to say, illusion has some existential import (that which appears in the illusion), as well as an existential support (*adhiṣṭhāna*, in place of which it appears). But appearance may not have this duality of 'something appearing as something else'. It may be just an appearance. Thus, while saying that no cognition can be proved to have ontological import, we are not asserting that every cognition is an illusion. For Jayarāśi any cognition is limited by its object.[37] It is like a sense-datum theorist saying that there cannot be sense-data that are not sensed. Any sense-datum is by definition an object of sensation and any sensation is by definition limited by its sense-datum. But sense-datum in this sense has only an epistemic status and not an

35. '*anenaiva vartmanā satyetara-vijñānayoḥ vibhāgābhāvaḥ abhyupagantavyaḥ*' (*TUS*, p. 11, lines 17–18). [By this very route one should uphold the non-distinction between true and false cognition.]

36. It is understood here that when Jayarāśi, like many other Indian philosophers, uses the words like *avabhāsa*, *vijñāna*, *jnāna*, and *buddhi*, it is not in the sense of the English word 'knowledge', which generally means true belief or true cognition, but it is in the sense of cognition understood in truth-value-neutral sense.

37. '*svaviṣayaparyavasāyinyo hi buddhayaḥ*' (*TUS*, p. 15, line 26). [Because, cognitions end up with their own objects.] The same idea is suggested by the statement, '*apohya-jñānāsambhavāt*' (*TUS*, p. 13, line 16; p. 27, line 9). The idea is that one cognition cannot be excluded by another cognition. Nor can it be supported by another cognition.

ontic one. Hence, no knowledge-claim can establish by itself the existence of anything beyond the level of appearance.

Jayarāśi Compared with Nāgārjuna and Śrīharṣa[38]

It may be interesting here to compare Jayarāśi's sceptical position with that of Nāgārjuna and Śrīharṣa. Nāgārjuna was a 2nd-century philosopher of Mādhyamika Buddhism and Śrīharṣa was an 11th-century poet and philosopher of Advaita–Vedānta.

Both of them, like Jayarāśi, develop a sceptical approach to pramāṇas. Nāgārjuna in *Vigrahavyāvartanī* (*VV*) argues that no pramāṇa can be established as authentic either intrinsically or extrinsically.[39] He claims that all forms of knowledge (pramāṇa) and their objects (prameya) are dependently originated and hence void (essence-less, *śūnya*). Śrīharṣa in *Khaṇḍanakhaṇḍakhādya* takes up definitions of pramāṇa presented in different schools and refutes them one after the other. Śrīharṣa also elaborately defends the method of negative debate (vitaṇḍā) as a legitimate philosophical method. He takes cognizance of Mādhyamika Buddhism and also of Bṛhaspati, the Lokāyata philosopher, as using the method of negative debate.[40] It is possible that Śrīharṣa was aware of Jayarāśi's work and considered Jayarāśi's sceptical interpretation of Bṛhaspati's aphorisms as authentic. We see in this way that the three philosophers, namely Nāgārjuna, Jayarāśi, and Śrīharṣa present similar positions on pramāṇas. They also use a similar method, namely the sceptical method under different names such as vitaṇḍā (negative debate) or *prasaṅga* (*reductio ad absurdum*, or, reduction to absurdity), or without calling it by any such name. Second, through the criticism of knowledge, they also criticize objects of knowledge; rather they are

38. The discussion that follows is a modified version of my paper (Gokhale 1999). The focus of that paper was to understand Nāgārjuna's scepticism. Here the focus has been changed.

39. *naiva svataḥ prasiddhir na parasparataḥ pramāṇair vā/*
Na bhavati na ca prameyaiḥ na cāpyakasmāt pramāṇānām// (*Vigrahavyāvartanī* [*VV*] 52)

[*Pramāṇas* are neither established by themselves, nor by each other, nor by their objects, nor accidentally.]

40. See note 5 in this chapter.

critical about the discourse of knowledge and its objects (pramāṇa–prameya–vyavahāra) in general. This, however, does not make the philosophical positions of all of them alike.

Now what is the difference among their philosophical positions? One way of understanding the difference is to see how they try to answer the sceptical paradox. Another way would be to see how they deal with the distinction between empirical truth (vyavahār) and ultimate truth (*paramārtha*).

Responses to the Paradox of Scepticism

Every sceptic has to face the charge that scepticism is self-defeating. There is a basic framework of common-sense beliefs or the beliefs concerning worldly practices, or practices concerning knowledge and its objects (loka-vyavahāra/pramāṇa–prameya–vyavahāra), which a sceptic too has to accept while presenting sceptical arguments. But sceptical arguments themselves are aimed at refuting all forms of knowledge and consequently the framework of common-sense beliefs. Sceptical arguments, in this way, try to refute the basic framework, which they presuppose. Hence, they defeat themselves. This means, in other words, that scepticism is paradoxical. Every sceptic has to come to terms with this charge of the paradoxical nature of scepticism. The way, in which a sceptic tries to overcome the paradox, may differ depending upon the sceptic's attitude towards the world and life, to be more concise, the sceptic's general standpoint. I am suggesting that the ways in which the three authors present and defend scepticism against the charge of being paradoxical; are different from each other in a significant way and this difference has something to do with their general standpoint. So let us consider their response to the sceptical paradox.

Nāgārjuna's Response

Nāgārjuna in his *Vigrahavyāvartanī* refers to the essentialists (*svabhāvavādins*) who charge Nāgārjuna with making a self-defeating argument. Essentialists argue, for instance, as follows:

1. If Nāgārjuna says that if everything is void (śūnya, *niḥsvabhāva*, essenceless), then this sentence is equally void and hence lacks persuasive force.[41]
2. Similarly, if Nāgārjuna denies everything then this denial must be based on some means to knowledge. If it is, then he has accepted at least one means to knowledge. If it is not, then his denial of everything is baseless.[42]

In response to these charges Nāgārjuna agrees that his statement, namely 'everything is void', is equally void.[43] So there is no problem if his statements have ontologically the same status as the statement of his opponents. His main point here would be that void-ness does not imply non-existence. It only implies non-essential or non-absolute existence (*niḥsvabhāvatva*).

On the other hand he is pointing out that his statements have logically different status from that of those made by his opponents, that is, the essentialists, because whereas the opponents are trying to prove something through their arguments, Nāgārjuna is not trying to prove anything.[44] Nāgārjuna interprets every assertion of the essentialists as an assertion of the essential nature of something.

41. *sarveṣāṁ bhāvānāṁ sarvatra na vidyate svabhāvaścet/*
tvadvacanamasvabhāvaṁ na nivartayituṁ svabhāvam alam// (*VV* 1)

[(The essentialist says to the non-essentialist): If anywhere anything in the world has no essence, then this statement of yours is also without essence and hence is not capable of refuting essence.]

42. In *Vigrahavyāvartanī* (*VV* 5–6), Nāgājuna's opponent claims that if Nāgārjuna wants to prove non-essentiality of all things, then he should first identify them with the help of pramāṇas such as perception and inference. But even perception has no essence according to him. So how can he identify the things? In *VV* (17–19), the opponent claims that in order to establish non-essentiality of things through arguments, one has to give some reason (*hetu*). But according to Nāgārjuna, reasons also have no essence. So how can he establish anything on the basis of them?

43. '*na svābhāvikametad vākyam*' (*VV* 24). [This sentence does not have own-nature.]

44. *yadi kācana pratijñā tatra syādeṣa me bhaved doṣaḥ/*
nāsti ca mama pratijñā tasmānnaivāsti me doṣaḥ// (*VV* 29)

[This fault would apply to me if I would have stated my thesis (to be proved). But I have no thesis. Hence I have made no fault.]

The non-essentialist's statements are not assertions in this sense. Though his statements have the same grammatical structure as those of his opponents, their logical structure is different. What exactly is that logical structure? Nāgārjuna does not clarify this. He only confesses that a non-essentialist is making statements purely for illumination.[45]

One is tempted to understand the situation on the lines of early Wittgenstein: the statements like 'Everything is non-essential' 'show' something without 'saying' anything.[46] Here the difference between the approaches of Nāgārjuna and early Wittgenstein too should be noted clearly. Wittgenstein holds that there is a set of statements which are significant and hence demonstrably true or false. The statements of natural sciences belong to this set.[47] Second, Wittgenstein does not seem to question the common-sense beliefs. Nāgārjuna on the other hand criticizes all sorts of statements whether they belong to science or common sense.

Nāgārjuna's arguments not only question the so-called scientific statements and common-sense statements but also language and logic in general. Through some arguments in *Madyamakaśāstra*, Nāgārjuna questions the laws of logic and also the function of language. He tries to balance his view by presenting a two-truth-theory and by giving instrumental status to conventional truth (vyavahāra). But he also shows through his arguments how the conventional truth is delusive and corrupt. Hence, he does not really transcend the paradox of scepticism, but tries to transform it in the form of the ultimate truth, that is, void-ness.[48]

45. *śūnyamiti na vaktavyam aśūnyamiti vā bhavet/*
ubhayaṁ nobhayaṁ ceti prajñaptyarthaṁ tu kathyate// (*Madhyamakaśāstra* [*MSN*] 22.11)

[One should not say that things are void; one should not say that they are non-void, or both or neither. But all this is said (at conventional level) for illumination.]

46. Mohanta (1997) brings out the similarity between Nāgārjuna and Wittgenstein on these lines. He, however, seems to have overlooked the differences between their approaches.

47. 'The totality of true propositions is the total natural science (or the totality of the natural sciences)' (Wittgenstein 1971: 4, 11).

48. For a detailed discussion on this issue, see Gokhale (2010).

Śrīharṣa's Response

When we move from Nāgārjuna to Śrīharṣa, we find that Śrīharṣa's answer to the so-called paradox of scepticism is more formal and technical than truly philosophical. Debate for him is a linguistic practice governed by certain conventional rules (vyavahāra–niyama–*samaya*).[49] This is true of the negative type of debate (vitaṇḍā) as of any other type. Now it is not one of the rules of the negative debate that the debater has to believe in some means to knowledge.[50] The conventional rules are to be accepted and followed, after all, only as a matter of convention and not for any deeper reasons.[51] This answer of Śrīharṣa does not really take the paradox of scepticism seriously. Because when all means to knowledge will be refuted and the whole world including the discourse of knowledge and its objects (pramāṇa-prameya-vyavahāra) will be treated as undeterminable (*anirvacanīya*), the debate and the so-called rules will also have the same status.

Śrīharṣa does not find this situation problematic perhaps because, for him, indeterminability of the discourse of knowledge and its objects is not an end in itself, but it is supposed to be a part of his Advaita–Vedāntic programme. So the dualistic practices are not totally unreal; only they are not real in the ultimate sense. They do have an existence—an ignorance-based existence (*avidyā-vidyamānatvam*).[52] The ultimate reality, namely the pure conscious-

49. '*tacca vyavahāraniyamasamayabandhādeva dvābhyām api tābhyāṁ sambhāvyate* ...', (*KKK*, 1970, Pariccheda I, p. 15) [And it (= fulfillment of the desire to ascertain the truth or to win in a debate) is possible by any of the two parties only by accepting the bond of the conventional rules of debate.]

50. '*na ca pramāṇādīnāṁ sattāpītthamevobhābhyām aṅgīkartumucitā, tādṛśa-vyavahāra-niyamamātreṇaiva kathāpravṛttyupapatteḥ/*' (*KKK*, 1970, p. 17). [It is not proper for the two parties to accept by the same token the existence of means to knowledge and so on, because the debate can occur merely by accepting the rules of debate of that type.]

51. '*etat taducyate, vyāvahārikīṁ pramāṇādisattām ādāya vicārārambha iti*' (*KKK*, 1970, p. 22). [This is what is meant. The debate starts by accepting conventional existence of means to knowledge, and so on.]

52. '*na vayaṁ bhedasya sarvathaiva asattvam abhyupagacchāmaḥ. kiṁ nāma? pāramārthikamasattvam. avidyāvidyamānatvaṁ tu tadīyam iṣyata eva*' (*KKK*, 1970, p. 112). [We are not denying existence of difference at all levels. What then? Only at the ultimate level. We do admit its ignorance-based existence.]

ness or Brahman, on the other hand, is beyond the duality of knowledge and its objects and does not get refuted even if all knowledge is refuted. Existence of this pure consciousness, according to him is self-evident.[53]

It may be noticed here that Śrīharṣa's sceptical approach is half-hearted as he criticizes common-sense practices as undeterminable (anirvacanīya) but makes room for the metaphysical reality of *ātman–brahman*, which is beyond the subject–object duality of knowledge.[54] While establishing the existence of Brahman, he sometimes takes recourse to the verbal testimony of *śruti* as well.[55] Let us now consider Jayarāśi's approach which is the matter of our main concern.

Jayarāśi's Response

Jayarāśi does not refer explicitly to the possible charge of paradoxical character of the sceptical exercise. But his acceptance of naive (pre-reflective or non-reflective) common-sense-based practices (*avicārita-ramaṇīyāḥ vyavahārāḥ*)[56] implies an answer to such a charge. Such

53. *'vastutastu vayaṁ sarvaprapañcasattvāsattvavyavasthāpanavinivṛttāḥ svataḥsiddhe cidātmani brahmatattve kevale bharamavalambya caritārthāḥ sukhamāsmahe'* (*KKK*, 1970, p. 67). [In fact we are happy, as we refrain from establishing existence or non-existence of all the worldly practices and are satisfied by relying on the absolute reality called Brahman, which is self-evident and has consciousness as its essence.] Śrīharṣa's identification of self-evident consciousness with Brahman could be debated. It is true that some kind of consciousness is epistemologically implied by the operation of cognitive faculties even if the latter is erroneous. (This seems to be the Vedāntic analogue of the Cartesian Cogito; 'I am conscious of something, therefore, consciousness exists.') But this epistemic necessity leads neither to ontological existence of pure consciousness nor to the thesis that the ontological pure consciousness is the same as the eternal all-pervasive Brahman.

54. *'svaprakāśe tu mānameyavyavasthāyā abhāvādeva tadāśrayā doṣā niravakāśāḥ'* (*KKK*, 1970, p. 43). [Because there is no operation of means to knowledge and objects of knowledge in the realm of the self-illuminating reality, the faults based on them have no scope.]

55. Śrīharṣa here seems to contradict his own scepticism about pramāṇas, when he says: *'astu vā praśno'yaṁ yathā tathā, śrutirevādvaite pramāṇamiti brūmaḥ'* (*KKK*, 1970, p. 73). [Or, let the question be what it is; we say that Vedas are the authority for non-dualism.]

56. *TUS*, p. 125.

practices, according to him, are equally accepted by ignorant and learned people.[57] But learned persons and especially philosophers do not stop at the naive common sense. They try to find out some metaphysical categories or principles (tattva, paramārtha) which exist behind or beyond appearances and try to establish them with pramāṇas. Jayarāśi focuses his whole argumentative exercise against such metaphysical categories and pramāṇas used for proving them. The principles or categories which he makes his target are not necessarily idealistic or transcendental in nature. Even the pramāṇas and prameyas (knowables) which constitute materialistic metaphysics or enlightened common sense become the object of his sceptical attack. What escape his sceptical attack are the pre-reflective common-sense practices which are practically unavoidable for all. Jayarāśi's general standpoint thus rests on the dichotomous or split co-existence of scepticism and common sense. Jayarāśi's scepticism, in this way, may be called fragmentary scepticism because though it pervades intellectual sphere, it does not influence the practical sphere. It leaves untouched the naive common-sense practices.

Of course a question can be asked here: Though Jayarāśi succeeds in avoiding transcendental metaphysics, does he succeed in avoiding *any* kind of metaphysics (even common-sense metaphysics) whatsoever?

Approaches to Empirical and Ultimate Reality

The other way of distinguishing among the three sceptics is to compare their attitudes to empirical reality (vyavahāra) and ultimate reality (paramārtha). Nāgārjuna and Śrīharṣa both criticize the empirical reality by refuting all the means and objects of knowledge. At the same time, they have to accept the empirical reality as conventional reality which is necessary for the possibility of intellectual, philosophical exercise leading to the knowledge of ultimate reality, which is the ultimate goal of life according to them. Both of them accept empirical reality as having instrumental value for reaching the

57. '*lokavyavahāraṁ prati sadṛaśau bālapaṇḍitau*' (*TUS*, p. 1). [The ignorant and the learned are similar with respect to the worldly practice.]

ultimate reality. But what is the ultimate reality? Here the two sceptics fall apart. For Nāgārjuna, the ultimate reality is not ontologically different from or independent of the empirical reality. Realization of the non-essential nature of the empirical reality is itself the realization of the ultimate reality for him. Śrīharṣa on the other hand believes in the pure and eternal consciousness as the ultimate reality. Jayarāśi differs from both of them in an important way. Jayarāśi approves of the worldly practices (vyavahāra) but does not try to give any justification of them. According to him, if one reflects upon them philosophically, one does not reach any essence or ultimate truth (tattva). Therefore, according to him, it is advisable not to reflect upon them but entertain them at surface level. That is why he describes them as enjoyable, insofar as they are not reflected upon (*avicāritaramaṇīya*). But the sceptical refutation of the empirical reality, which induces Nāgārjuna and Śrīharṣa to transcend the level of empirical reality and embrace the ultimate reality, does not induce Jayarāśi to do so; rather it leads Jayarāśi to deny ultimate reality which he terms as tattvas. That is why Jayarāśi entitles his work '*Tattvopaplavasiṁha*' which means '(vigorous like) a lion in the act of refuting (all) tattvas'.

We saw that the ways in which the three sceptics respond to the paradox of scepticism are different. These differences are also related to the differences between the ways in which the empirical and ultimate reality are related in their philosophical schemes. This, I believe, throws light on the fact that even a sceptic while leading the life as a human and as a philosopher has to come to terms with common sense and that he may do so in the light of his general standpoint about life and the world. It partly explains how Nāgārjuna, Jayarāśi, and Śrīharṣa, in spite of their sceptical attitude towards the means and objects of knowledge, show an affinity to Buddhism, Lokāyata, and Advaita–Vedānta respectively.

The theme can be presented and formulated in a more general way. The affinity of a sceptic to specific philosophical school could be determined by many historical, intellectual, and psychological factors. Hence, the labels of the three schools of Indian philosophy, namely Buddhism, Lokāyata, and Advaita–Vedānta related to the three sceptics may not be that essential. What is more essential about them is that the different forms of scepticism they are advocating are three different configurations of the three concepts: scepticism, common sense, and metaphysical reality.

If the three forms of scepticism are understood in this broad sense, then we can find their analogues even in the history of Western scepticism. In what follows, I will give a brief sketch of the Western analogues of the three forms of scepticism.[58]

Locating Jayarāśi on a Global Map of Scepticism

Now, let us consider the three models of scepticism as they are found in the West. I have characterized them as: (*a*) scepticism subservient to transcendental revelation, (*b*) concerned scepticism, and (*c*) the dichotomous co-existence of scepticism and common sense:

Scepticism Subservient to Transcendental Revelation

Many sceptics who emerged in the Renaissance and Reformation periods represented what can be called fidelity-based scepticism. Here we find a combination of scepticism and faith. Erasmus (16th century), for instance, 'recommended the skeptical attitude of suspension of judgment along with acceptance of the churches view'.[59] Another philosopher, Michel de Montaigne, 'showed why all of man's rational achievements up to that point were seriously in doubt.' But, at the same time, 'he kept repeating that only through faith and revelation can real knowledge be gained'.[60]

Pierre Bayle, a sceptic, insisted that 'the point of his sceptical attack was to make men see that philosophy was an unsatisfactory guide and could only lead to doubts. Then perhaps, he insisted, they would abandon reason and turn to faith'.[61]

58. The sketch that follows is based on Richard Popkin (1967: 449–61).

59. Popkin (1967: 451).

60. Popkin (1967: 452).

61. Popkin (1967: 455). Some of the thoughts of Bayle overlap with what I have called concerned scepticism, when, for instance, he employs his scepticism as a justification for complete toleration. Second, he does not seem to insist on faith so much as other fideistic sceptics do.

Among existentialists, Kierkegaard can be identified as a fidelity-based sceptic.[62] This type of scepticism could be studied as the Western analogue of the Advaitic 'scepticism' of Śrīharṣa.[63]

Concerned Scepticism

The other variety of scepticism would be more concerned or engaged by its nature in the sense that it is an intellectual exercise aimed at the solution of the problem of human life through the development or maturation of scepticism itself.

Sextus Empiricus, the Pyrrhonian sceptic, for instance, by giving his sceptical argumentation tried to:

> lead mankind to the Pyrrhonian goal of *ataraxia* (unperturbedness). As long as people try to judge beyond appearance and to gain knowledge in the dogmatist's sense, they will be frustrated and worried. By setting forth the evidence pro and con, they will be led to suspension of judgment and peace of mind and thereby will be cured of the dogmatist's disease, rashness.[64]

Apart from various differences in details, the broad points of contact between the concerned scepticism of Sextus Empiricus and that of Nāgārjuna are interesting. Nāgārjuna held that to judge something as existent leads to eternalism and to judge something as non-existent to nihilism.[65] Both are expressions of fundamental craving.[66] He also refers to an essentialist viewpoint (*dṛṣṭi*) as a kind

62. 'Campus built on the fideistic skepticism of Kierkegaard and Leon Shestov ...' (Popkin 1967: 459).

63. The two also differ in that the fideistic scepticism of the West insists on faith as the source of divine knowledge whereas the Advaitic scepticism insists on direct awareness of revelation (*aparokṣajñāna* or *sākṣātkāra*) as the source. But I have pointed out in note 55 in this chapter that Śrīharṣa also takes recourse to *śruti* as the source of the knowledge of Brahman.

64. Popkin (1967: 450).

65. '*astīti śāśvatagrāhaḥ, nāstītyucchedadarśanam*' (*MSN* 15.10). ['Is' (that is, thinking about something that it is) is adherence to eternality. 'Is not' (that is, thinking of something that it is not) is the view of annihilation.]

66. Nāgārjuna correlated judgments concerning existence and non-existence with the two kinds of craving namely *bhavatṛṣṇā* and *vibhavatṛṣṇā* (that is, craving for becoming and craving for destruction) respectively (*MSN* 25.10).

of disease and realization of non-essentiality of everything as freedom from the disease.[67]

But there are important differences between Pyrrhonian sceptics and Nāgārjuna. While responding to the charge that the sceptical attitude may make living impossible, Pyrrhonians held that they were not doubting the world of appearances and that one could live peacefully and un-dogmatically in that world by following natural inclinations and the laws and customs of society.[68] Nāgārjuna's defense was different. Appearance and reality are not the basic pair-concepts in his scheme, as are conditional and absolute (*pratītya* and *a-pratītya*), and essential and non-essential (*sasvabhāva* and niḥsvabhāva). So, he would accept everything as conditional and non-essential and deny its status as absolute and essential. Second, though Nāgārjuna may accept customs, traditions and natural inclinations as conventional truths (*lokasaṁvṛti-satya*), he may accept them only provisionally and superficially. His philosophical exercise aims at transcending conventional truth and reaching ultimate truth. A Pyrrhonian sceptic would be satisfied with conventional truth; he will only avoid dogmatic adherence to it. To that extent, a Pyrrhonian sceptic would come closer to Jayarāśi, who accepts worldly practices at their surface level (the level un-reflected-upon).[69] This brings us to the third model of scepticism.

The Dichotomous Co-existence of Scepticism and Common Sense

The possibility of, or rather the need for the dichotomous or split co-existence of scepticism and common sense was indicated by David Hume. 'Hume showed that man was caught between a total Pyrrhonism that he could not refute and natural compulsion to believe in the future course of events, the reality of external world, the existence of some kind of personal identity, and possibly in some kind

67. Nāgārjuna equates *dṛṣṭi* (essentialist viewpoint) with a disease in *MSN* (13.8). This is suggested by his claim that those who hold *śūnyatā* itself as a dṛṣṭi are incurable. Also see Candrakīrti's commentary on this verse.

68. Popkin (1967: 450–1).

69. Matilal (1986: 68) has noticed similarity between Jayarāśi and Sextus Empiricus on the same line.

of intelligent force in the world.'[70] So reasoning or philosophizing leads to complete scepticism. Nature, on the other hand, prevents us from believing in or accepting the doubts that result from sceptical reasoning.

This dichotomous approach indicated by Hume seems to have been operationalized by George Santayana. He reduced common sense to animal faith when he said,

> I have imitated the Greek skeptics in calling doubtful everything that, in spite of common sense, anyone can possibly doubt. But ... life and even discussion forces me to break away from a complete skepticism ... I have frankly taken nature by the hand, accepting as a rule in my farthest speculations, the animal faith I live by from day to day.[71]

It is easy to see how Jayarāśi's scepticism would be an example of this kind. His notion of 'worldly practices [being] enjoyable insofar as they are not reflected upon' (*avicārita-ramaṇīya* vyavahāra) is closely comparable with Santayana's notion of animal faith.

***

Cārvākas in general were opposed to dogmatic beliefs of the religious philosophies of India. Jayarāśi joins other Cārvākas on this point when he criticizes the doctrines like that of other worlds and the soul. But his anti-dogmatic stance assumes an extreme form when he regards the possibility of knowing something for certain itself as a dogma. In this way he resembles the Western sceptics like Sextus Empiricus and David Hume.

Hume himself, however, was not a Pyrrhonian sceptic. He can be called a mitigated sceptic, whose scepticism, to a large extent, stemmed from his extreme form of empiricism. Unlike Pyrrhonian sceptics, Hume seems to accept the possibility of empirical knowledge to minimum extent. The closest Indian analogue of David Hume would be 'the extreme-empiricist Cārvāka' which is the theme for the next chapter.

70. Popkin (1967: 456).
71. Popkin (1967: 459); I have abridged the original quotation.

3

Extreme Empiricism in Cārvāka-darśana

Cārvāka-darśana is popularly known to accept extreme-empiricist epistemology, materialist ontology, and hedonistic–egoistic ethics. In this chapter, I will concentrate on the nature of extreme empiricism, according to which perception is the only means to knowledge and inference is not a means to knowledge at all. My main purpose here is to understand the extreme empiricism of Cārvākas with special reference to their refutation of inference as *pramāṇa*. Having done that, I will consider the implications of this extreme empiricism with respect to other aspects of the philosophy of Cārvākas, namely their ontology, axiology, and also their epistemology in general.

Some modern scholars such as Debiprasad Chattopadhyaya and Ramkrishna Bhattacharya have held that extreme empiricism (that is, the view that perception is the only pramāṇa) was not the genuine view of Cārvākas at all.[1] Bhattacharya claims that extreme empiricism was attributed to Cārvākas by their opponents. He also claims that the Cārvākas invariably accepted a certain kind of inference as pramāṇa. According to him it was the grammarian Bhartṛhari who criticized inference as pramāṇa and his criticism was wrongly attributed to Cārvākas by

1. Chattopadhyaya (1978: 22–4); Bhattacharya (2012: 80, 55–63).

Naiyāyikas and others. He claims that Naiyāyikas like Jayanta, while presenting Cārvāka criticism of inference, included verses from Bhartṛhari's *Vākyapadīya* (*VP*) without distinctly acknowledging their source.[2] Bhattacharya's claim is an exaggeration. Though Jayanta includes a few verses from Bhartṛhari's criticism of inference in his presentation of Cārvāka position, those verses are very few in proportion.[3] The Cārvāka criticism of inference presented by Jayanta contains many other critical arguments which must be having a source other than Bhartṛhari's philosophy of grammar. That other source is likely to be the Lokāyata tradition. In fact Bhattacharya himself, who otherwise refuses to attribute the criticism of inference to Cārvāka-darśana, acknowledges two aphorisms as genuine Cārvāka aphorisms, one of which restricts pramāṇa-hood to perception and the other which criticizes the pramāṇa-hood of inference.[4] To quote:

1. *pratyakṣam (ekam) eva pramāṇam.*
   [Perception is the only (single) authoritative means to knowledge.]
2. *pramāṇasya agauṇatvād anumānād arthaniścayo duralabhaḥ.*
   [An object can hardly be ascertained through inference because an authoritative means to knowledge is not secondary.][5]

Though the second aphorism seems to be an incomplete statement (and that is permitted in an aphorism), the intended meaning is clear.

2. Bhattacharya (2012: 151–2).

3. Out of twenty verses of the Jayanta's criticism of pramāṇa-hood of inference, (*Nyāyamañjarī* [*NM*], part I, pp. 108–9) only three verses are borrowed from *Vākyapadīya* (*VP*, v. I.32, I.34, and I.42).

4. Bhattacharya (2012: 80).

5. Jayanta quotes this passage that Chattopadhyaya and Gangopadhyaya translate as: 'Since pramāṇa must be non-secondary, and inference is secondary, it is very difficult to have ascertainment regarding an object through inference' (Chattopadhyaya 1990: 128). The statement has been explained in different ways. According to Jayanta's explanation, Cārvāka claims that the definition of *anumāna* in terms of *pakṣadharma*, *vyāpti*, and so on has to be interpreted by referring to secondary senses whereas the definition of *pratyakṣa* can be interpreted in its primary sense. Hence anumāna becomes secondary and ceases to be pramāṇa. Even in this explanation, the Cārvāka does not claim that inference is secondary pramāṇa. The editor of *Nyāyamañjarīgranthibhaṅga* (*NMGB*, p. 62, fn. 2) points out that this aphorism has been mentioned in a Buddhist text, Karṇagomiṭīkā, where the term *agauṇa* (non-secondary) is interpreted as *abhrānta* (non-erroneous). This interpretation is closer to my interpretation.

The meaning of this statement can be unpacked as follows: 'A pramāṇa (an authoritative means to knowledge) is non-secondary in its status; that is, a pramāṇa is worth its name only in the literal or strict sense of the term. It cannot be called pramāṇa in a secondary sense. Hence, inference is not a pramāṇa. Consequently, ascertainment of an object is not possible through inference.' Here I have translated the word 'pramāṇa' in the strict sense as an 'authoritative means to knowledge'. The aphorism implies that inference is not pramāṇa in the strict sense of the term. Hence, if this is a genuine Cārvāka aphorism, then the view of Chattopadhyaya and Bhattacharya that extreme empiricism is not a genuine Cārvāka view is one-sided and biased.

Bhattacharya interprets the earlier mentioned aphorism to mean that inference can be accepted as secondary pramāṇa (*gauṇa*-pramāṇa). Such an interpretation would be incorrect because the aphorism does not imply any distinction between primary and secondary (*mukhya* and gauṇa) pramāṇa. It simply denies the possibility that pramāṇa can be secondary. Hence, the aphorism does not support Bhattacharya's position. In order to allow the possibility of inference being secondary pramāṇa, the aphorism has to be set aside (not to be discarded altogether, but to be attributed to another school of Cārvākas) and other statements attributed to Cārvākas are to be considered, which explicitly accept inference as a means to knowledge. I will provide a detailed analysis of this in the next chapter, where I explore the possibility of using the term pramāṇa in both the senses, a strong one and a weak one, and then claim that those Cārvākas who accept a certain kind of inference as pramāṇa were using the word pramāṇa in a weak sense. In this chapter, however, I am concerned with the stronger sense of the word pramāṇa, which is accepted in the earlier discussed aphorisms.

It is true that there are also other schools besides that of Cārvāka that criticize inference as pramāṇa. Bhartṛhari does so in *VP* as mentioned previously. Śaṅkarācārya, in the commentary on the section called *Tarkāpratiṣṭhāna* (non-respectability of reasoning), points out many intrinsic defects in reasoning or inference (*tarka*), as a means to knowledge.[6] But there is a difference between the Cārvāka

6. Śaṅkara's commentary on the *Brahmasūtra*: '*tarkāpratiṣṭhānādapyanyathānu meyam iti ced evamapyavimokṣaprasaṅgaḥ*' (*Brahmasūtraśāṅkarabhāṣyam* [*BSSB*] 2.1.11).

approach to inference on the one hand and the approaches of Bhartṛhari and Śaṁkara, on the other. When Cārvākas criticize inference, they weigh its strength against perception and not against verbal testimony. On the other hand, when Bhartṛhari and Śaṁkara criticize inference, they weigh it against verbal testimony, particularly the testimony of Vedas.[7] The problem before the latter was that their opponents can use reasoning for challenging the 'truths' conveyed by the Vedas. So they point out the weaknesses of inference as pramāṇa and assign a limited role to it, namely that of supporting Vedic insights by reasons. Naturally they expected that an inference is acceptable if it is not contradicted by Vedic authority.[8] The view of the extreme-empiricist Cārvāka on the other hand, would be (and this would also be the view of mitigated-empiricist Cārvāka) that verbal testimony, if at all it is a genuine candidate for pramāṇa-hood, is an indirect means to knowledge. Hence, it is reducible to inference so that no special treatment needs to be given to it. Extreme empiricists would further say that all the objections against inference as pramāṇa would also be applicable against verbal testimony. Hence, I will now concentrate on the criticism of inference, made by the extreme-empiricist Cārvākas.

The extreme empiricism of Cārvākas can be stated in two statements:

1. Perception is pramāṇa.
2. There is no other pramāṇa.

7. Bhartṛhari stresses the importance of verbal testimony (*āgama*) against reasoning (tarka) in *VP* (v. I.30 and I.31). He asserts the importance of transcendental 'direct' knowledge of *Ṛṣis* and others as superior to inference and ordinary perception in *VP* (v. I.36–8 and I.41). Similarly Śaṅkara in *BSSB* (2.1.11), after criticising inference or reasoning for being essentially controversial, makes Vedas an exception to this defect: '*vedasya tu nityatve vijñānotpattihetutve ca sati vyvasthitārthaviṣayatvasyopapat teḥ tajjanitasya jñānasya samyaktvam atītānāgatavartamānaiḥ sarvairapi tārkikairapahnotum aśakyam.*' [(Unlike knowledge derived from inference,) the truth of the knowledge generated by Vedas cannot be denied by any logician, whether past, future, or present, because, that the Vedas have well-established content is evident from the fact that they are eternal and are the cause of knowledge.]

8. This was the approach of Manu also. '*ārṣaṁ dharmopadeśaṁ ca vedaśāstrāvirodhinā/ yastarkeṇānusandhatte sa dharmaṁ veda netaraḥ//*' (*Manusmṛti* [*MS*] 12.106). [No one else, but only he knows dharma, who corroborates the religious preaching of the *Ṛṣis* by reasoning which does not contradict with the Vedic system.]

Here the word 'pramāṇa' means an authoritative means to knowledge. It is not just a means to knowledge that *can* give a true cognition, but a means which *necessarily* provides true cognition. Cārvākas deny the status of pramāṇa to inference in this sense. They probably do not deny that inference can sometimes give us true cognition. For instance they do not deny that if one sees smoke on a hill and infers that there must be fire, it is quite possible (or 'probable') that one will actually find fire if one goes there. What they are denying is that there is a 'necessity' by which one 'must' find the fire there. 'Wherever there is smoke, there is fire' may be a fact of the limited, observed world, a fact which we have observed so far, but it cannot be established as universal or necessary truth, according to Cārvāka.

If such a universal or necessary statement of the concomitance between smoke and fire is not established as true, the inference of fire from smoke will remain unsound. It should be noted, however, that such an inference may not be invalid. Here we have to note the distinction between validity and soundness. By validity of inference we mean that characteristic of an inference on account of which its conclusion necessarily follows from its premises (whether the premises are true or false). By soundness of an inference, on the other hand, we mean that characteristic of an inference on account of which it is not only valid, but has true and only true premises. As a result, a sound inference is such that it necessarily yields a true conclusion. We cannot say so with respect to an inference, which is only known to be valid. Given that an inference is valid, it does not necessarily follow that its conclusion must be true.

Many 'standard' books on Indian philosophy spread a misunderstanding about Cārvākas that when they criticize inference as pramāṇa, they question the validity of inference. A cursory look into the works of well-known writers on Indian philosophy such as Hiriyanna, Radhakrishnan, Jadunath Sinha, and Chandradhar Sharma reveals this fact.[9] This misunderstanding is probably the consequence of a more general misunderstanding about the notion of *anumāna-pramāṇa* according to which it is translated as 'valid inference'. It is also about the notion of pramāṇa which is translated

9. Hiriyanna (1973: 190); Radhakrishnan (1996: 279); Warder (1971: 128); Sinha (1999: 266); Sharma (1973: 42–4).

as 'means of valid knowledge'. Of course these authors were probably using the term 'valid' in a very general and vague sense, such as 'acceptable', 'authentic', or 'error-free'. But this usage of the word in a vague sense becomes misleading particularly when one is talking about inference which is 'acceptable' in more than one ways. It may be formally acceptable when it is valid in the sense in which modern logic uses the word. It may also be suitable in another sense, if it yields a true conclusion (whether it is formally valid or not). It may be acceptable in a stronger sense when it is sound, that is, it is valid and all its premises are true. So when the extreme-empiricist Cārvākas maintain that inference is not pramāṇa, the sense in which they claim that inference is 'not acceptable' becomes an important issue. To interpret this view as the notion that 'inference is invalid' becomes thoroughly misleading. It becomes even more misleading when comparatively modern scholars like Chattopadhyaya,[10] Bhattacharya,[11] and Eli Franco[12] speak the language of pramāṇa-hood as validity, inference as being invalid, or inference as having 'limited validity' and so on. It should have been kept in mind, at least when modern logic uses the word valid in a special sense, that the notion of pramāṇa is primarily concerned with 'truth' and not with 'validity'. Further, the Cārvāka objection against inference as pramāṇa is not primarily about validity of inference, but about the question whether a formally valid inference (of a particular kind) necessarily yields truth. Even a valid inference may fail to yield a true conclusion if at least one of its premises is false. It is well known that Cārvākas raise the question about truth of one of the premises, namely, the statement of universal concomitance.

Second, it should also be noted that the Cārvāka criticism of inference (anumāna) *as* pramāṇa should not be taken as their criticism of inference in general. The word anumāna is generally translated in English as inference. But this translation is misleading. What is called anumāna in classical Indian epistemology is a special variety of 'inference', as it is understood in Western logic. Inference could be inductive or deductive and the latter too can be of various

10. Chattopadhyaya (1978: 22), for example, reports the 'generally assumed' view about Lokāyata that 'the Lokāyata denied the validity of inference'.

11. Bhattacharya (2012: 58, 63).

12. Franco (1987: 8).

kinds. For instance, the valid inferences in propositional logic and quantification logic differ from each other and those in relational logic differ from both (though they mix with each other to a large extent). Out of the varieties of inferences dealt with in different branches of Western logic, anumāna of Indian tradition would be close to BARBARA of syllogistic logic.[13] In quantification logic, it would be close to the inference, the proof of which involves the rules like universal instantiation, *modus ponens* and *modus tollens*.[14] In an inference of this kind one of the premises is a universally general statement which is the analogue of the statement of universal concomitance (*vyāpti*) in the 'inference for others' (*parārthānumāna*). Cārvāka criticism pertains to this type of inference. It is the criticism of a specific type of deductive inference, which is based on inductive generalization.

Hence, many scholars of Indian philosophy seem to have misconstrued the Cārvāka criticism of inference at least in two ways. First, it is construed as the criticism of inference in general or reasoning in general. Second, it is construed as a challenge to validity of inferences. We clearly see this confusion in Chattopadhyaya's

13. 'BARBARA' refers to a valid mood in the first figure in Aristotelian Syllogistic, in which both the premises and the conclusion are 'A-propositions' (that is, universal affirmative propositions). ['In medieval times each valid form of syllogism was given a name, the vowels in the name indicating the mood. Thus, AAA in the first figure was called Barbara' (Barker 1974: 67).] An example of BARBARA would be: 'All men are mortal. All Greeks are men. Therefore all Greeks are mortal.' Here 'all Greeks' stands for the class of all Greeks. It could be uniformly replaced by a unit class like 'Socrates'. In Indian logic, such an argument would be said to be based on positive concomitance (*anvaya-vyāpti*). Indian logicians would also recognize an equivalent formulation in which the major premise (concomitance premise) is replaced by its transposition such as: 'No immortal things are men.' The inference, which in this way involves negative concomitance as the major premise, will resemble the valid mood of the second figure CESARE of Aristotelian Syllogistic (see Randle [1924], as included in Ganeri [2001]).

14. Modus ponens and modus tollens are two valid forms of argument which are used as principles of deduction. In modus ponens, one is given conditional statement as the first premise. In the second premise one asserts its antecedent and thereby derives its consequent as conclusion. This resembles the inference based on positive concomitance. In modus tollens too, a conditional statement is given as the first premise. In the second premise one denies its consequent and thereby derives the negation of its antecedent as the conclusion. This resembles the inference based on negative concomitance (see Barker 1974: 122).

discussion of the alleged Cārvāka criticism of inference. This has given rise to further confusion between what he calls 'employing arguments for destructive purpose' and 'negative or destructive attitude to the validity of reasoning as such'.[15] It is true that Cārvākas made a destructive use of inference. (But such a use was made by all systems against their rival systems.) While doing so they did not necessarily have destructive attitude to arguments themselves. When they upheld a destructive attitude towards inference it was not against 'reasoning as such', but its particular form, namely deductive inference based on inductive generalization. And again this destructive attitude to inference did not pertain to its validity, but to soundness. Moreover, although Cārvākas were questioning soundness of inferences, they were not questioning the pragmatic utility of them (particularly of verifiable inferences and those justifying common sense). Conversely, although Cārvākas would allow verifiable inferences and common-sense inferences for practical purposes, their theoretical criticism of the soundness of inferences does not become out of place. It is important therefore to understand Cārvāka criticism of inference in its proper perspective.

Cārvāka criticism of inference as pramāṇa is found as the 'position to be refuted' (*pūrvapakṣa*) in many works by non-Cārvākas. Jayarāśi, a sceptic Cārvāka thinker, also advances arguments against inference as a means to knowledge as a part of his criticism of all means to knowledge. Philosophically, Cārvāka criticism of inference can be divided into two parts:

1. Dilemma of Inference: Cārvākas raise a dilemma which renders inference as problematic.
2. Arguments against Universal Concomitance: Cārvākas point out how universal concomitance, which is the basis of any inference (anumāna) cannot be ascertained.

Though these two parts of Cārvāka criticism are interconnected, each one of them has a distinct conceptual pattern. Hence it is elegant and also convenient to discuss them separately. So let us first discuss the dilemma of inference.

15. See Chattopadhyaya (1978: 22–33, particularly, 25–7).

Dilemma of Inference

Jayantabhaṭṭa in *Nyāyamañjarī* (*NM*) states the dilemma of inference as follows:

> Where is the case for inference? Because in the case of particular (*viśeṣa*) there is no connection; in the case of universal (*sāmānya*) there is redundancy [*siddhasādhana*, 'proving the proved']; and a particular qualified by universal is not tenable.[16]

This version of the dilemma is also found in *Nyāyakumudacandra* (*NKC*) of Prabhācandrasūri.[17] It can be understood as a trilemma concerned with the object of inference. The question raised here is whether the object of inference is (*a*) a particular, (*b*) a universal, or (*c*) a particular characterized by a universal.

Cārvākas point out that every alternative is riddled with some difficulty. Let me explain with reference to inference of fire from smoke.

1. Let us suppose that what one infers is a particular fire-item on the hill. Let us also suppose that one is inferring it on the basis of the particular fire-items one has seen in the kitchen and elsewhere. Now Cārvākas argue that the particular fire-items one has seen before and the particular fire-item one is inferring are all discrete items and there is no connection (*anugama*/*anvaya*) among them on the basis of which one can arrive at the knowledge of the particular fire-item on the hill from those seen in the kitchen and elsewhere.
2. Suppose somebody says that it is not a particular fire-item, but universal fire ('fire in general' or fire-ness) that we are inferring. Further, since universal fire is common to all particular fire-items, the connection among them can be established. Then the Cārvākas can be said to uphold that 'the (so-called) fire in general' is already proved (when we saw fire before). Hence, it is redundant to prove it again.

16. *viśeṣe'nugamābhāvāt sāmānye siddhasādhanāt/ tadvato'nupapannatvād anumānakathā kutaḥ//* (*NM*, part I, p. 108)

17. *NKC*, part I, pp. 69–70.

3. At this stage the opponent may come out with the third alternative that what we prove is not just a particular fire-item nor universal fire but a particular fire-item as characterized by the universal fire-ness. On this, Cārvākas say that 'the particular characterized by universal' is untenable, because there is no real thing called 'universal'.[18] Here Cārvākas seem to be joining hands with the Buddhists (such as Diṅnāga and Dharmakīrti) who claim that only particulars really exist, universals do not, as they are simply mental constructs. So particulars and universals cannot exist together such that one characterizes the other.

Jayarāśi's Version

Jayarāśi gives a slightly different version of the dilemma and uses it as an argument against different definitions of inference advanced by philosophers of rival schools.[19] He does not present it in the form of a trilemma, but as a dilemma consisting of the first two horns as follows:

1. If the object of inference is exclusively (viśeṣa) that of inference, then its concomitance with the mark (which is known through empirical observation) cannot be known and the knowledge of target-property will not *follow* from the knowledge of reason-property.[20]
2. If on the other hand the object of inference is common (sāmānya) to perception and inference, then it is redundant because the inference attempts to prove that which is already proved by perception.[21]

It is note-worthy here that although by the terms viśeṣa and sāmānya Jayarāśi is referring to the alleged objects of inference, now 'viśeṣa' means 'exclusive' (something which is exclusively the object of inference) and sāmānya means common (something which is common

18. *'vāstavaṁ hi na sāmānyaṁ nāma kiñcana vidyate/'* (*NM*, part I, p. 109). [There exists no real thing which is called 'a universal'.]
19. *TPS*, pp. 72–3, 82–3, and 89.
20. *'viśeṣe'nugamābhāvaḥ'* (*TPS*).
21. *'sāmānye siddhasādhyatā'* (*TPS*).

object of perception and inference). So the dilemma in Jayarāśi's version gets addressed to the relation between perception and inference. Jayarāśi applies this dilemma against the conceptions of inference presented by Naiyāyikas, Buddhists, as well as Mīmāṁsakas.

In Western logical tradition, we find some logicians presenting a dilemma of inference which is similar in some respects to the dilemma presented by Cārvākas. Cohen and Nagel, for instance, have presented the dilemma in the following words:

> If in an inference, the conclusion is not contained in the premise, it cannot be valid and if the conclusion is not different from the premises, it is useless; but the conclusion cannot be contained in the premises and also present novelty. Hence inferences cannot be both valid and useful.[22]

This dilemma differs from the dilemma presented by Cārvākas in two important respects:

1. The dilemma in Western tradition applies to any type of deductive inference whether purely propositional or quantificational or relational. But the inference to which Cārvāka's dilemma applies is a kind of quantificational inference where a particular conclusion is drawn from a universally general statement (that is, the statement of universal concomitance).
2. The dilemma in Western tradition focuses on validity of inference. As against this, the Cārvāka's dilemma is mainly concerned with pramāṇa-hood of inference, which, as observed before, is more about soundness than simple validity.

In spite of these differences there is a basic similarity between the two dilemmas. Both talk about deriving a proposition as conclusion from a given set of propositions which can be called premises. The questions they raise also have a basic similarity: either there is no sufficiently strong connection between premises and conclusion such that the conclusion necessarily follows from the premises, or the connection is too strong to assure any novelty in the conclusion.

Out of the two horns of the dilemma, the question of novelty or redundancy can be handled by bringing in psychological or practical

22. Cohen and Nagel (1976: 173).

considerations and by pointing to the limitations of human intellect to grasp complex necessary relations. What is logically obvious may not be psychologically so and hence a complex inference, though logically valid, may yield a 'novel' or non-superfluous conclusion (from psychological point of view). Similarly in Indian tradition, if universal concomitance (vyāpti) is given, the conclusion in its 'general form' follows necessarily because the universal concomitance is a general relation between reason-property (*hetu-dharma*) and target-property (*sādhya-dharma*) and the conclusion, if it too is of a general nature, is contained in it. Proving such a conclusion will be a case of 'proving the proved' (*siddhasādhana*). The question of unconnectedness (or that of there being no sufficiently strong connection between premises and conclusion) arises in the Western tradition if the argument is invalid. Such a question generally does not arise in Indian tradition, because the valid form of 'inferential statement' (whether it is a five-limbed formula or three-limbed formula) is more or less taken for granted (at least in Dharmakīrtian and post-Dharmakīrti stage of Indian logic).[23] But the question of unconnectedness or (of there being no sufficiently strong connection) arises between reason-property and target-property. This is the question of availability of universal concomitance (vyāpti/*avinābhāva*) which is one of the major issues raised by extreme-empiricist Cārvākas. In fact, this is the form ultimately assumed by Cārvākas' argument against pramāṇa-hood of inference.

Cārvākas' Arguments against Universal Concomitance

With the development of the theory of inference, universal concomitance (vyāpti) between reason-property and target-property assumed a more central and important position. It was accepted as the ground of inferential knowledge by all the systems, which accepted inference as pramāṇa. Hence, the Cārvāka criticism of inference also focuses on the notion of universal concomitance at this developed

23. I have tried to show in Gokhale (1992) that the nature of inference in the pre-Dharmakīrti stage of Indian logic was akin to analogical reasoning, whereas it assumed the form of a valid inference with the introduction of universal concomitance statement by Dharmakīrti.

stage. Inference can serve the purpose of an authentic means to knowledge if universal concomitance, which is its ground, can be ascertained. At this stage, Cārvākas argue that universal concomitance cannot be ascertained. We find this approach recorded and discussed in many Nyāya-Vaiśeṣika and Jaina epistemological and logical works.[24] In what follows I will state and discuss the argument presented in *NM*. The Cārvākas' argument recorded in *NM* can be formulated in two stages. At the first stage the Cārvāka argues that there probably are no laws of nature at all. At the second stage, this argument upholds that even if there are laws of nature, they cannot be known apodictically.

Stage One: There Are No Laws of Nature

Those who accept inference as pramāṇa presume that there is absolute regularity in nature. The idea behind this is that each thing in this world has its own nature or essence (*svabhāva*). That is why we can classify things according to their essences. For example, material elements were classified into four gross elements in accordance with their essential nature. Water has natural fluidity; fire is essentially hot; air has a non-hot-non-cold touch accompanied by colourlessness; earth has odour as its essence. In this way, all the elements have their essential characteristics and the former function and interact with each other according to the latter. Due to the essential nature of things, events occur in the world in an orderly way.

This view can be perceived as a form of the doctrine of essence (*svabhāvavāda*). Interestingly enough, svabhāvavāda is a view generally attributed to Lokāyatikas. The following aphorismic statement is quoted in this context:

> Laukāyatikas call self-nature as the cause of the world.[25]

24. To cite a few: *Nyāyabhūṣaṇam* (*NBu*, pp. 216ff.); *NM* (part I, pp. 112ff.); *NKC* (part I, pp. 69ff.).

25. '... *laukāyatikāḥ svabhāvaṁ jagataḥ kāraṇamāhuḥ*', quoted by Athavale (1997: fn. 54) from *Bṛhatsaṁhitā-vṛtti* (*BSV* 1.7). The sentence is followed by

> *svabhāvādeva jagad vicitramutpadyate, svabhāvato vilayaṁ yāti. tathā ca tadvākyam- kaḥ kaṇṭakānāṁ prakaroti taikṣṇyaṁ, vicitrabhāvaṁ mṛgapakṣiṇāṁ ca/ mādhuryamikṣoḥ kaṭutāṁ ca nimbe, svabhāvataḥ sarvamidaṁ pravṛttam//* (*BSV* 1.7)

This statement is not to be interpreted as providing a causal explanation of the world, or as denying causation in reducing it to chaos. Rather, it should be interpreted as the denial of theism. The main point here is that the orderly function of things and diversity among them is all due to their essential nature. The things possess their natures intrinsically; their respective natures are not conferred upon them by an external agency like God. So it is not necessary to seek a transcendent cause like God for explaining diversity and orderliness in the world. The doctrine of own-nature in this form denies the popular theistic causal explanation. If it can be said to offer a causal explanation, it does so in a minimal way.

The criticism of universal concomitance that we are considering now, however, questions even this minimalistic causal explanation of the world. Cārvāka as depicted here by Jayanta is denying the essential nature of things. This scepticism about the doctrine of own-nature can be explained as follows.

The basic idea in the notion of own-nature of a thing is that it is something constant or non-changing. For instance, we say that to burn is the very nature of fire. It implies that fire will cease to be fire if it stops burning. We also say that fire has the capacity to burn as a part of its very essence. However, contrary to this presupposition it is observed that the so-called capacities of things or essences of things change with the change in space, time, and states of

---

[The diverse world arises due to the own-nature and it ceases to exist too due to own-nature. This is what they say: Who causes sharpness in thorns and varied nature of animals and birds? (Who causes) sweetness of the sugarcane and bitterness of the Neam-fruit? All this has happened due to own-nature (of things).] *Sarvasiddhāntasaṅgraha* (*SSS* 2.4–5) contains similar statements of Cārvākas:

> *na kalpyau sukhaduḥkhābhyāṁ dharmādharmau parairiha/*
> *svabhāvena sukhī duḥkhī jano'nyannaiva kāraṇam//4//*
> *śikhinaś citrayet ko vā, kokilān kaḥ prakūjayet/*
> *svabhāvavyatirekeṇa vidyate nātra kāraṇam//5//*

[As for the pleasure and pain, the opponents should not imagine merit and demerit (as their causes). People become happy or unhappy by their own nature. There is no other cause.
Who makes peacocks colourful? Who makes cuckoos sing? There is no cause other than own-nature in this case.]

things.[26] Can one say, for instance, that fluidity and downward flow is the very nature of water? Contrary to this general presupposition it is also observed that water, if cooled down to zero degree centigrade, becomes solid, and if heated up to hundred degrees centigrade, becomes airy. So its fluidity and tendency to flow downwards change according to circumstances. Even the fact that heated water starts boiling does not occur uniformly as the temperature at which it boils varies according to its altitude. This would be the position of the accidentalist (*yadṛcchāvādin*) camp of Cārvākas who would question the belief in the uniformity of nature. It is like David Hume saying that we think that the future will resemble the past because of our belief in the uniformity of nature, which is rooted not in reason, but in habit or custom.[27]

It is possible to answer this sceptical argument from another camp of Cārvākas who are naturalists (*svabhāvavādin*) and not accidentalists. That things act differently at different times, locations, and states does not show that there are no laws of nature—only that they are complex. How exactly a thing functions differently in different circumstances itself becomes a part of the nature of the thing. In order to acknowledge and bracket this complexity scientists use the expression 'other things being equal' while giving an account of a law of nature.

Accidentalism (*yadṛcchāvāda*) is ontological scepticism and naturalism (svabhāvavāda) is ontological realism in relation to the laws of nature. But whether we accept ontological scepticism or realism, the epistemological scepticism with regard to the so-called laws of nature can still be maintained. This leads us to the second stage.

26. *deśakāladaśābhedavicitrātmasu vastuṣu/*
avinābhāvaniyamo na śakyo vastumāha ca//
avasthādeśakālādibhedād bhinnāsu śaktiṣu/
bhāvānām anumānena prasiddhir atidurlabhā// (*NM*, part I, p. 108)

[Things have varying nature subject to the difference of space, time, and state. Therefore it is not possible that there would be universal agreement. It has thus been said that since the various things differ in their powers (*śakti*) due to the change of the state, time, and space, it is hardly possible to determine the things by inference.]

This argument is also found in *VP* (I.32), which is an idealistic text in philosophy of grammar. Cārvākas might have borrowed it from that. It is also possible that this was not a part of the criticism of anumāna presented by extreme-empiricist Cārvākas, but Jayanta attributed it to them.

27. Hume (2007: 32, section 5.1.5).

Stage Two: Even If There Are Laws of Nature, We Cannot Know Them for Certain

At this stage, the Cārvākas accept for the sake of argument that there are laws of nature and that events happen not accidentally but according to certain laws. The question that they now raise is whether one can know any such law for certain. A law of nature would generally assume the form of an invariable or 'necessary' relation between two types of things/events, such that if α type of thing/event occurs, β type of thing/event must occur (or 'must have occurred' [in the past] or 'will occur' [in future]). This interrelation between two types of things/events was supposed to be natural (*svābhāvika*) and/or unconditional (*nirupādhika*). It is expressed in a negative way (*vyatireka*) as 'α cannot occur without β'. It is also expressed as a relation of pervasion (vyāpti) where α is said to be pervaded by β—which can be interpreted as a set-subset relation between the set of α-possessing entities and a set of β-possessing entities. If we designate the two sets as $S(\alpha)$ and $S(\beta)$ respectively then the relation can be expressed as $S(\alpha) \subset S(\beta)$.

Such a relation is said to hold, for example, between smoke and fire. The different expressions of the relation would be:

Wherever there is smoke there is fire.
If there is smoke there must be fire.
Smoke cannot exist without fire.
Smoke is pervaded by fire.

All Indian philosophical systems except Cārvāka-darśana believe that such a relation holds between smoke and fire and that it can be known for certain. Systems differ in their explanation of the exact nature of this relation and the way the relation is known. For Buddhism it is essentially a causal relation;[28] for other systems the relation of invariable concomitance need not necessarily be based on a causal relation. Similarly different systems suggested different ways of ascertaining the relation, to which I will turn soon. The most common element of these different ways was 'observation and non-observation'; that is, for example, observation of smoke with fire

28. This is the approach of the Buddhist logicians such as Dharmakīrti. It will be discussed in this chapter under the title 'Mental Construction of Universal Concomitance'.

(*sahacāra-darśana*) and non-observation of smoke without fire (*vyabhicāra-adarśana*). It was held on the basis of this dual method that we can ascertain that smoke cannot exist without fire.

As against this, the Cārvākas point out that even if one observes smoke a hundred times with fire and never sees smoke without fire, one cannot rule out the possibility that smoke may exist without fire.[29] By repeated observation one gets, at the most, a high probability of smoke existing with fire,[30] but no necessity in it. For knowing fire for certain on the basis of smoke, what one needs is the ascertainment of a necessary relation between them, but that is not possible.

This is the gist of the Cārvāka scepticism above the knowledge of universal concomitance as found in the works like *NM*. It highlights the basic limitations of human knowledge concerning the laws of nature.

The Cārvāka scepticism about the knowledge of universal concomitance closely resembles Hume's scepticism about induction.[31] Hume questions rationality of our belief in the uniformity of nature, which implies that the future will resemble the past. He also questions causation that is regarded as a matter of necessity. According to him, when we observe two events occurring in sequence, they cause an impression of their conjunction. One may go beyond a single case and experience constant conjunction of similar pairs of events. But this constant conjunction, Hume argues, cannot produce a necessary connection. He explains this in terms of the three modalities: necessity, possibility, and impossibility. All these elements of Hume's account of the problem of induction are found in the Cārvākas' criticism of inference.

Hume's theory of induction has two aspects, negative and positive. The discussed account of the problem of induction constitutes the negative aspect of his theory. The positive aspect consists of his psychological explanation of induction, which he gives in

29. 'By repeated observation this much only may be ascertained, that smoke is associated with fire; but it can never be established by repeated observation that smoke is never present in a place where there is no fire' (Chattopadhyaya 1990: 131). For the translation of the detailed argument, see Chattopadhyaya (1990: 128–32).

30. This view will be discussed towards the end of the chapter.

31. My account of Hume's problem of induction is based on the article 'David Hume' by Morris (2013). Cārvāka argument against the knowledge of universal concomitance appears on the scene in 7th or 8th century and Hume's argument against inductive knowledge in the 17th century. But I am concerned here with the similarity of argument and not with the chronological gap.

terms of habit, custom, and association of ideas. One does not find any such element in the Cārvāka criticism of inference. Another positive element in Hume's theory was his introduction of the notion of probability, which acquired importance in due course as a part of the scientific method. As I will indicate later, the germs of the theory of probability are also found in the Cārvāka criticism of inference.

Responses to Cārvāka Scepticism about Universal Concomitance

As against the Cārvāka scepticism about the knowledge of universal concomitance, the opponents of Cārvākas, such as Sāṅkhyas, Nyāya-Vaiśeṣikas, Buddhists, and Jainas claimed that the certain knowledge of the laws of nature is possible. They explored different ways to show how that was possible. It is possible to consider critically these different ways from Cārvāka point of view. The problem of the knowledge of universal concomitance needs to be considered in this broader perspective.

In the context of the Indian philosophical tradition, when we talk about the knowledge of universal concomitance, the first question that would be asked is, if the universal concomitance can be known, by what means (pramāṇa) can it be known? To be more precise, can the universal concomitance be known through perception or inference or verbal testimony? Do we need an independent means to the knowledge of universal concomitance, or, can it be ascertained without any pramāṇa? Some of the above alternatives were proposed by certain philosophical systems. Some are not actually proposed by any one, but they can be considered as theoretical possibilities. We will discuss them all in order to get a comprehensive view of the matter. Let us consider the case of verbal testimony, it being the weakest, and then turn to other alternatives.

Verbal Testimony (Śabdapramāṇa)

Can verbal testimony be regarded as the means to the knowledge of universal concomitance? There are two major difficulties in doing so.

1. Suppose one grants that sometimes one does know universal concomitance on the basis of verbal testimony. The question

is whether one can universalize this. Suppose I know from my father, who is a reliable person (RP_1) for me, that wherever there is smoke, there is fire, and suppose my father knew it from another reliable person (RP_2) and he again from some third (RP_3), then this will go on ad infinitum (because we have presumed that universal concomitance can be known only through verbal testimony). To break this infinite chain, we have to presume that someone must have known the universal concomitance from a source other than verbal testimony.

2. The second difficulty arises because verbal testimony is reducible to inference, and if the view that universal concomitance is knowable through inference is not acceptable, so is the view that it is knowable through verbal testimony. We will soon see how the former view is not acceptable. That verbal testimony is reducible to inference can be shown in the ensuing paragraph.

In fact, two inferences are involved in the process of knowing a fact from the sentence uttered by a reliable person. At the first stage, the listener infers the meaning intended by the speaker on the basis of the words uttered. In this inference, the word–meaning relation, though conventional, serves as concomitance relation. At the next stage, the listener infers that the meaning intended by the speaker corresponds to facts. Here the listener's belief that whatever the speaker says (in the relevant situation) is true to facts (that is, the speaker is a knowledgeable person and does not deceive others), serves as the judgement of the concomitance relation which could be based on the listener's prior experience about the speaker. (The two inferences are made so rapidly that even the listener may not recognize that he is making two logically distinct inferences.)

Perception

There are systems which hold that universal concomitance can be known through perception. Primarily, there are two positions which come under this. According to one position, universal concomitance can be known by ordinary perception which has external particulars as its objects. Mīmāṁsakas[32] and some Naiyāyikas uphold this view. The other position would be that universal concomitance can be known through a kind of extraordinary perception. This view was again held by some Naiyāyikas. Hence the question whether universal concomitance is knowable through perception can be split into two:

1. Is it knowable through ordinary perception?
2. Is it knowable through extra-ordinary perception?

Let us consider these alternatives.

1. Ordinary Perception

While examining this view one has to also consider non-perception. According to this view, one can ascertain a universal relation between smoke and fire because one has perceived smoke with fire several times but has not seen smoke without fire. This view is held by Mīmāṁsakas and Naiyāyikas with some variation. Mīmāṁsakas are known for their view that if we repeatedly observe (*bhūyodarśana*) smoke with fire and never observe smoke without fire, then we can legitimately form the statement of universal concomitance, 'Wherever there is smoke, there is fire.'[33] Naiyāyikas do not accept 'repeated observation' as the means to the knowledge of universal concomitance on technical grounds. It cannot be decided as to how many times one has to observe the co-existence of smoke and fire, whereas the knowledge of the concomitance relation occurs at one point of time and not several times. So technically, only one perception of co-existence, which may be preceded by such several perceptions, ascertains universal concomitance.

32. As Kumārilabhaṭṭa says, '*bhūyodarśanagamyā ca vyāptiḥ*' (*Ślokavārtikam* (*SV*), Anumāna-pariccheda, 12). [The pervasion (between reason-property and target-property) is knowable by repeated observations.] And Vācaspatimiśra in *Nyāyavārtikatātparyaṭīkā* (*NVTT*) says, '*bhūyodarśanajanitasaṁskārasahitam indriyam eva dhūmādīnāṁ vahnyādibhiḥ svābhāvikasam-bandhagrāhi iti yuktam utpaśyāmaḥ*' (*NVTT* 1.1.5, p. 140). [We think it right that it is nothing but the sense organ accompanied by the impression caused by repeated observations, which grasps the natural connection of things like smoke with those like fire.]

33. See Kumārila's view in note 32 in this chapter.

The main difficulty with the proposal that we ascertain universal concomitance on the basis of ordinary perception—whether one occurrence or many occurrences of it—is that through a single ordinary perception we can observe only a single, specific case of co-existence (and by a group of ordinary perceptions, a group of specific cases of co-existence), whereas the very nature of the universal concomitance is that it is universal, referring to all particulars (past, present, and future) of a kind. For example, when one says 'wherever there is smoke there is fire', one is referring to all the locations in the world—past, present, and future—where there is smoke. Similarly since the statement implies that 'wherever there is no fire, there is no smoke', one is also referring to all locations—past, present, and future—where there is no fire. By ordinary perception (or by a group of such perceptions) one cannot grasp all these locations.

This objection is raised mainly by Cārvākas, but it is also indicated by Buddhists, particularly by the Buddhist logician Dharmakīrti. Having raised the objection that we cannot ascertain invariable concomitance by perception and non-perception, Dharmakīrti comes out with an alternative proposal that it is causality and identity which are the grounds of an invariable relation. Dharmakīrti's proposal will be discussed later. Cārvākas, however, consider their objection as conclusive and final. As against this, some Naiyāyikas[34] try to make a case for 'perceptual knowledge of all particulars of a kind' by introducing a kind of extraordinary perception (*alaukikapratyakṣa*). This suggestion of these Naiyāyikas needs to be examined.

2. Extra-ordinary Perception

Naiyāyikas in their development of the theory of perception, classify perception as follows:[35]

In the knowledge of universal concomitance, one is concerned with the first type of extraordinary perception, that is, perception based on universal as the extraordinary sense-object contact. The idea behind this type of extraordinary perception will now be discussed.

34. Chatterjee (2008: 192, 228).

35. This classification is accepted in the Nyāya-Vaiśeṣika works like *Tarkasaṁgraha* of Annambhaṭṭa and *Nyāyasiddhāntamuktāvali* of Viśvanātha-Nyāyapañcānana.

According to Naiyāyikas, we can see smoke (a particular line of smoke) by ordinary perception. Almost every particular according to them has a universal characteristic in terms of which we identify the particular as a member of a class. For example, when one sees a smoke item, one can identify it as belonging to the class of smokes. In Nyāya language, this means that one identifies it as possessing the universal (sāmānya/*jāti*) called 'smoke-ness'. This universal smoke-ness being a universal has special ontological features according to Naiyāyikas. It is all-pervasive and eternal because smoke-ness is the common property shared by all smokes—past, present, and future—belonging to all locations in the universe. In this way, smoke-ness which the observer sees in one smoke-particular connects him, as it were, to all smoke-particulars in the world. Knowledge of all smokes through the knowledge of 'smoke-ness' in one smoke is a case of extraordinary perception according to Naiyāyikas. Here smoke-ness in one smoke itself serves as the sense-object-contact. Naiyāyikas also submit that by this extraordinary perception of all smokes, one does not know all the smokes with their specific characteristics, but only as having the general characteristic, namely smoke-ness.

In this way, Naiyāyikas try to make a room for perceptual knowledge of 'all smokes' and 'all fires' in order that the knowledge of the universal truth 'wherever there is smoke, there is fire' becomes possible. Whereas this kind of knowledge cannot be explained in terms of ordinary perception, they explain it in terms of extraordinary perception. It can be doubted, however, whether a satisfactory

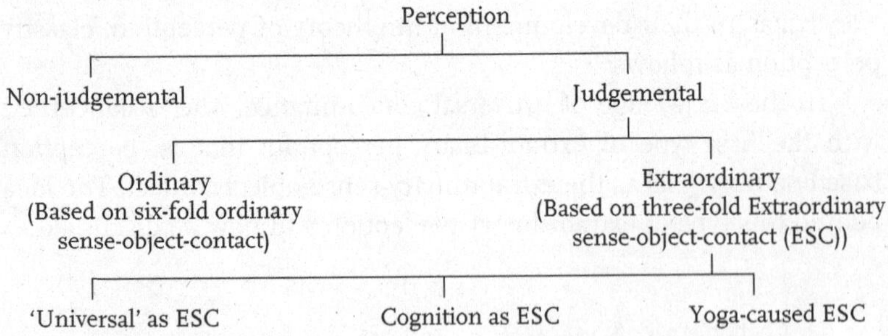

FIGURE 3.1 Nyāya-Vaiśeṣika Classification of Perception
Source: *Tarkasaṁgraha* (*TSa*: 211–20).

explanation of the knowledge of universal concomitance can be given by taking recourse to extraordinary perception of the kind mentioned earlier. By universal-based extraordinary perception, if at all it makes sense to say that it is a kind of genuine veridical perception, one can perhaps know all smokes (as smoke) and all fires (as fire). But one will not know any of their other characteristics. Hence one will not know whether all these smokes are accompanied (or preceded) by fire. Similarly one will not know that there is a necessary relation between smoke and fire such that smoke cannot exist without fire. And unless one knows these things, one cannot be said to have known the invariable relation between smoke and fire.

More basically, the idea of extraordinary perception is itself not acceptable to Cārvākas. In the universal-based extraordinary perception, with which we are concerned here, Naiyāyikas presuppose the existence of universals, which are eternal and all-pervasive. Only because of that, a universal connects one particular in which it inheres with all particulars of its kind. The existence of universals is not acceptable to Cārvākas.[36] As a result, there is no 'knowledge' of all the things of a kind based on the knowledge of 'universal' belonging to one thing of that kind. When one sees smoke and identifies it as smoke, one is able to imagine or conceive how other things in the world, which are called smoke, would be like. But this does not mean that one 'knows' all the smokes that are (and were and will be) there in the world. Hence, the Nyāya view that universal concomitance can be known by universal-based extraordinary perception is not satisfactory.

Inference (Anumāna-pramāṇa)

While examining this possible explanation of the knowledge of universal concomitance, it should be made clear once again that by inference, what is understood here is not inference in general but a special variety of inference in which one of the premises is a statement of universal concomitance. So, here one is asking a question whether universal concomitance can be ascertained on the basis of an inference which is itself based on the statement of universal concomitance. In other words, one is asking whether a universal

36. See note 18.

concomitance can be ascertained only on the basis of another universal concomitance. The answer is that though there are occasions when one universal concomitance can be derived from another one, we cannot accept it as a universal rule. One can even have a chain of concomitances in which the earlier one is derived from the next one; this chain must stop somewhere, where the last one cannot be further derived from another concomitance. The point can become clear from the following chain of arguments:

1. (a) All humans are mortal.
   (b) Socrates is human.
   (c) Therefore Socrates is mortal.
2. (a) All animals are mortal.
   (b) All humans are animals.
   (c) Therefore, all humans are mortal.
3. (a) All conditioned things are perishable.
   (b) All animals are conditioned things.
   (c) Therefore, all animals are perishable (mortal).

Here we have three arguments (1), (2), and (3). In each argument, the step (a) is a statement of universal concomitance (vyāpti), while (b) states the existence of reason-property in the subject (*pakṣadharmatā*), and (c) is the conclusion.

[(1) (a)] which is the concomitance-statement of the first argument is the conclusion [(2)(c)] of the second argument. The second argument is based on the concomitance-statement [(2) (a)], which is the conclusion [(3) (c)] of the third argument. The third argument contains a concomitance-statement, [(3) (a)]: 'All conditioned things are perishable.' This can be regarded as an identity statement in Buddhist framework, but it is not a conclusion of another inference. Hence, the process of deriving one concomitance from another concomitance comes to an end here. This implies that there must be at least a few statements of universal concomitance which are not established by inference, but are established, if at all they can be, by some other means to knowledge. For example, Jainas suggested that tarka should be accepted as an independent form of knowledge through which we know general truths such as the universal concomitance.

Tarka-pramāṇa

Jaina logicians after Siddhasena-Divākara (6th century AD) became clearly aware of the problem about the knowledge of universal concomitance. They became aware that if inference is an authoritative means to knowledge and that knowledge of universal concomitance is a necessary pre-requisite of inferential knowledge, then we have to regard the knowledge of universal concomitance as a different type of knowledge not subsumable under the already accepted forms of knowledge, such as perception (ordinary or extraordinary), inference, and verbal testimony. They called this new form of knowledge 'tarka'.

Jainas defined tarka as the knowledge arising from observation and non-observation, of the relation between the terms such as reason-property and target-property which exists in all the three time periods?[37]

Now the question is whether introduction of tarka as an independent form of knowledge can give satisfactory explanation of the knowledge of universal concomitance. It can be noticed in the given definition of tarka that it again refers to observation and non-observation as the basis of the knowledge of universal concomitance. It appears that observation and non-observation are necessary for the knowledge of universal concomitance (except when the latter is understood as analytic relation or the relation based on identity). Given that in smoke–fire case one has observed smoke only with fire and never without fire, the question that now arises is how does tarka, which is an independent form of knowledge, lead one to the universal and necessary statement that wherever there is smoke, there must be fire? Jainas do not give any explanation of this. One could either say here that on the basis of observation and non-observation one has an intuitive grasp of the universal relation or that one conducts an exercise in reasoning (inductive reasoning) based on the data collected

37. Consider for example Vādidevasūri's definition of tarka as given in *Pramāṇanayatattvāloka*: '*upalambhānupalambhasambhavaṁ trikālīkalitasādhyasādhanasambandhādyālambanam idamasmin satyeva bhavatītyākāraṁ saṁvedanam ūhāparanāmā tarkaḥ.*' ['Knowledge of the form, "this being this is", etc., arising from apprehension and non-apprehension, and consisting of the establishment of a relationship which subsists in all the three times, such as the relationship between the proven and the mark, is tarka or inductive reasoning otherwise known as *ūha*.'] See Antarkar, Gokhale, and Katarnikar (2011: 83).

from observation and non-observation. Jainas do not say any of these things and hence the logical status of tarka as pramāṇa remains unclear.[38] Modern scholars, have a tendency to interpret tarka–pramāṇa of Jainism with inductive reasoning. But it is doubtful whether inductive reasoning can be regarded as an adequate means to the knowledge of universal concomitance.

Inductive Reasoning

In Western logic and philosophy of science, it is generally held that we reach the general truths such as 'all men are mortal' or 'wherever there is smoke there is fire' by inductive reasoning. In the Indian tradition too, inductive reasoning or generalization is accepted in some form or other, but it is rarely given the status of pramāṇa. Modern scholars, as mentioned earlier, have a tendency to interpret tarka-pramāṇa of Jainism with inductive reasoning. Similarly *yukti-pramāṇa* introduced in *Carakasaṁhita* (*CS*)[39] can be regarded as a form of inductive generalization.

38. Jainas must have borrowed the term 'tarka' with its cognate term 'ūha' from Gautama's *Nyāyasūtra* where tarka is accepted as one of the sixteen basic concepts of Nyāya and is defined as a kind of ūha (reasoning). Naiyāyikas explained 'tarka' as a kind of 'ūha' related to a cause–effect relation or sign-signified relation in general, leading to the knowledge of truth. Later on, the Nyāya philosopher Udayana developed the notion of *reductio ad absurdum* (*aniṣṭa-prasaṅga*) and identified tarka with it. Tarka at this stage was treated as hypothetical reasoning indicating how a thesis, if accepted, leads to undesirable consequences. Naiyāyikas regarded this tarka as a useful tool for ascertaining invariable concomitance, but never gave it the status of pramāṇa. This could have been due to their dogmatic adherence to the theory of four (and only four) pramāṇas. As compared to this, Jainas developed a more elastic and open approach to pramāṇas. They recognized the forms of knowledge like memory (*smṛti*), recognition (*pratyabhijñā*), and inductive reasoning (tarka) as pramāṇa, which were not acknowledged as pramāṇa in other systems. For explaining inductive generalization as a form of knowledge, they adopted the Nyāya notion of tarka as a tool for knowing universal concomitance, and elevated its status to an independent pramāṇa. However, the question remains whether Jainas brought out the logical status of tarka clearly.

39. '*buddhiḥ paśyati yā bhāvān bahukāraṇayogajān/yuktistrikālā sā jñeyā trivargaḥ sādhyate yayā//*' (*Carakasaṁhitā* [*CS*], Sūtrasthāna, 11.24). [The cognition which sees things as arising from collocation of multiple causes should be known as *yukti* which has (things in) all the three times (as its object). It is the one by which the class of the three (goals) is achieved.] Here also the expression 'paśyati' (sees, intuits [?]) is significant. The word 'yukti' can also mean reasoning/argument. But Caraka seems here to associate the word 'yukti' with *yoga* (collocation) than with reasoning.

Modern scholars tend to translate 'tarka' as inductive reasoning because the word 'tarka' (or its cognate term 'ūha') in its primary sense means reasoning. Even if we grant that according to Jainas, 'tarka' means the knowledge of universal concomitance based on inductive reasoning, the problem of induction (raised by Cārvākas in the East and David Hume in the West) remains insuperable. Pramāṇa should give us certain, indubitable knowledge. But tarka, understood as inductive reasoning, cannot give us certain or indubitable knowledge of invariable concomitance. Hence it will cease to be a pramāṇa.

As against this, one might say that 'tarka' is defined by Jainas as the resultant knowledge of universal concomitance and not as the process which leads to it. The process could have the form of inductive reasoning. The resultant knowledge, however, may not be of the nature of reasoning; it could be just a kind of intuition into which the inductive reasoning culminates. But now there are some basic questions about intuition.

Intuition or Internal Perception

Though this view is not conclusively held by any system of Indian philosophy, the Nyāya logicians like Jayantabhaṭṭa regarded mental perception (*mānasa-pratyakṣa*) as the means to the ascertainment of universal concomitance.[40] The role of intuition is acknowledged by some Western logicians in inductive generalization.[41]

Here one takes recourse to intuition because one cannot have sensory perception of 'the general truth' (vyāpti) with which one is concerned. One has sensory perception of the co-existence between a

40. *tatra kecidācakṣate mānasaṁ pratyakṣaṁ pratibandhagrāhīti pratyakṣānupalambhābhyām analasahacaritam anagneśca vyāvartamānaṁ dhūmam upalabhya vibhāvasau niyato dhūma iti manasā pratipadyate* (*NM*, part I, p. 110)

[On this issue some say that mental perception causes one to grasp the connection. Having cognized through perception and non-perception the smoke as concomitant with fire and as excluded from non-fire, one knows by mind that smoke is necessarily related with fire.]
That this was Jayanta's own view is substantiated by Jayanta's concluding remark as '... *manasā niyamajñānasiddherityalaṁ nirbandhena*' (*NM*, part I, p. 112). [... because it is proved that the necessary relation is known by mind. So don't insist any more.]

41. Cohen and Nagel (1976: 275) cite W. E. Johnson who understands induction as intuition and calls it intuitive induction.

particular smoke and a particular fire, but not of the universal relation between smoke and fire. The intuitive cognition of a general truth may be psychologically caused by the sensory perception (and non-perception) of individual cases and also the rational process of inductive generalization, but it is not logically necessitated by these empirical and rational processes. Hence, the intuitive grasp of universal concomitance will not have the necessity and objectivity that one expects from pramāṇa. Suppose there are two persons, each one of whom observes smoke and fire together several times—they see neither smoke without fire nor fire without smoke—then it is possible that one of them will form on the basis of this common background a universal statement of the form 'wherever there is smoke there is fire' and the other one might form the converse of the above universal statement, that is, 'wherever there is fire, there is smoke'. Here the first one has intuition of a correct universal statement whereas the second one has intuition of an incorrect universal statement. Intuition here has no role in judging as to which one is correct and which is not correct. Jayantabhaṭṭa's proposal that universal concomitance can be ascertained through mental perception (mānasa-pratyakṣa) is defective for the same reason.

I have tried to argue that the Jainas' proposal that universal concomitance can be ascertained by an independent pramāṇa called tarka is not clear enough and it does not provide a stronger alternative to the other views concerning the knowledge of universal concomitance. The proposal is not satisfactory whether one interprets tarka as 'inductive reasoning' or 'intuitive or mental perception based on inductive reasoning'.

Hence, the proposals for explaining the knowledge of universal concomitance, such as those in terms of repeated observation, observation and non-observation, intuition, inductive generalization, and mental perception are all unsatisfactory mainly because they fail to provide logically sufficient grounds for forming statements of universal concomitance and making inferences. This was the main objection Cārvākas raised against the theory of 'repeated observation' as we have seen in Jayantabhaṭṭa's exposition in *NM*. I have tried to show previously that this objection can be levelled against other theories of the knowledge of universal concomitance as well. This brings us to the last alternative according to which the universal concomitance is not 'known' through any pramāṇa, but it is mentally constructed in terms of necessity.

Mental Construction of Universal Concomitance

Buddhist logicians since Dharmakīrti were aware of the defect in the theory of 'observation and non-observation'. But unlike Cārvākas, they tried to provide a logical ground to the possibility of forming a statement of universal concomitance. According to the Buddhist logician Dharmakīrti, the law of invariable relation (*avinābhāva-niyama*) is mentally constructed by us on the basis of necessity (in the form of causation or identity). Though this mental construction is the basis of inference as pramāṇa; this itself, for technical reasons, cannot be given the status of pramāṇa.

According to Dharmakīrti, though one may not reach a universal truth just on the basis of observation and non-observation of limited number of cases, it may be possible to reach universality through a different route—the route of necessity. If somehow one comes to know the necessary connection between α and β such that α cannot be there without β, then we can be sure that in every case of α there must be β. In that case it is not necessary to observe innumerable cases of α and β. As he says in *Pramāṇavārtika* (*PV*):

> The universal law of invariable relation [avinābhāva-niyama] is not established on the basis of observation and non-observation, but by either of the two principles (i) effect–cause relation (ii) identity of two essential aspects of a thing.[42]

These two principles suggested by Dharmakīrti give two forms of necessity. He claims that if a necessary relation holds between the reason-property and the target-property, such that they are two numerically different objects, then they are necessarily linked with each other through causality. The relation can be brought out by saying that the reason-property exists only because of (that is, only as caused by) the target-property. Hence the relation between the two properties would be called causality (*tadutpatti*). If, on the other hand, the two

42. *kāryakāraṇabhāvād vā svabhāvād vā niyāmakāt/*
avinābhāvaniyamo'darśanānna na darśanāt// (*Pramāṇavārtikam* [*PV*] 3.31)

properties are not distinct but are two aspects of one and the same thing, then they can be necessarily related to each other if the thing cannot have the reason aspect without having the target aspect. In this case, the relation between the two aspects would be identity (*tādātmya*). Out of the two types of relations, smoke-fire case belongs to the former kind. Accordingly, the existence of fire is inferred from the existence of smoke not on the basis of their observed co-existence and non-observation of smoke without fire, but on the basis of causal necessity which holds between the two.

The latter type of necessary relation is a kind of containment relation between two aspects of one and the same thing. A narrower aspect is said to be contained in ('pervaded by'—vyāpta) the broader aspect such that if a thing has the former, then it must have the latter. The stock example given by Buddhists is, 'This must be a tree, because it is a *śiṁśapā*.' Śiṁśapā is a species of a tree. Suppose there is a śiṁśapā tree before us. Then, 'being a śiṁśapā' is its narrower aspect, contained in (pervaded by) the broader aspect namely 'being a tree'. We can also say that there is partial identity between the two so that 'every śiṁśapā is a tree, but every tree need not be a śiṁśapā'. In the Western philosophical tradition, a statement like 'every śiṁśapā is a tree' would be called an identity-statement or analytic statement. It can be compared with the statements like: 'Every brother is a male' and 'every human being is an animal'. These statements are true in virtue of the meanings of the terms contained in them. We are not required to observe the relevant facts in order to confirm the truth of these statements.[43]

When Cārvākas raise objections against the ascertainment of universal concomitance, they do not refer to the type of examples discussed where the relation between reason-property and target-property is conceptual, but the examples like smoke and fire where the relation is supposed to be empirical or causal and not just conceptual. This suggests that the scepticism of the extreme-empiricist Cārvākas is not against all types of concomitance-relations. It is against the concomitance-relation based on causation, or such other synthetic relations, and not against that based on identity or analytic

43. For my detailed discussion on 'necessity' in Dharmakīrti's theory of inference, see Gokhale (2006).

relations. This suggests that Cārvākas do not have objection against analytic necessity, though they have reservations about causal necessity.

The Cārvāka objection against the Buddhist belief in causal necessity can be spelt out in the following way. Buddhists claim that the universal concomitance between any two things/events is not determined by observation and non-observation, but is rooted in a cause–effect relation, which is necessary. Against this, Cārvākas ask how the so-called necessary relation between an effect and its cause is determined after all. It seems that Buddhists have no other way than to refer to observation and non-observation. Hence, the Cārvāka objections against observation and non-observation as the determiners of universal concomitance will be equally applicable here.

The controversy between Cārvākas and Buddhists on the issue of causation can be compared with a similar 'controversy' between Hume and Kant (or Humeans and Kantians).[44] Historically the difference between the two controversies would be that in the Western tradition, Hume preceded Kant whereas in the Indian tradition, Cārvāka presents his reaction against the Buddhist Dharmakīrti. But the historical differences apart, the debates are similar in their essence. Dharmakīrti and Kant maintained that analytic necessity is not the only necessity; there is also synthetic necessity and that causation is an important kind of synthetic necessity.[45] (Dharmakīrti maintained that it is the only kind.) As against this, Cārvākas and Hume maintained that though the so-called causal connection is synthetic, it is not a necessary relation. Though there may be constant conjunction of event α and event β (as Hume would put it), or repeated

44. This discussion draws on the Stanford Encyclopedia article 'Kant and Hume on Causality' (De Pierris and Friedman 2008).

45. Though the laws of Newtonian physics, which are causal in nature, are cases of synthetic a priori knowledge, there are other varieties of synthetic a priori knowledge according to Kant, which are not based on causation. For example the laws of pure arithmetic are not analytic and yet they are necessary, but they are not causal either. In '2 + 2 = 4' the predicate is not contained in the subject (hence the statement is not analytic), nor are 2 and 2 together the cause of 4 (because there is no temporal order), and yet the proposition is necessarily true. For Dharmakīrti, however, it seems that all synthetic necessity is causal. He would have said that the statements of pure arithmetic are true in virtue of the very nature (identity, svabhāva) of things and hence they may fall in the category of the statements based on tādātmya.

observation of co-existence of α and β and non-observation of α without β (as Cārvākas would put it), causal connection between α and β cannot be proved to be a necessary relation.

As against this, Kant would say that the succession between cause and effect is necessary; the effect does not merely follow upon the cause, but is posited through it and follows from it. Similarly, Buddhists would say that causality is so deep-rooted in the nature of things that a real thing (*sat*) is defined as the one having causal efficacy (*arthakriyāsamartha*).[46]

The way the problem arises in Indian philosophy can also be stated as follows. Naiyāyikas maintained that the relation between sign and the signified should not be irregular, which means that the counter-example of the form 'sign exists, but what is signified by it, does not' should not be available. They believed that such a relation can be established on the basis of observation and non-observation. Dharmakīrti did not agree with this. According to him, the relation between the sign and the signified should not be just 'regular' but 'necessary'. The counterexample should not be just non-available, but impossible. Such a necessary relation between two distinct objects is possible only through causality. Cārvākas agree with the Buddhists on the point that the relation between the sign and the signified should not be just regular, but it should be 'necessary'. But they disagree with the Buddhists on obtainability of such a necessary relation.

One could grant for the sake of argument Kant's view that causality is a category necessary for understanding events. Similarly one could grant Dharmakīrti's view that a real thing has causal efficacy. But the question is whether this helps us in ascertaining authenticity of any particular inference based on causation. There is a difference between accepting causation in general or causal efficacy of things in general and accepting causal connection between two specific types of things or events. One can say from the side of Cārvākas that former type of belief does not imply the latter type of belief. Moreover, it could

46. '*arthakriyāsamarthaṁ yat tadatra paramārthasat*' (*PV* 2.3). [Here a real in true sense is that which has capacity to do something.] One important difference between the Indian and Western understanding of causation needs to be noted here, though it does not affect the general point I am making. The concept of cause in the West is generally understood as the sufficient condition of the effect, whereas in Indian philosophical discussions, it is generally understood as a necessary condition.

be granted that belief in causality is practically and psychologically necessary for human life, but this does not imply that it is also logically necessary. This is a possible Hume-like response to Kant and Cārvāka-like response to Buddhists.

Probability Thesis

The Cārvāka view that statements of universal and necessary relation cannot be ascertained may imply that their approach to acceptability of inference is purely negative and destructive. But that is not the case. Some Cārvākas, while denying the authenticity of inference, said that inferences can give probable conclusions.[47] This is significant. When other schools accept inference as pramāṇa, they regard it to be a source of certain or indubitable knowledge. And when the schools like Vyākaraṇa and Advaita–Vedānta doubt certainty or indubitable character of inference, they do it in order to support scriptural testimony which would be regarded as equally, if not more, dubitable by Cārvākas. Non-Cārvāka schools believe in the possibility of indubitable and certain knowledge not mainly because they are interested in establishing worldly practices, but because they are interested in establishing transcendental/metaphysical phenomena like soul, God, other worlds, rebirth, ritualistic practices with the guarantee of their fruits, and also the absolute and permanent emancipation as the ulti-

47. *atra cārvākāḥ, yogyatāviśeṣaṇena kim? yanna pratyakṣaṁ tannāsti iti anupalabdhimātram eva bādhakaṁ syāt. anumānavilopaśca iṣṭa eva. dhūmadarśanānantaraṁ vahnyartha-pravṛttiśca sambhāvanāmātrāditi* (*Nyāyakusumāñjali* [*NK*], chapter III, Haridāsa-Bhaṭṭācārya's preamble to v. 6)

[Here Cārvākas say, '(When you say that absence of a thing is known through non-apprehension of a capable, that is, apprehensible object) what is the use of 'capability' as the qualifying condition? Whatever is imperceptible does not exist; in this way non-apprehension itself will be the sublating condition. And the disappearance of inference as an authentic means to knowledge is quite desirable (for us). Our act of proceeding towards fire, having seen smoke, is simply based on probability.']

loke dhūmādidarśanottaraṁ vahnyādikavyavahārastu prāyeṇa vahnirbhaviṣyati ityādi sambhāvanā iti bhāvaḥ (Yādavācārya's commentary on Jānakīnātha's *Nyāyasiddhānta-mañjarī*, quoted by Athavale 1997: 39, fn. 3).

[The intended meaning is this: the activity concerning fire and such like, after the perception of smoke and so on, takes place among people with the thought that there is a likelihood, that probably there would be fire.]

mate goal of life. For asserting the transcendent reality, some of them are ready even to keep in suspense the fundamental source of knowledge, namely the sensory experience. Cārvākas are not interested in ascertaining—or rather, they are challenging the existence of—the so-called transcendent realities. They are in search of certainty within the mundane practical world. Extreme-empiricist Cārvākas like to attribute the title 'pramāṇa' in the sense of 'source of certainty' only to perception. Other so-called sources of knowledge according to them can give us only probability, not certainty.

Naiyāyikas rule out the Cārvāka's appeal to 'probability' by reducing the latter to doubt.[48] But even as doubt, it should be understood as a special kind of doubt where one of the options is stronger than the other (*utkaṭaikakoṭika saṁśaya*). Such a doubt has a constructive pragmatic role. Hence an inference, though it gives only probability and not certainty, can lead us to take positive steps and also can lead us to success. In other words, even if one uses the terminology of doubt, one has to distinguish between 'doubting that' and 'doubting whether'. The Nyāya category of doubt refers to the latter whereas probability (*sambhāvanā*) refers to the former.

The given approach reflects the scientific temper of Cārvākas. In the Western knowledge tradition, the doctrine of probability developed as a part of the methodology of science and this methodology boosted science. In India, while philosophers were running after certainty and making tall claims about it, even scientists making discoveries in astrology, medicine, and psychology were treated as seers, as men of unerring intuitions, not as fumblers making probable conjectures subject to verification and modification. Naturally probability theory could not be imagined as a theory of scientific knowledge but was taken to be a weaker position of the heretics, to be set aside quickly. This attitude seems to have hindered scientific progress in India.

The position that science gives probable knowledge, that scientific knowledge claims are subject to verification and falsification and are never strictly certain, underlines in a humble way the limitations of human knowledge. The position of a scientist is humble in this sense in contrast with the position of a metaphysician.

48. '*sambhāvanā hi saṁśayaḥ*', Haridāsa-Bhaṭṭācārya's commentary on *NK* (III.6). [Because probabilistic thought is a doubt.]

The development of scientific knowledge consists in achieving greater and greater probability and approximating certainty. But this journey of knowledge is an unending process. The methodological position of the extreme-empiricist Cārvāka is conducive to scientific attitude and scientific growth in this way. The absolutist and definitive concept of knowledge accepted by other systems is generally detrimental to the growth of science.

Implications of Extreme Empiricism on Other Aspects of Cārvāka-darśana

In the foregoing discussion, I have tried to show that the opponents of Cārvāka do not have a logically satisfactory answer to extreme empiricism, which denies the authenticity of inference. However, this raises an issue at another level. The popular version of Cārvāka-darśana attributes an extreme-empiricist position to Cārvākas. But according to the same version, materialistic ontology and egoistic–hedonistic ethics are attributed to the same Cārvākas. Now the question is, do these theories cohere with extreme empiricism?

Materialistic ontology implies that there are only four gross elements in the world and living bodies, sense organs, and empirical objects are their combinations. Consciousness arises from the combination of matter like intoxicating power arises from the fermentation of molasses or red colour arises from chewing of the leaves of piper-betel with other ingredients. Now, that consciousness arises in this way from the combination of matter is the conclusion of an inference—a metaphysical type of inference.[49]

The egoistic–hedonistic ethics implies that maximization of one's own pleasure and minimization of one's own pain is good for all. This is a universal generalization—a universal concomitance implied by the hedonistic ethics. But belief in such a universal concomitance is inconsistent with extreme empiricism.[50]

This inquiry can continue further. Cārvāka materialism implies that there are material elements that exist independently of their

49. See Chapter 5.
50. For the discussion on Cārvāka hedonism, see Chapter 4.

appearances. But is extreme empiricism consistent with this view? Cārvākas deny inference as pramāṇa because its truth cannot be guaranteed, as there is a permanent possibility of error. By the same token, the authenticity of ordinary perception also can be questioned. While accepting perception as pramāṇa, Cārvākas do not take into account the possibility of perceptual error. Now the question can be asked: isn't illusion or hallucination a permanent possibility with regard to perception? And if that is so, the Cārvāka insistence on perception as the only pramāṇa cannot be accepted without analyzing perception. Such an analysis of perception could lead to phenomenalism. This is a sense-data theory that upholds that perception could be pramāṇa with respect to its direct object. The latter could be called a sense datum, or a phenomenon, or—to borrow a Sautrāntika Buddhist concept—a unique particular (*svalakṣaṇa*) and to accept the possibility of error with reference to the judgemental cognition (*savikalpakajñāna*) that judges or interprets the direct object in terms of the preconceived universal ideas. In this context, even the so-called judgemental perception can be regarded as an inference and the Cārvāka criticism of inference as pramāṇa can be consistently extended to judgemental perception, in which case, illusion can be explained not as an error in 'seeing' but that in 'seeing as' or 'interpretation', which is a kind of inference.

I suggest that the extreme-empiricist epistemology of Cārvākas, if extended to its logical end, leads to phenomenalism and not to materialism. Can the extreme-empiricist epistemology be called a truly Cārvāka epistemology then? It can be called a Cārvāka epistemology because of its negative role, which functions as a strategy for excluding any kind of otherworldly theory of reality or values. But does it fulfill this role satisfactorily? In fact, the position of extreme-empiricist Cārvākas leads to a dilemma:

1. If perception alone is accepted as pramāṇa then the statements regarding God, other worlds, and so on, can be rejected, but the materialistic thesis will also have to be rejected.
2. If, on the other hand, perception along with inference is accepted as pramāṇa, then the materialistic thesis can be defended, but the arguments for metaphysical entities such as God and soul will also have to be accepted.

It reminds one of a similar dilemma faced by the logical empiricists in the West as a result of the verifiability theory of meaning:

1. Weak verificationism leads to acceptance of scientific propositions as meaningful, but also to the acceptance of some metaphysical statements as meaningful, which is not desirable.
2. Strong verificationism helps in discarding metaphysical statements as meaningless, but it also makes us discard some scientific propositions (involving theoretical terms) as meaningless, which is not desirable.[51]

***

The dilemma of the extreme empiricism of the Cārvākas underlines the need for a more accommodative and yet stronger epistemology which will preserve its negative or destructive elements but will be more constructive in its theory of reality and values. Such an epistemology was referred to as belonging to 'more learned' (*suśikṣitatara*) Cārvākas by Jayantabhaṭṭa and was attributed to Cārvākas in general by Purandara as mentioned by Kamalaśīla. This brings us to what can be called the position of a mitigated-empiricist Cārvāka, which is the subject matter of the next chapter.

51. Carl Hempel in his article 'The Empiricist Criterion of Meaning' (see Ayer 1959: 108–29) points out that the requirement of complete verifiability in principle rules out all sentences of universal form and hence along with metaphysical statements, many statements which are the integral part of scientific theory are also ruled out. Similarly he points out the disadvantages of 'complete falsifiability' as the criterion and concludes, 'Interpretations of the testability criterion in terms of complete verifiability or of complete falsifiability are inadequate because they are overly restrictive in one direction and overly inclusive in another' (Hempel 1959: 114). I am aware that the problem that logical positivists faced is more complex than I have stated. It is also a fact that debates in analytic philosophy have gone way beyond the parameters of logical positivism. I only want to indicate that the problem that extreme empiricists of India and those of Europe face is similar in a broad way.

4

Mitigated Empiricism in Cārvāka-darśana

I have discussed so far two epistemological positions within Cārvāka-darśana. The second chapter discussed scepticism, while the third engaged with extreme empiricism. In this chapter, I will discuss mitigated empiricism advocated by some Cārvākas. By the term 'mitigated empiricism', I refer to the position that though perception is the major instrument of knowledge, a certain kind of inference too can be accepted as a means to knowledge.

As I have suggested in the first chapter, the acceptance of a kind of inference as a means to knowledge is not a later development of Cārvāka epistemology. Such an approach was well known and respected even before the term Cārvāka was associated with Lokāyata philosophy. Kauṭilya in his *Arthaśāstra* prescribes the study of philosophy, which consisted of three disciplines—Sāṅkhya, Yoga, and Lokāyata[1]—

1. ... Kauṭilya says that the branches of learning are four and only four. The (common) essential character of all the branches of learning (*vidyātva*) consists with them as the means, one can learn the (nature of) *dharma* and *artha*. Logic-based philosophy (*ānvīkṣikī*) (is represented by the following three): Sāṅkhya, Yoga, and Lokāyata. Dharma and *adharma* belong to Vedic lore; gain and loss belong to *vārtā*; good policy and bad policy belong to *daṇḍanīti*. (*Arthaśāstra* [*AK*] 1.2.8–10, quoted in translation in Chattopadhyaya 1990: 74)

to the children of royal families. He termed philosophy as ānvīkṣikī, which involved the application of reasoning (*hetu*) for investigating into strengths and weaknesses of other disciplines, namely scriptures (*trayī*), polity (*daṇḍanīti*) and economy (*vārtā*). This implies that application of reasoning (hetus) is a mark not only of Sāṅkhya and Yoga, but also of Lokāyata. Further, this application is not merely destructive or critical, but also constructive.

Lokāyatikas used reasoning in a variety of ways. They questioned the authenticity of the Vedas with a critical or destructive use of reason[2] for which they were criticized by believers as heretic (*nāstika*[3]), argumentative (*haituka*[4]), and also nihilist or sceptic (*vaitaṇḍika*[5]). Though it is possible that some Cārvākas ('sceptic Cārvākas') used reasoning only for refutation, there must have been others who also had a constructive agenda. They used reasoning to support materialist ontology and the worldly way of life. These Lokāyata thinkers were in all probability different from sceptic Lokāyata thinkers. Arguably, different Lokāyatikas adopted different policies in ontology, epistemology, and axiology in order to combat other-worldly metaphysics, axiologies, and epistemologies supporting them. With the development of epistemological theory by other Vedic and non-Vedic systems, the Cārvākas must have reexamined and reformulated their

2. Destructive use of reason means the use of reason only for refutation.

3. *yo'vamanyeta te mūle hetuśāstrāśrayād dvijaḥ/*
sa sādhubhirbahiṣkāryo nāstiko vedanindakaḥ// (*Manusmṛti* [*MS*] II.11)

[The one who dishonours these two roots (of dharma) (namely Vedas and Smṛtis) by taking recourse to the science of reasoning, is a heretic (nāstika) and a blamer of the Vedas and hence should be excommunicated by the good persons.]

4. '*pāṣaṇḍino vikarmasthān baiḍālavratikāñchaṭhān/haithkān bakavṛttīṁśca vāṅmātreṇāpi nārcayet//*' (*MS* 4.30). [One should not honour even by words the heretics, those following prohibited professions (those pretending to be virtuous and humble, but are not), behaving like a cat or a crane, wicked ones, and logicians (*haituka:* those who use reasoning for criticising Vedas).]

5. *na hi lokāyate kiñcit kartavyamupadiśyate/*
vaitaṇḍikakathaivāsau na punaḥ kaścidāgamaḥ// (*Nyāyamañjarī* [*NM*], part I, p. 247)

[In Lokāyata no duty is prescribed. It is just talk in refutation (of others without making any constructive claim). There is no scripture (it upholds).] Here Jayanta is not talking about Vaitaṇḍika school of Cārvākas, which he has elsewhere referred to as the school of Cārvāka-dhūrtas, rather he is making an allegation that all Cārvākas are vaitaṇḍika.

own epistemological theory. Systematic forms of scepticism, extreme empiricism (narrow empiricism), and mitigated empiricism (broad empiricism) of Cārvākas might have been the result of it. In this chapter we will concentrate on the mitigated empiricism, which was attributed to some Cārvākas. We will also consider the implications of this empiricism for the ontology and axiology attributed to them.

Here a question can be asked: Is there any continuity between extreme empiricism and mitigated empiricism? The fact that extreme-empiricist Cārvākas do not accept inference as *pramāṇa* at all, whereas mitigated empiricists do accept a certain kind of inference as pramāṇa would imply that some of the major objections raised by extreme-empiricist Cārvākas against the authenticity of inference (for example, non-availability of universal concomitance) were withdrawn by the mitigated empiricists. It would imply that the two positions are more discontinuous than continuous.

But this is not the only way to understand the relationship between the two positions. There is an alternative way which would imply continuity between the two positions rather than discontinuity:

1. When the extreme-empiricist Cārvākas criticize inference, they are questioning its authoritative character. They are not denying its usefulness completely. They are admitting that many a time inferences do give pragmatically successful results. They sometimes explain it in probabilistic terms.
2. On the other hand, when mitigated-empiricist Cārvākas accept inference as pramāṇa, they too do not accept it in the sense of authoritative means to knowledge. They are not withdrawing the criticism of inference, particularly the one in terms of impossibility of ascertainment of universal concomitance.
3. Non-Cārvāka systems accept inference generally in order to defend the existence of transcendent entities which are supported by scriptures rather than experience. When mitigated-empiricist Cārvākas accept inference, they do it mainly in order to explain and justify the facts of the empirical world. Consequently they do not accept all inferences, but those which are testable by ordinary human experience or necessary for the explanation of such experience. Hence primacy of perception is the doctrine commonly accepted by extreme-empiricist and mitigated-empiricist Cārvākas.

Of course these points of similarity or continuity do not obliterate the difference between the two 'schools' of Cārvāka. However, two points of difference are significant in this context.

1. One difference is obviously in terms of the thrust they attach to acceptance of inference as a means to knowledge. The thrust of extreme-empiricist Cārvākas is on criticism of inference. They are more concerned about the authoritativeness attributed to inference by the idealist, theist, and dualist metaphysical systems than with the defense of alternative ontology through inferences. As against this, the mitigated-empiricist Cārvākas are more concerned about justification of worldly existence and common-sense beliefs. This difference between the two kinds of Cārvākas may be temperamental rather than philosophical.
2. The philosophically significant difference between the two schools is that the criticism of inference advanced by extreme-empiricist Cārvākas is indiscriminate; it applies to all inferences based on inductive generalization indiscriminately. In comparison, when mitigated Cārvākas accept inference as a means to knowledge, they do not accept all inferences indiscriminately. We will see later, some mitigated-empiricist Cārvākas accepted only empirically testable inferences. Other mitigated-empiricist Cārvākas accepted only commonsensically acceptable inferences. This was their advancement over extreme empiricism.

In the previous chapter I have referred to the Cārvāka aphorism according to which, since the word 'pramāṇa' is used in its strict (*agauṇa*, non-secondary) sense, it cannot be applied to inference.[6] This is how some Cārvākas must have justified their extreme-empiricist approach. But this allows the possibility that one can use the word pramāṇa in a weaker or secondary sense and then apply it to inference. When some Cārvākas uphold that inference can give us probability but not certainty, they make room for such a possibility within the Cārvāka framework.

6. '*pramāṇasya agauṇatvād anumānād arthaniścayo duralabhaḥ/*' [An object can hardly be ascertained through inference (anumāna) because an authoritative means to knowledge (pramāṇa) is not secondary.] See Chapter 3 for more details.

The term pramāṇa in its secondary sense would refer to the means of knowledge, which gives at least probable knowledge if not certain. While accepting such a possibility, one has to go beyond the previously mentioned Cārvāka aphorism and claim that Cārvāka-darśana was not always restricted to the so-called Cārvāka aphorisms. Cārvākas took such liberties either by giving deviant interpretation of the aphorisms or bypassing them.[7] Hence, one comes across the mitigated-empiricist Cārvākas who take the secondary sense of the word 'pramāṇa' seriously and then deal with the question as to which kind of inference can be accepted in the secondary sense of the word pramāṇa.

Here I want to suggest that although extreme-empiricist Cārvākas prefer to use the word 'pramāṇa' univocally, in the strict or primary sense, the word as a matter of fact has been used, in Indian epistemological parlance, in more than one sense. Sometimes it is used in its strict or primary sense, sometimes in its loose or secondary sense. I have suggested in the last chapter that the strict or primary or non-secondary sense of the term 'pramāṇa', in which the extreme-empiricist Cārvāka wanted to use the word, was that pramāṇa means an authoritative means to knowledge.

The question of the two senses of the word 'pramāṇa' is not restricted to Cārvākas' use of the word. It is a general issue in Indian philosophical literature. S. S. Barlingay brings out the ambiguity in the use of the word pramāṇa:

> ... since the root *mā* or *pramā* is a synonym of the root *jñā*, the ambiguity in respect of the root 'jñā' also occurs in respect of the root 'mā'. The word pramāṇa is, thus, sometimes used as a means to knowledge (which cannot be false) and sometimes used as a means of cognition (which can also be illusory). Of course this ambiguity is not quite apparent and protagonists of Indian logic usually do not accept that they are using the word pramāṇa in more than one sense.[8]

Barlingay refers to the the first sense as the strict sense and explains it in terms of authority. In this light we can make the distinction between primary and secondary sense of the word 'pramāṇa' as follows:

7. For a detailed comment, see the section on Bārhaspatya-darśana in Chapter 1.
8. Barlingay (1976: 14–15).

1. According to primary sense of the word, 'pramāṇa' means 'an authoritative means to knowledge' or 'an authority'. Pramāṇa in this sense necessarily yields true cognition and that is how it becomes a reliable source of knowledge. This sense of the word 'pramāṇa' can also be called its strict sense or stronger sense.
2. 'Pramāṇa' also implies 'a means to cognition' in which case it is not an 'authoritative means to knowledge'. Pramāṇa in this sense is a useful means to knowledge, in the sense that it can be used for attaining knowledge, but there is no guarantee that it must yield knowledge. Depending upon other conditions it can yield false cognition instead. I call this sense the secondary sense of the word pramāṇa. This sense of the word 'pramāṇa' can also be called a loose sense or a weaker sense.

The distinction between the two senses has wider implications. It can be broadly correlated to two theories of truth (*prāmāṇya*), namely the theory of intrinsic truth and that of extrinsic truth. When, for example, Mīmāmsakas maintain that the Vedas have intrinsic truth or intrinsic authenticity (*svataḥ-prāmāṇya*), or some Buddhists claim that the cognition of pragmatic function (*arthakriyā*) is intrinsically true,[9] they refer to pramāṇa-hood in the strong sense, which stands for unerring or authoritative character of pramāṇa. When, on the other hand, Naiyāyikas claim that sense organ is *pratyakṣa-pramāṇa*, they mean that a sense organ is the instrument of perceptual knowledge, though there is no guarantee that it will give knowledge (that is, true cognition) and knowledge alone. A sense organ in itself does not have unerring or authoritative character. This does not mean that, according to Naiyāyikas, such an unerring or authoritative character of knowledge was not available in the case of perception. Veridical perception could, for example, be guaranteed if all the necessary conditions are fulfilled, that is, if the eyes are in a so-called standard working condition, if the object is at an appropriate distance, there is sufficient light, and the mind is not under the spell of

9. See, for example, the schemes of Devendrabuddhi, Dharmottara, Kamalaśīla, and Manorathanandin regarding svataḥ-prāmāṇya (what the author translates as intrinsic validity) as enlisted in Madhumita Chattopadhyay (2007: 67–70). This will have implications on the Cārvāka theory of prāmāṇya. Also see note 11 in this chapter.

hallucinations. Similarly, in the case of inference, if the reason-property (hetu) fulfilled all the five conditions (*'pañca-rūpa/pañca-lakṣaṇa'*, or, as Buddhists would say, three conditions, *'tri-rūpa/tri-lakṣaṇa'*), then the existence of target-property (*sādhya*) in the locus could be guaranteed. The Naiyāyikas and Buddhists believed that those five or three conditions (respectively) could actually be fulfilled in many cases and one can be certain that they are fulfilled. This allows for inference as pramāṇa in the strong sense of the term. When Cārvākas claim that inference is not pramāṇa, they question this possibility. As against this, Naiyāyikas and Buddhists, in spite of accepting the theory of extrinsic truth, claimed that inference can be called pramāṇa in the strong sense of the term. This is, however, not the main point here. The main point is that the extrinsic theory of truth (*parataḥ–prāmāṇya–vāda*) makes room for the use of the word pramāṇa in its weak sense.[10]

In the light of these two senses of the word 'pramāṇa', we can say that the mitigated-empiricist Cārvākas accept inference (of a certain kind) in secondary sense, but not in the strict sense.

Several questions emerge at this juncture: While interrogating the authenticity of inference, the extreme-empiricist Cārvākas assert the authenticity of perception. But can perception be called pramāṇa in the strict sense of the term? Does it necessarily yield true cognition? Can there not be error in perception, by way of illusion or hallucination?

The extreme-empiricist Cārvāka may respond by claiming that even when one commits an error in perception, the error can be corrected by referring to another perception, a veridical perception.

However one could object to this saying that the method of discerning that one perception is veridical and the other is erroneous involves reasoning, that is, the use of inference. Cārvākas would argue against this that after all inference is not possible independently of perception. Suppose, for instance, one infers that water that one is observing is real and not a mirage because it has capacity to quench thirst. Such a person proves his perception of water to be veridical on the basis of the pragmatic success to which it leads. But the inference from pragmatic success is based on the experience of such a success, which has been accepted without inference. For example, the perception of water from

10. To avoid the problem of scepticism, Norman Malcolm (1999: 67–74) distinguished between the strong and weak sense of the word 'knowledge'. Mitigated-empiricist Cārvākas seem to be employing a similar strategy.

distance may be doubtful. But the experience of satisfaction of thirst when one is drinking water cannot be doubted. In other words, there are some basic perceptions—like the experience of pragmatic success (or failure) or the experience of a sense-datum—which are accepted without any support other than the perceptions themselves; nevertheless, these basic perceptions provide the grounds for deciding whether a given perception is veridical or illusory. In this sense, there are at least some perceptions (which could be called basic or ultimate perceptions), which can be called pramāṇa in the strict sense of the term. Inference, on the other hand, always needs support from experience and hence, cannot be regarded as pramāṇa in the strict sense of the term.[11]

As it has been argued, mitigated-empiricist Cārvākas claim that inference of a certain kind can be accepted as pramāṇa in the secondary sense of the term. Naturally, they do not accept any and every kind of inference as pramāṇa in this sense. This leads to a three-tier classification of means of cognitions: (*a*) pramāṇa in the strict sense of the term (authoritative means to knowledge), (*b*) pramāṇa in the secondary sense of the term (means to knowledge but not authoritative means), and (*c*) pseudo-pramāṇa (pseudo-means to knowledge or the means to pseudo-knowledge).

At first sight, this three-tiered approach to pramāṇa resonates with the Jaina approach to knowledge, which consists of three central notions: pramāṇa, *naya*, and *durnaya* (or *nayābhāsa*). But the three-tier approach to knowledge introduced by the Jainas substantially differs from the Cārvāka trio. The three notions introduced by Jainas refer to complete knowledge, partial knowledge (viewpoint), and pseudo-knowledge/pseudo-viewpoint respectively,[12] whereas the three-fold classification accepted by mitigated-empiricist Cārvākas

11. This has implications to the question whether the empiricist Cārvākas would accept intrinsic truth or extrinsic truth of cognition (*svataḥ-prāmāṇya* or *parataḥ-prāmāṇya*). The answer is, they would accept intrinsic truth of at least basic perceptual cognitions whereas extrinsic truth of non-basic-perceptual and inferential cognitions. Here I differ from Kar (2013: 23) who claims, 'Cārvāka standpoint, it seems ... cannot support the intrinsic validity of any empirical knowledge-claim.'

12. *sadeva, sat, syātsaditi tridhārtho,*
mīyeta durnītinayapramāṇaiḥ/
yathārthadarśī tu nayapramāṇa-
pathena durnītipathaṁ tvamāsthaḥ// (*Anyayogavyavacchedadvātriṁśikā* [*AVD*]: 28)

refers to (*a*) true and certain cognition, (*b*) possible true cognition (*c*) essentially false cognition (pseudo-cognition). Thus, though both Jainism and Lokāyata make reference to the notion of pseudo-knowledge, the Jaina notion stands for 'partial view-point posing itself as complete knowledge'. In the Cārvāka scheme on the other hand, pseudo-knowledge stands for something unintelligible or nonsensical. The Cārvāka scheme is perhaps more closely comparable with that of logical empiricists who provide a three-fold classification of propositions in the following manner:

1. Certainty/Necessity: Under this head we can consider logically necessary propositions, analytic propositions, and also empirically necessary propositions such as sense-data statements.
2. Contingency/Possibility: Under this head we can consider empirically true statements which happen to be true, but being contingent, could have been empirically false.
3. Non-sense/Impossibility: Under this head we can consider pseudo-propositions of metaphysics and ethics, in addition to logically/analytically false statements (such as contradictions).[13]

This classification is broad and also vague. But I have given it in this form in order to throw some light on the Cārvāka approach. Pramāṇa, in the strict sense of Cārvāka classification, would give certainty or necessity. Pramāṇa in the secondary sense would give contingency or possibility; whereas the third category, namely pseudo-pramāṇa, would give nonsense or impossibility. (The difference would be that

---

[An object can be cognized in three ways: by way of wrong view as, 'It is only existent (and not at all non-existent)', by (right but partial) view as, 'It is existent', and by right knowledge as 'In a way, it is existent'. (Oh Mahāvīra!) you, the one who sees rightly, reject the path of wrong view by following the path consisting of (right but partial) view and right knowledge.]

13. Wittgenstein (1971) in *Tractatus Logico-Philosophicus* distinguishes between tautologies, contradictions, significant statements, and metaphysical and ethical/aesthetic statements. He terms tautologies and contradictions as senseless (1971: 4.461), while metaphysical and ethical/aesthetic statements are seen as nonsensical or pseudo-propositions (1971: 6.42, 6.53). It should be noted that analytic or logical truths are called necessary in the analytical tradition, while basic observation statements can be called 'certain', but not 'necessary'. I have clubbed them together for the sake of brevity.

Cārvākas would generally take necessity and possibility in an empirical sense whereas logical empiricists take them in logical sense.)

Logical empiricists regard the metaphysical statements about the 'transcendent realities' such as God as non-sense or as pseudo-statements. In true sense of the term they are not significant statements at all and hence the question of their being true or false does not arise. They refer to 'impossibility' in its broader sense, though they are not logical contradictions and hence they do not refer to 'logical impossibility'. Now I want to suggest that when Cārvākas are criticizing speculative inferences such as those for the existence of God or other worlds, they are suggesting that they are pseudo-pramāṇa leading to pseudo-knowledge. In other words, the conclusions of these inferences are not cognitively meaningful statements—they are nonsensical. The Cārvāka ridicule of sacrifices and *śrāddha* rituals,[14] hints at absurdity or meaninglessness of these beliefs, rather than their simple falsehood. The non-speculative inferences, on the other hand, which give empirically verifiable conclusions, can be called scientific inferences in a broad sense. They do not yield necessarily true conclusions, but possibly or probably true conclusions. Such inferences can be accepted by Cārvākas as pramāṇa in the secondary sense of the term.

At this point, one needs to ponder over the basis on which the mitigated-empiricist Cārvākas distinguish between inferences that can be accepted and those which are worth rejecting. Here two different proposals have been made from the side of Cārvāka.[15] I call one proposal positivistic and the other common-sense oriented. I am suggesting that the mitigated-empiricist approach which Jayantabhaṭṭa in *Nyāyamañjarī* (*NM*) attributed to 'more learned Cārvākas', can be called positivistic whereas the approach that Kamalaśīla in *Tattvasaṅgrahapañjikā* (*TSP*) attributes to Purandara can be called common-sense oriented. I am going to discuss them in this order not

14. That is, rituals addressed to the departed ancestors. For Cārvākas' criticism of the *śrāddha* rituals, see note 6 in Chapter 6.

15. I have discussed the two proposals and their implications in Gokhale (1993). The present chapter can be called a development of that paper. An earlier version of some points made in the chapter was presented to the University Grants Commission as the module (Module No. 39 of the paper Logic-1) entitled 'An Empiricist Approach to Classification of *Anumāna*' prepared under its e-PG-Pathshala programme in Philosophy.

because they were presented in this historical order—it is possible that both the views existed simultaneously—but because, I will argue, they follow a logical order. The positivist proposal leaves certain questions unanswered which the common-sense-oriented proposal seems to address more satisfactorily.

In what follows, the two proposals will be discussed in some detail.

First Proposal: Positivist Approach to Inference

Jayantabhaṭṭa, in his *NM*, refers to the view that inference is of two kinds: *utpanna-pratīti* and *utpādya-pratīti.*[16] The inference of fire from smoke belongs to the former kind. The inference of transcendent entities like God belongs to the latter. Hence, the former kind of inference is acceptable as pramāṇa, but the latter is not. Jayantabhaṭṭa attributes this view to those, whom he calls more learned (*suśikṣitatara*) Cārvākas.[17]

Jayantabhaṭṭa in *NM* acknowledges three categories of Cārvākas. (*a*) Knave Cārvākas whom he also calls learned Cārvākas,[18]

16. Though Bhattacharya refers to this distinction several times in his exposition of Cārvāka epistemology, it is doubtful whether he is clear about it. Take, for instance, his statement: 'The Cārvākas were quite prepared to accept inference as a means to valid knowledge in so far as it was preceded or verifiable by perception' (2012: 74). In fact 'inference preceded by perception' and 'inference verifiable by perception' refer to two different types of inference. The latter refers to a stronger one whereas the former to a weaker one. To attribute the acceptance of the former type of inference to Cārvākas is unacceptable. Naiyāyikas define inference as the knowledge preceded by perception. They even try to prove the existence of God by the inference based on perception. For example, that a pot is produced by a potter is a matter of common experience on which their argument for God is based. This does not make the inference acceptable to Cārvākas.

17. *'suśikṣitatarāḥ prāhuḥ, dvividhamanumānaṁ, kiñcidutpannapratīti, kiñcid utpādya-pratīti; īśvarādyanumānaṁ tu utpādya-pratīti'* (*NM*, part I, p. 113). [More learned ones say: Inference is of two kinds. Some are such that experience of them (that is, their objects) has already arisen. Some are such that experience of them (that is, their objects) has yet to arise. The inference of God and such like is of the latter type.]

18. Jayanta also refers to Cārvāka-dhūrtas as Suśikṣita-Cārvākas. *'aśakya eva pramāṇa- saṅkhyāniyama iti suśikṣitacārvākāḥ'* (*NM*, part I, p. 33). [According to learned Cārvākas it is impossible to fix the number of pramāṇas.] Jayanta attributes the same position to Cārvāka-dhūrtas in *NM* (part I, p. 59). For a discussion on this, see Chapter 2.

(*b*) traditional Cārvākas (or permanent Cārvākas as referred to by Cakradhara),[19] and (*c*) more learned Cārvākas. Knave Cārvākas, as we have seen in Chapter 2, deny any kind of certainty with regard to number and defining characteristics of the means and objects of knowledge. Traditional Cārvākas accept only perception as the means to knowledge and criticize inference. The more learned Cārvākas accept what they call utpanna-pratīti inference in addition to perception and deny utpādya-pratīti inference.

Now what is this distinction between utpanna-pratīti and utpādya-pratīti inference? Literally, 'utpanna-pratīti' means that, the experience of which has already arisen and 'utpādya-pratīti' means that, the experience of which is yet to be generated. Apparently, the two terms are used as the qualifications of inference. But they should not be taken literally in that sense. That is because whether an inference itself is experienced or not is not an issue. The issue is whether the object of inference, that is, the target-property, is already experienced in the past or it is yet to be experienced. Naturally, one who had made the distinction is referring to two situations: one in which the object of inference is already known through perception and the other where the object of inference is yet to be experienced.

The distinction can be clarified with examples. The inference of fire based on smoke is utpanna-pratīti because it is about an experienced object. The inference of God is utpādya-pratīti because its object is yet to be experienced.

Of course, when one says that the target-property in the case of utpannapratīti inference is already experienced, one is not saying that the same individual object which is being inferred is already experienced. One is not saying, for example, that the individual fire which the knower is inferring to be there on the mountain has already been seen by the knower. Still the inference is called utpanna-pratīti because one who is inferring the existence of fire has experienced

19. '*pratyakṣamevaikaṁ pramāṇamiti cārvākāḥ*' (*NM*, part I, p. 26). [According to Cārvākas there is only one pramāṇa, namely perception.] Here Jayanta refers to Cārvākas without qualification. This popular category could be the same as what Cakradhara refers to as 'Cirantana-Cārvāka' (permanent Cārvāka). Cakradhara refers to Cirantana-Cārvākas such as Bhāvivikta who interpret the aphorism of Bṛhaspati namely '*bhūtebhyaścaitanyam*' in a traditional way (*Nyāyamañjarīgranthibhaṅga* [*NMGB*], p. 197).

some fire, say, in the kitchen. In other words, fire here is not the experienced (individual) object, but experienced type of object. More generally, the object of this inference is an empirical object. As against this the inference of the existence of God is called utpādya-pratīti. It is so called not simply because its object, namely God, is not experienced before, but because even the object of same type as God is not experienced. In other words, this inference is called utpādya-pratīti because its object is non-empirical. In view of this distinction, we can say that utpanna-pratīti inference is inference of an empirical object whereas utpādya-pratīti inference is inference of a non-empirical object, For the sake of brevity we will call them empirical inference and non-empirical inference respectively.

On the basis of this analysis, the mitigated-empiricist Cārvāka position on inference as pramāṇa can be restated as follows: empirical inference is pramāṇa in the secondary sense of the term pramāṇa, but non-empirical inference is not pramāṇa even in the secondary sense. We can call this form of mitigated empiricism as 'positivist form of mitigated empiricism'.

Similar Classifications in Vaiśeṣika, Sāṅkhya, and Nyāya

Here I want to point out that the Cārvāka classification of inference just discussed need not be taken in isolation as a classification peculiar to Cārvākas. In fact the classification was explicitly or implicitly made by many other systems. For example, it is parallel to the Vaiśeṣika classification of inference into 'seen (in particular)' and 'seen in general' (*dṛṣṭa* and *sāmanyato-dṛṣṭa*).[20] Similarly, the threefold

20. In *Vaiśeṣikasūtra* (*VS*) this classification is suggested (as the classification of *liṅga*, that is, the inferential mark) in the following aphorisms: '*vāyusannikarṣe pratyakṣābhāvād dṛṣṭaṁ liṅgaṁ na vidyate//15//sāmānyatodṛṣṭāccāviśeṣaḥ//16//*' (*VS* 2.1.15–6). [There is no perceived mark for proving the existence of air, because the properties associated with air (such as motion, number, and size) are not perceptible (*VS* 2.1.15). And from a 'generally cognized' mark, the specific characteristics (of the target property) are not proved (*VS* 2.1.16; also see *VS* 3.1.6–7).] Jayarāśi has mentioned this classification as: '*atha anumānena anumīyate; dve anumāne, dṛṣṭaṁ sāmānyatodṛṣṭaṁ ca*' [If you say that it can be inferred by an inference, there are two types of inferences: 'seen' and 'seen in a general way'.]

classification of inference presented by Naiyāyikas[21] and Sāṅkhyas,[22] as *pūrvavat, śeṣavat,* and *sāmānyatodṛṣṭa,*[23] can be interpreted as an expansion of the two-fold Vaiśeṣika classification and hence can be compared with the Cārvāka classification. Before entering into the comparison of these classifications and its implications in detail, it is important to note a major distinction between Cārvāka classification and the classification of others. The classifications of inferences that Vaiśeṣikas, Naiyāyikas, and Sāṅkhyas are presenting are classifications of acceptable inferences according to them. But the classification that Cārvākas are presenting, though formally similar to these, is meant to be the one between acceptable and non-acceptable inferences.

Now coming back to the question of comparison between different classifications, I want to suggest that logically speaking empirical and non-empirical can be regarded as two basic types of inferences. In Nyāya–Vaiśeṣika–Sāṅkhya context they may be termed as 'dṛṣṭa and adṛṣṭa' and in Cārvāka context they may be termed as 'utpanna-pratīti and utpādya-pratīti'. I also suggest that the three-fold classification introduced by Naiyāyikas and Sāṅkhyas can be rearranged around the two-fold classification. This is possible in two ways.

1. Pūrvavat and śeṣavat of the threefold classification would be the two varieties of the empirical inference and the other type namely non-empirical may be identified with sāmānyatodṛṣṭa of the three-fold classification. To illustrate with a diagram:

21. *'atha tatpūrvakaṁ trividhamanumānaṁ, pūrvavat, śeṣavat, sāmānyatodṛṣṭaṁ ca/'* (*NS* 1.1.5). [Now inference is the one which is preceded by it (= perception). It is of three kinds: 'like the prior', 'like the remaining', and 'seen in a general way'.]

22. *'trivdham anumānam ākhyātam; talliṅga-liṅgi-pūrvakam'* (*Sāṅkhyakārikā* [*SK(G)*] 4). [Inference is said to be of three kinds. It is preceded by (the knowledge of) the mark and the bearer of the mark.] Īśvarakṛṣṇa, the author of *SK(G)* mentions only the third type, namely *sāmānytodṛṣṭa* by name. The other two, namely *pūrvavat* and *śeṣavat* are mentioned by the commentators.

23. The threefold classification, particularly the first two kinds, have been interpreted in diverse ways. For the discussion see Barlingay (1976: 156–7) and Gokhale (1992: 225–7).

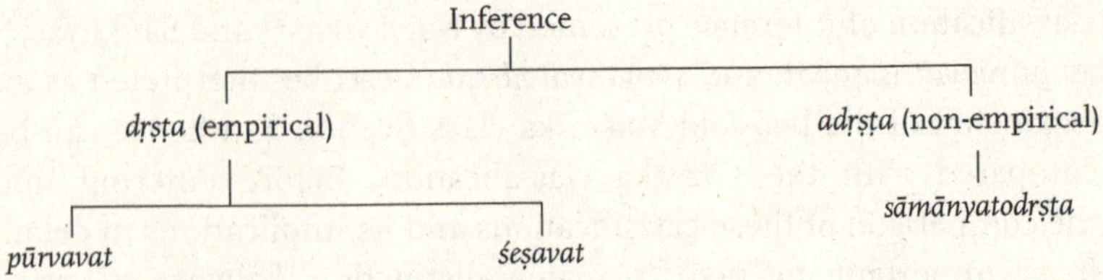

2. The twofold classification may be interpreted as the one between empirical and non-empirical, but out of them empirical may be identified with pūrvavat and non-empirical may be classified further into śeṣavat and sāmānyatodṛṣṭa. This second alternative can be illustrated with the figure as follows:

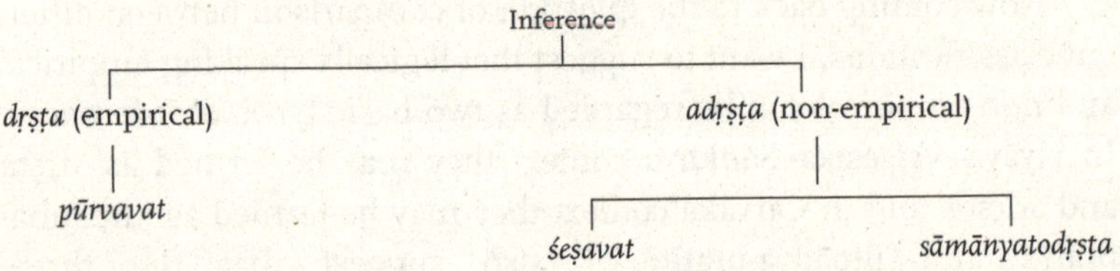

Which alternative one accepts, that is, how one correlates two-fold classification with the three-fold, will depend upon how one interprets pūrvavat and śeṣavat inferences. If one interprets them as causal inferences (that is, that of effect from its cause and of cause from its effect respectively[24]) then both of them can be considered as the varieties of empirical inference. Similarly if pūrvavat is interpreted as the inference based on prior observation and śeṣavat as the inference about the character of a uniform whole from a character of its part,[25] then too both can be called empirical.[26] But if śeṣavat is

24. '*pūrvavaditi yatra kāraṇena kāryamanumīyate...śeṣavat tad yatra kāryeṇa kāraṇamanumīyate...*' (*Nyāyabhāṣya* [*NBh*] 1.1.5, pp. 146 and 148). [Pūrvavat means where the effect is inferred on the basis of cause ... śeṣavat is that in which cause is inferred on the basis of effect.]

25. This interpretation of pūrvavat and śeṣavat was suggested by Gauḍapāda in his commentary of *Sāṅkhyakārikā* (*SK[G]*: 4).

26. It is not the rule that inference of whole from its part is always empirically verifiable. If the whole being too vast is imperceptible and only its parts are perceptible, then the inference of a property of the whole based on a property of its parts will not be verifiable.

understood as 'argument from difference'[27] and is identified with purely negative inference,[28] then it will deviate from the empirical and be closer to sāmānyatodṛṣṭa. Rather than further intricacies, what is more relevant and logically more important here is the distinction between empirical inference and non-empirical inference. If one is inferring the object of the same type as we have experienced before, then the inference will be called empirical. If on the other hand one infers the object of a kind which has not been experienced before, then the inference will be called non-empirical.

Non-empirical inference according to the second alternative discussed could be either sāmānyatodṛṣṭa or śeṣavat. The nature of these two types of non-empirical inference needs to be understood with illustrations so that it may become clear as to why some mitigated-empiricist Cārvākas are critical about non-empirical type of inference. The discussion will also throw light on the possible difficulties in the positivist proposal of these Cārvākas.

Sāmānyatodṛṣṭa Inference

The term 'sāmānyatodṛṣṭa' means 'seen in a general way'. In the case of sāmānyatodṛṣṭa inference, the inferring person has not experienced the type of object that is being inferred before, but has experienced something of a much more general kind. The idea can be clarified with the help of a few illustrations.

1. **Inference of the sun's motion:** Like people of all other ancient cultures, Naiyāyikas too believed that sun rotates around the earth. But the problem was that we do not see the sun 'moving'. What we see is that sun's position in the sky changes over a period of time. Hence the movement of the sun, which one

27. Śeṣavat, meaning *pariśeṣānumāna* (inference about the residual), was one of the interpretations suggested by Vātsyāyana (*Nyāyabhāṣya* [*NBh*] 1.1.5).

28. This identification was suggested first by Vācaspatimiśra by denying the genuineness of the example suggested by Vātsyāyana and Uddyotakara. '*idaṁ tu pariśeṣasyodāharaṇaṁ nādaraṇīyam. vyatirekiṇo hi nāmāntaramidaṁ pariśeṣa iti*' (*Nyāyavārtikatātparyaṭīkā* [*NVTT*] 1.1.5, p. 156). [This example of *pariśeṣa*, however, is not to be honoured, because pariśeṣa(-anumāna) is another name of *vyatireki* (-anumāna).]

never sees, is to be inferred on the basis of the change of its position.[29] How does one infer it? One sees many moving things and also sees that they change positions. Hence, one forms a general rule associating 'change of position' with 'movement'. On the basis of this general rule, one infers sun's movement, though the latter is imperceptible. Hence the inference of the sun's movement is a case of sāmānyatodṛṣṭa inference.

2. **Inference of the visual sense organ:** One sees a table with one's eyes, but one cannot directly perceive the visual sense through which one perceives it. The visual sense organ, which is not the same as the physical eyes but is supposed to be located in them, is supposed to be the means to visual perception. One experiences visual perception (rather, 'perceiving visually') as an act, but does not perceive the means through which it is performed. The means of this act, namely the visual sense organ, is inferred on the basis of the general rule, 'whichever is an act, is performed through some means'.[30] One forms this rule of act-means-relation on the basis of observable instances—where both act and means are observable. The act of writing is possible through a pen, the act of cutting fruit is possible through a knife, and so on. Similarly, one infers that the act of visual perception must be possible through some means. This means is called visual sense organ. The inference for visual sense organ is not directly about 'visual sense organ' but about 'some means' or 'the property of being caused through some means'. 'knives, pens, and so on' are visible means whereas 'visual sense organ' is an invisible means.

It can be noticed here that a sāmānyatodṛṣṭa inference of the kind mentioned earlier has a peculiar feature. In such inferences

29. '*vrajyāpūrvakam anyatra dṛṣṭasyānyatra darśanamiti, tathā cādityasya, tasmād asti apratyakṣāpyādityasya vrajyā*' (*NBh* 1.1.59, pp. 148–9). [Perception of a thing in one place after being seen in another place is preceded by its movement. The perception of sun is of similar kind. Hence there is movement of the sun.]

30. Vacaspatimiśra in *Sāṅkhyatattvakaumudī* gives this instance of *Sāmānyatodṛṣṭa-anumāna*. '*aparaṁ ca vītaṁ sāmānyatodṛṣṭam adṛṣṭa-svalakṣaṇa-sāmānya-viṣayam. yathendriya-viṣayamanumānam*' (*Sāṁkhyatattva-kaumudī* [*STK*] 5). [The other type of positively-connected inference is 'seen in general' which has an unseen universal belonging to a particular as its object; for instance, the inference about sense organs.]

one takes a leap from one type of entity as instances to another type of entity which is the object of inference. In this sense such inferences can be called type-crossing inferences. They can also be called analogical inferences, because the 'instances' (*dṛṣṭānta*) there serve only as analogies or metaphors and not as examples proper. For example, in the present case the things like knife and pen are only analogies for a visual sense organ which is to be proved. In an empirical inference, such as that of fire from smoke, the fire that one sees in the kitchen is a proper example of what is to be proved, namely the fire on the mountain. Here the instance and the instantiated belong to the same type; there is no leap from one type of entity to another.

Sāmānyatodṛṣṭa inference is a type-crossing inference and analogical inference as explained earlier. These features are also found in the Nyāya inference for God, which will be discussed now.

3. **Argument for the existence of God:** One of the oft-quoted versions of the Nyāya argument for the existence of God is as follows:

> The things like trees and mountains have a maker, because they are products.
>
> Whatever is a product has a maker, like a pot.[31]

With reference to this inference we can say that we have seen the maker of a pot, namely the potter, whereas God is not the same type of maker as the potter. A potter is an empirical object whereas God is not. One has never experienced God nor can one experience Him in future. But there are many more categorical differences between the two 'makers'. God as a maker is not an embodied person like a potter who has imperfect knowledge which he obtains through senses and the

31. Jayanta gives his argument for God as follows: '*pṛthivyādi kāryaṁ dharmi tadutpatti-prakāra-prayojanādyabhijña-kartṛpūrvakam iti sādhyo dharmaḥ kāryatvād ghaṭādivat*' (*NM*, part I, p. 178). [The effects such as earth—the property-bearer (in this inference)—are preceded by a being which knows well their origination, types, purpose (behind their creation), and so on—this is the property to be proved—because they are effects, like the things such as pot.]

mind, but an omniscient being who has perfect knowledge which he has without sense organs or mind. Second, the potter produces the pot by using his hands whereas God creates things without possessing a body. In this sense, potter is not *an instance* of what we want to prove, unlike fire in the kitchen which is the *perfect instance* of the fire on the hill. Potter is just an analogy (and a thoroughly incomplete analogy) for God. The inference involves a leap from one kind of entity to another. Hence, this inference too is a type-crossing inference.[32]

4. **Sāṅkhya argument for the existence of the soul:** The well-known Sāṅkhya argument for the existence of soul (*puruṣa*)[33] also belongs to the sāmānyatodṛṣṭa type. The argument can be stated as follows:

> The things such as the eyes are meant for something other than them, because they are composite (*saṅghāta*). All composite things are meant for something other than themselves. For example the things like bed are not meant for themselves, but for persons, who use them.[34]

In this argument, what is ultimately intended to be proved is the soul (puruṣa), for whose consumption/use the organs such as eyes are meant. This soul is regarded as essentially non-composite whereas the organs are essentially composite. The soul as an essentially non-composite being is intended to be proved, but this is not stated in the argument itself. That is because the universal concomitance on which the argument is based is substantiated by the examples like bed and seat, where these things as well as the beings for which they are meant (namely persons) are all composite. In other words, although the

32. This confirms the conceptual link between 'non-empirical inference' and 'inference seen in a general way'. We have seen that the Cārvākas, whom Jayanta calls 'more learned ones', include the inference of God under 'utpādya-pratīti' (non-empirical). Jayanta himself, while discussing the inference, calls it *sāmānyatodṛṣṭa*. '*sāmānyatodṛṣṭaṁ tu liṅgamīśvarasattāyām idaṁ brūmahe...*' (*NM*, part I, p. 178). [We state, however, the reason, seen in a general way (*sāmānyatodṛṣṭa*), for the proof of the existence of God.]

33. '*saṅghātaparārthatvāt*' (*Sāṁkhyakārikā* [*SK*] 17). [Because, composite things are meant for something other than themselves.]

34. '*cakṣurādayaḥ parārthāḥ saṅghātatvāt śayanādivat*' (*NMGB*, p. 63).

universal concomitance in this inference is, 'Whatever is composite is meant for something else', it assumes the form, 'Every composite thing is meant for some other composite thing'. As a result, the soul for which the organs are meant, if at all it exists, turns out to be a composite thing. But this is contrary to what Sāṅkhyas intend to prove. With this idea Diṅnāga, the Buddhist logician, accuses Sāṅkhyas of committing the fallacy called *iṣṭavighātakṛt* ('the reason destroying the intended target').[35]

It can be claimed that the fallacy called iṣṭavighātakṛt is a common fallacy of all sāmānyatodṛṣṭa inferences, because of their type-crossing nature. That is because in such inferences the universal concomitance is found applicable to entities of one type, say T1, but the entity that is intended to be proved belongs to another type, say T2. The universal concomitance as it is substantiated by the known instances implies that the target property too should belong to the type T1, which is contrary to what is intended.

Śeṣavat Inference

If śeṣavat inference is understood, following Vātsyāyana's first interpretation, as the inference of cause from effect, then it will be an empirical inference and mitigated-empiricist Cārvākas may not have an objection to it. But śeṣavat, according to Vātsyāyana's second interpretation, is sometimes equated with purely negative inference which is not based on any positive evidence and hence is often non-empirical. Similarly 'explanatory implication' (*arthāpatti*) accepted by Mīmāṁsakas as an independent means to knowledge, but reduced to purely negative inference by Naiyāyikas is often used for proving transcendent entities. These different types of reasoning form a group on account of structural similarity. They will be the object of Cārvākas' criticism. They will be discussed in what follows.

Inference of the Residual and Negative Inference

Śeṣavat inference, according to the second interpretation given by Vātsyāyana, is understood as inference of the residual

35. Gokhale (1992: 104).

(*pariśeṣānumāna*).[36] When two or more alternatives are prima-facie available and all but one are denied, the remaining one is taken to be proved. Here, what gets proved is said to be proved not on the basis of positive evidence, but only negative one. Inference of the residual can be presented as a disjunctive syllogism of the following type:

$$\begin{array}{c} p \lor q \lor r \\ \sim q \\ \underline{\sim r} \\ \therefore p \end{array}$$

Disjunctive syllogism is logically equivalent to *modus tollens*, subjcct to definition of implication in terms of disjunction and negation. That is:

$$(p \lor q) \equiv (\sim p \supset q) \equiv (\sim p \supset \sim\sim q)$$

Hence $p \lor q$

$\sim q \,/\, \therefore p$

will be a case of disjunctive syllogism, whereas,

$\sim p \supset \sim\sim q$

$\sim q \,/\, \therefore p$

will be a case of modus tollens.

Inference of the residual can be formally presented as disjunctive syllogism, which is logically equivalent to modus tollens which is nothing but a kind of negative inference (*vyatireki*-anumāna). On this formal basis, pariśeṣānumāna can be taken to be equivalent to vyatireki-anumāna.[37]

36. '*śeṣavan nāma pariśeṣaḥ, sa ca prasaktapratiṣedhe anyatra aprasaṅgāt śiṣyamāṇe sampratyayah*' (*NBh* 1.1.5, p. 155). [Śeṣavat means the inference about the residual. It means ascertaining the remaining alternative, because we are not forced to deny it when we are forced to deny other alternatives.]

37. Here, I have shown how there is formal equivalence between pariśeṣānumāna and vyatireki-anumāna (that is between disjunctive syllogism and modus tollens). From the material point of view, however, it may not be equivalent to what is called 'kevala-vyatireki' (purely negative), it could be 'anvaya-vyatireki' (positive-negative) instead. For instance, the example of pariśeṣānumāna given by Vātyāyana (by which *ākāśa* was proved as an independent substance) was that of anvaya-vyatireki according to Vācaspatimiśra (*NVTT* 1.1.5, p. 156).

Explanatory Implication and Purely Negative Inference

In explanatory implication (arthāpatti), which was accepted by Pūrvamīmāṁsakas as an independent pramāṇa, we get a similar situation. Consider a stock example of arthāpatti: 'Devadatta has become fat, but he does not eat at day time. It follows from this that he must be eating at night.' Here there are two alternatives about the fat Devadatta. He must be eating during the day or at night. The first alternative is negated, while the second is inferred on the basis of this negative evidence. This has led Naiyāyikas to reduce explanatory implication (arthāpatti-pramāṇa) to purely negative inference (kevala-vyatireki-anumāna).[38]

The point that I am trying to make is that in the above types of reasoning, one is trying to establish something on the basis of negative evidence, when one does not have any positive empirical evidence. Since in these types of inference the target-property is not yet experienced, they can be subsumed under the category of non-empirical inference and would be the target of criticism by the more learned Cārvākas. In this context, two types of inferential reasoning deserve special attention: (*a*) purely negative inference (kevala-vyatireki-anumāna) and (*b*) explanatory implication (arthāpatti).

Purely Negative Inference (Kevala-Vyatireki-Anumāna)

In the later development of the Nyāya logic, inference was classified into three kinds as positive–negative, purely positive, and purely negative.[39] In the first type only positive concomitance is available; in the second type only negative concomitance is available, and in the third type both positive and negative concomitances are available. Here I am concerned with the second type. In purely negative inference one is not proving something of the same type as, or even

38. For example Jānakīnātha discusses *arthāpatti*-pramāṇa (*NSMn*, pp. 121–2) and concludes, '*arthāpattipadaṁ kevalavyatirekina eva nāmāntaram iti saṅkṣepaḥ*' [In brief, the word 'arthāpatti' is another name of purely negative inference].

39. '*liṅgaṁ trividham, anvayavyatireki, kevalānvayi, kevalavyatireki ca*' (*Tarkasaṁgraha* [*TSa*]). [The mark (reason-property) is of three kinds: positive–negative, purely positive, and purely negative.] The three-fold classification of the mark corresponds to the three-fold classification of inference.

similar to, what one has experienced, but one is trying to prove something very different from or dissimilar to it. For instance, Naiyāyikas explain purely negative inference with the illustration of an argument for the existence of soul as follows: The living bodies of beings must be possessing souls, because they possess the act of breathing, and so on.[40]

The point that the given argument is trying to make is as follows. The activities such as breathing are found in living bodies; they are not found in the insentient things such as a pot, cloth, or rock. Hence there must be something in the living bodies because of which they exhibit such distinctive signs. This distinguishing factor must be that living body possesses a soul (*ātman*). By positing the entity called soul we can say that a living body is able to breathe because a soul is associated with it; it stops breathing, that is, it dies, when the soul is dissociated from it.

The examined inference is different from the inferences that have been discussed under sāmānyatodṛṣṭa inference in that in the latter what one wanted to prove was available in our experience in a very general form. Thus, God was known before as 'some maker', sense organ was known as 'a means of an act'. But in the present inference, the soul that a Naiyāyika wants to prove is not experienced before even in a most general form. We have here, according to Naiyāyikas only negative concomitance of the type—'Whatever lacks soul, does not possess the acts such as breathing, for example, pot, cloth, and rock'.[41] We do not have positive concomitance of the type, 'Whatever breathes, possesses a soul', because existence of the soul is itself being argued for in this inference.

When the more learned Cārvākas oppose non-empirical inference, their opposition also applies to purely negative inference of the type discussed previously.

40. Keśavamiśra in *Tarkabhāṣā* (*TB*) illustrates purely negative inference as follows: '*kaścid hetuḥ kevalavyatirekī ... yathā jīvaccharīraṁ sātmakaṁ prāṇādimattvāt*' (*TB*, p. 97). [A kind of reason is purely negative ... for example, a living body possesses soul, because it contains breath and so on.]

41. In fact even negative concomitance is problematic in this example because in order to notice that there is *no* ātman in the things like pot, cloth, and rock, ātman should be an observable entity.

Explanatory Implication (Arthāpatti)

Explanatory implication, what Mīmāṁsakas call arthāpatti, will also be covered by the purely negative inference mentioned earlier. I have indicated before that Naiyāyikas, while denying the status of explanatory implication as independent pramāṇa, sometimes reduce it to purely negative inference.[42] Hence, Cārvākas, who are opposed to purely negative inference, are also likely to be opposed to explanatory implication. In order to examine the Cārvāka attitude to explanatory implication, let us try to understand its nature in more details.

In the case of an explanatory implication, a certain phenomenon (say, A) is sought to be explained and for a satisfactory explanation of that phenomenon, some other phenomenon (say, B) is claimed to be necessary. In this way B is derived from A on the basis that A cannot be explained satisfactorily without accepting B.

To refer back to the example of 'fat Devadatta' we have mentioned before, Devadatta in the last fifteen days has put on weight, but he is never seen eating at day time during these days. This phenomenon can be explained satisfactorily only if we accept that he must be eating at night.

This example is just a model example for understanding the nature of explanatory implication as pramāṇa. There are more serious examples for which in fact Mīmāṁsakas accept explanatory implication as an independent pramāṇa. Two such examples can be considered.

1. Mīmāṁsakas accept power (potency, *śakti*) as an independent category (*padārtha*) which they try to prove by using explanatory implication. We observe, for example, that fire burns. This observational fact can be explained satisfactorily only if we accept that fire has the power to burn. The burning power of fire is something that we never see with our naked eyes, but we have to accept its existence. Mīmāṁsakas claim that we know it on the basis of explanatory implication.[43]

42. See note 38 in this chapter.

43. *'tatra pratyakṣato jñātāt dāhād dahanaśaktitā'* (*Ślokavārtikam* [*SV*], Arthāpatti-paricchedа, 3). [Among them, (the example of explanatory implication from perceptually known phenomenon is:) 'the capacity of fire to burn (is known) from the act of burning known by perception'.]

2. Mīmāṁsakas believe that the performance of a sacrificial rite generates power which in its turn gives the performer the fruit of the sacrifice. They claim that the existence of this power can be proved on the basis of explanatory implication. Their line of argument is explained below.

There is a Vedic injunction: 'one who has desire for heaven should perform *Jyotiṣṭoma* sacrifice.' Being a Vedic injunction, it must be authentic. Now the question is how we can explain it satisfactorily. The performance of the Jyotiṣṭoma sacrifice will be over within a limited period of time. The heaven will be attained after death. How can the performance of the sacrifice complete in this life cause attainment of heaven after death? The time gap between cause and effect is not acceptable. A cause–effect relation with a time gap can be explained satisfactorily only if we accept an intermediate entity which links cause with the effect. In the case of Jyotiṣṭoma sacrifice, it is the power called *apūrva*, generated anew by the sacrifice. Apūrva is an intermediate entity and links 'performance of sacrifice' with 'attainment of heaven'. According to Mīmāṁsakas this power called apūrva is established through explanatory implication.[44]

So far I have discussed different types of non-empirical inferences of unobservable entities—including explanatory implications accepted by Mīmāṁsakas in order to clarify the view of the 'more learned' Cārvākas, that an empirical inference may be accepted but a non-empirical inference may not. The non-empirical inferences that Cārvākas want to reject include different types of speculative, analogical, and transcendental inferences that Naiyāyikas, Mīmāṁsakas, and others are accepting and using for their ideological aims. Accepting inference as pramāṇa is not a naive or innocent move on the part of non-Cārvāka systems because all inferences are not of the same type, nor are they on the same level of acceptability. Some are

44. *śrutārthāpattirevaikā pramāṇaṁ tasya veṣyate/*
śabdaikadeśabhāvācca svārtheṣvāgama eva naḥ// (*Tantravārtika* [TV] 2.1.5, p. 364)

[Specially because we also hold only such apparent inconsistency to be the means of knowing the apūrva and inasmuch as this apparent inconsistency forms a part of verbal testimony, our sole authority for the apūrva is the scripture itself (translation by Ganganath Jha (1998: 504); Jha translates arthāpatti as apparent inconsistency).]

stronger and hence more easily acceptable, whereas some are weaker and not so easily acceptable. Opponents of Cārvākas might have been aware of this, but because of their dogmatic attachment to the doctrines of God, soul, other worlds, and ritualism, they were trying to defend even weaker types of inferences.

The refusal of the more learned Cārvākas to accept non-empirical inferences is basically the refusal to accept such weaker types of inferences. This is the sum and substance of the given discussion.

Difficulties in the Positivist Proposal

The position of the 'more learned Cārvākas' has to face some difficulties. By rejecting non-empirical inferences including sāmānyatodṛṣṭa inferences, purely negative inferences, and explanatory implications, Cārvākas succeed in rejecting God, soul, and the power of rituals, but they may also have had to reject many things which they did not want to. It was seen, for instance, that according to Naiyāyikas even the movement of sun (which can extend to stars and planets) can be inferred through sāmānyatodṛṣṭa inference. Since this movement is too subtle, it is not perceived through eyes, the inference which proves it can be called non-empirical. Can Cārvāka afford to reject this kind of inference?

One could say that the so-called motion of the sun is a false appearance caused by the rotation of the earth. But this would only mean that sun's motion is relative and not absolute. As relative motion it is real. The point is that even this relative motion is not noticed by our physical eyes and hence it has to be inferred and the inference by which one knows it is not strictly empirical. One can go one step further and ask, how does a scientist know that earth is rotating around itself, which causes the illusion of sun moving around the earth? It is again by inference and that inference too has to be analogical and non-empirical.

This problem has another side. Though the inference of the motion of planets is 'analogical', it is different from other analogical inferences. Other analogical inferences cross types in that there the gap between evidence and the provable object is radical; here it is not so radical. The difference between the motion of a car and the motion of a star is only quantitative, not qualitative. This means that all analogical inferences are not alike; some of them could be closer to empirical verifiability and hence more acceptable.

A similar question arises about the inference of sense organs. We perceive with the help of sense organs, but we never perceive the sense organs. We have to infer their existence and the inference we use has to be of the non-empirical or analogical type. But can we discard this inference simply because it is non-empirical? Can we deny the existence of sense organs because they cannot be proved by empirically testable inference?

The explanatory implication of Mīmāṁsakas also gives rise to similar questions. We have considered two cases of explanatory implication: one proving the existence of 'power' (śakti) of fire to burn and the other proving an intermediate entity called apūrva, which is a kind of power generated by the performance of a sacrifice. The two examples pertain to two different types of explanatory implication: (*a*) the implication drawn from an empirically known fact (*dṛṣṭārthāpatti*)[45] and (*b*) implication drawn from the 'fact' known from scriptures (*śrutārthāpatti*). Now it is easy to understand that Cārvākas will not be ready to accept the second kind of implication because they do not accept (Vedic) scriptures as an authority. But can we say the same thing about the first kind? That fire burns is an empirical fact which Cārvākas are not inclined to deny. But can they easily deny that fire must be having power/capacity to burn?[46]

45. '*Dṛṣṭārthāpatti*' literally means explanatory implication drawn from a perceived or known phenomenon in general, but Kumārilabhaṭṭa defines it to be the phenomenon known from the sources other than verbal testimony (*SV*: Arthāpatti-pariccheda, v. 2).

46. Whether śakti can be regarded as an independent padārtha is a controversial issue in Indian philosophy. Accepting śakti means accepting something as potential which may or may not be actualized. We can say, for instance, that seed has śakti (power) to produce sprout. This does not mean that a seed must necessarily produce the sprout, but it will do so if other conditions (such as soil, heat, light, and moisture) are favourable. But if any necessary condition is unfavourable, then, it will not produce the sprout. Here Nyāya-Vaiśeṣikas would say that the situation can be explained without accepting the entity called śakti. In other words, the statement, 'Seed has a power to produce sprout' can be translated completely without using a synonym of 'power'. For example, 'Seed will produce a sprout if all other causal conditions are present with the seed; it will not produce a sprout if one of the necessary favourable conditions is lacking.' This is an issue which one may come across in philosophical science. A scientist may have to accept some theoretical entities for explanatory purpose. But whether those entities have ontological existence or not may be doubtful.

There are many things whose existence in some sense needs to be accepted as a part of our individual and social life in this world. The question is whether 'the more learned Cārvākas' would be inclined to accept it and whether their epistemological apparatus enables them to do so. For instance:

1. All Cārvākas except the sceptic ones believe that there are four material elements: earth, water, fire, and air. They are not saying that there are just sense-data, but they are claiming that there are material objects which exist beyond such data. Can material objects be established by empirical inference? It seems that Cārvākas, as they are popularly described, have a naive realist conception of perception according to which we can directly perceive material elements. But Cārvākas here ignore the argument from illusion. At the same time one can also see that Jayarāśi's scepticism leads us to a kind of phenomenalism, which is possible, at least in principle, to be shared by extreme-empiricist and even mitigated-empiricist Cārvākas.
2. Non-sceptic Cārvākas believe that consciousness arises from four material elements. This belief is neither established by perception nor by empirical inference. One has never perceived consciousness arising from the combination of four material elements nor can we see it arising in that way. One could have experienced intoxicating function arising from molasses when they are processed or fermented. But intoxicating function arises in a being which is already conscious. Second, the examples of new qualities arising from chemical combinations (like red colour in a betel leaf) are only analogies and not instances proper of origination of consciousness. Hence, the Cārvāka argument for the materialistic (rather, epiphenomenalistic) explanation of consciousness[47] ultimately turns out to be an argument from analogy, a non-empirical inference which the more learned Cārvākas have in fact denied.
3. Cārvākas also accept a social–political set-up in which worldly pleasure (*kāma*) and wealth (*artha*) are pursued as legitimate

47. This argument will be discussed in detail in Chapter 5.

human goals. A social set-up presupposes the acknowledgement of the conscious beings other than oneself. Even a simple communication situation, which Cārvākas have to accept when they enter into argument with their opponents, presupposes the belief in the existence of other minds. Now, existence of other minds is not a fact given in direct experience; it can be established only by an argument from analogy, which is a non-empirical inference.

4. There are other non-empirical categories such as 'space' and 'time' which are to be accepted in order to explain our common daily life. For explaining these categories properly one has to transcend the limits of perception and empirical inference.

Cārvākas who were opposed to otherworldly metaphysical beliefs, but at the same time had the task of explaining and justifying beliefs like the ones stated above, had to enrich their epistemology further. The proposal of Cārvākas like Purandara, which accepts 'commonsensical inference' in place of 'empirical inference', seems to make this possible.

Second Proposal: Common-sense-oriented Approach to Inference

In *TSP*, Kamalaśila quotes Purandara's statement that Cārvākas do admit *lokaprasiddha* inference, but the kind of inference which is made by transcending the worldly way (*laukika-mārga*) is denied by them.[48] Some modern Cārvāka scholars such as Debiprasad Chattopadhyaya and Ramkrishna Bhattacharya regard this as the authentic Cārvāka view on inference. But as I have suggested in the first chapter, though it can be regarded as the view of a dominant school of Cārvākas, it cannot be regarded as the representative view of all Cārvākas. Similarly these scholars do not distinguish between the two proposals; the one attributed to the more learned Cārvākas by Jayanta and the other attributed to Purandara. They have a tendency

48. '*purandarastu āha, lokaprasiddham anumānaṁ cārvākair api iṣyata eva. Yattu kaiścit laukikaṁ mārgam atikramya anumānam ucyate tan niṣidhyate*' (*TSP*, on *Tattvasaṅgraha* [*TS*] 1481).

to assimilate them or club them into one proposal. Here I want to argue that the two proposals are essentially different and have different implications. Therefore they should be considered separately.

Purandara contrasts 'lokaprasiddha inference' with 'the inference which is made by transcending the worldly way'. Apparently, this opposite pair is different from the pair we discussed before, namely empirical and non-empirical. But what Purandara must have meant by the pair he introduced needs to be elucidated. He introduces the notion of lokaprasiddha inference, but he does not explain the exact meaning of the term. One will have to see what consistent sense the term can convey. Let us consider the possible meanings of the term 'lokaprasiddha'.

1. According to one interpretation, 'loka' means 'perception' or 'sense organ' and 'lokaprasiddha' means 'known by perception' or 'known through sense organs'. 'Lokaprasiddha' in this sense would be almost synonymous with 'empirical' of the previous classification. However, this interpretation is not acceptable in the present context. Here, one has to take into account the complete statement of Purandara. He asserts lokaprasiddha inference and rejects certain kinds of inferences that contrast with it. He claims that some people accept inference which transgresses the worldly way (laukika-mārga) and that Cārvākas reject inference of that type. The word 'laukika-mārga' does not mean just 'perception', but a way of life which accepts this world (loka) as real—in this sense it is a this-worldly way of life. This is consistent with Cārvāka's denial of other worlds.[49] Naturally lokaprasiddha inference is to be contrasted with 'inference which transgresses the worldly way'.

49. The word 'laukika-mārga' can also literally mean 'the course of perception' or 'empirical way'. But the words 'loka' and 'laukika' are not generally used in that sense. This use of the word 'laukika-mārga' can be compared with the word 'lokavyavahāra' in the saying '*lokavyavahāraṁ prati sadṛśau bālapaṇḍitau*' [Both ignorant and learned people have similar attitude to worldly practices], quoted by Jayarāśi in the beginning of *TUS*. Loka-vyavahāra or laukika-mārga are not based just on 'experience' but also some of our beliefs about the world which are necessary presuppositions of our daily life. For example, the belief in the existence of material objects, our own mind, other minds, space, and time. The beliefs constituting loka-vyavahāra are comparable with what G. E. Moore calls common sense (see Moore [1959]: 'A Defence of Common Sense').

2. Another interpretation of the term lokaprasiddha is 'well-known in the world'. Bhattacharya has suggested this meaning in his work.[50] 'Lokaprasiddha' in this sense means 'popular' or 'accepted by people'. This meaning is wider than the one suggested earlier, but it is too wide to be acceptable. Cārvākas do not accept any and every inference which is acceptable to people. People accept the ideas like *karma*, life after death, and God and there are some popular arguments in favour of these beliefs. 'You reap as you sow' is a popular argument given in support of karma-doctrine. 'Like a pot has a potter as its maker, a painting has a painter as its maker, the world has God as its maker',[51] is again a popular argument for the existence of God. Cārvākas are not ready to accept these popular inferences. Hence, this second alternative is not acceptable.
3. While discussing the first alternative I suggested that 'lokaprasiddha inference' has to be contrasted with 'the inference which transgresses the worldly way'. This leads to the third possible meaning. Accordingly 'lokaprasiddha' can mean 'strongly established within the framework of this-worldly way of life'. Here I interpret the term 'loka' as related to this-worldly or secular way of life and the term '*prasiddha*' as 'strongly established' (pra-siddha). In other words lokaprasiddha inference is an inference which proves something within the framework of this-worldly way of life. I think that this is the most plausible meaning of the word.
4. Bhattacharya draws attention to the distinction made by some Cārvāka thinkers between lokaprasiddha inference and *tantrasiddha* inference. The latter term seems to refer to the inference which is specific to a philosophical/metaphysical system (*tantra*).[52] As against this 'lokaprasiddha' would mean com-

50. Bhattacharya (2012: 57).
51. The popular argument runs:

jagatāṁ yadi no kartā, kulālena vinā ghaṭaḥ/
citrakāraṁ vinā citraṁ svata eva bhavet tadā//

[If the world does not have a maker, a pot will arise by itself, without a potter and a picture will arise by itself, without a painter.]

52. This meaning of the word 'tantra' is consistent with the Nyāya usage of the terms such as '*sarvatantra-siddhānta*' and '*pratitantrasiddhānta*' (see *Nyāyasūtra* [*NS*] 1.1.26–9).

monly acceptable by all. It should be noted here that 'lokaprasiddha' here does not mean 'what happens to be commonly accepted by all', but 'what should be commonly accepted by all'. It can be taken to mean 'commonsensical' in a strong sense of the term.

5. Guṇaratna in his commentary on *Ṣaḍdarśanasamuccaya*, refers to a kind of inference sometimes (*kvacana*) accepted by Cārvākas which he describes as 'engaged in carrying out worldly affairs' and contrasts it with transcendent inference which establishes the things like heaven and the unseen.[53] I think Guṇaratna by the former type is referring to the same type of inference as referred to by the term 'lokaprasiddha' by Purandara.
6. Guṇaratna's statement underlines the connection between 'lokaprasiddha' inferences and common sense. Common-sense view of the world makes day to day worldly affairs possible and intelligible. This is the role of lokaprasiddha inferences also. Common-sense beliefs are supported by strong pragmatic grounds; they contain a pragmatic necessity whereas their rejection leads to pragmatic contradiction. Similarly it can be said that lokaprasiddha inferences help us in avoiding pragmatic contradictions. By accepting them and denying the other-worldly inferences, these Cārvākas are introducing a pragmatic criterion of acceptability of inference.

In view of these considerations discussed, I propose that the term 'lokaprasiddha-anumāna' can be conveniently translated as commonsensical inference. In this light, Purandara's mitigated empiricism can aptly be called common-sense empiricism.

I want to suggest here that commonsensical inference as interpreted earlier is conceptually different from the empirical inference accepted by the 'more learned' Cārvākas. But at the same time, it is

53. While commenting on *'mānaṁ tvakṣajameva hi'* (*Sarvadarśanasaṅgraha* [*SDS*] v. 83), Guṇaratna explains the significance of the word *'hi'* as follows: *'hi-śabdo'tra viśeṣaṇārtho vartate. viśeṣaḥ punaścārvākairlokayātrānirvāhaṇapravaṇaṁ dhūmādyanumānamiṣyate kvacana, na punaḥ svargādṛṣṭādiprasādhakam alaukikam anumānam iti'* (*SDSam*, p. 457). [The word 'hi' (in the given verse) is meant for qualification. The qualifier here is that Cārvākas sometimes accept the inference from the things like smoke and other things, which is engaged in carrying out the worldly affairs. But they do not accept a transcendent inference which establishes the things like heaven and the unseen (result of actions).]

wide enough to include the latter. In addition to empirical inferences, it includes a class of non-empirical inferences under the condition that they are necessary for making worldly affairs possible and intelligible. Their acceptability is not restricted to any particular dogma or a metaphysical system (tantra), but they are commonly acceptable by all.

In fact commonsensical inference as understood in the present context need not be considered as a singular type of inference, but it can be considered as a group of different types of inferences. These different types will not be on the same logical level. I suggest that it primarily includes three basic types:

1. The empirical inferences based on empirical generalizations (regarding causal relations) which give highly probable, though not certain, conclusions. The conclusions of these inferences are supposed to be empirically testable.
2. Inferences based on logical or conceptual necessity. They would include identity-based inferences accepted by Buddhists and mathematical/logical inferences of axiomatic systems.
3. Common-sense inferences involving explanatory necessity or pragmatic necessity. Existence of space, time, other minds, matter, and so on, follow from our daily life by way of explanatory necessity or pragmatic necessity. In this sense they are derived by commonsensical (lokaprasiddha) inferences.[54]

One can ask how it is theoretically possible for Cārvākas to arrive at lokaprasiddha inference understood as discussed. It is possible, I think, in the following way. Empiricist Cārvākas begin their epistemological enterprise by accepting perception as the authoritative means to knowledge. But perception as an authority, that is, an error-free form of cognition, may amount to non-judgmental perception. But this is not sufficient, as these Cārvākas have as strong theoretical and practical commitment to our mundane life. So, at least a broad framework of our

54. For example, when I am writing, it follows that material objects like paper and pen exist. When I am communicating with others, it follows that there are other minds. Similarly when I am writing, it follows that there are space and time. When I am writing, I am moving the pen from left to right. Right and left being spatial concepts, it follows that space exists. Since writing is an act which begins at one point of time and ends at another, it follows that time exists. All these forms of reasoning were introduced or suggested by G. E. Moore (1959: 53–4) in the 20th century as a part of his defense of common sense.

life in this world is also something that is given according to the Cārvākas. But that the latter is given is more a part of pragmatic necessity than epistemic necessity for them. This pragmatic necessity becomes now an overarching concept under which are accepted empirical inferences, analytic reasoning, and commonsensical inferences.

In fact, in this framework, Cārvākas are always concerned with the question of the dividing line between common-sense metaphysics and transcendent metaphysics; what is empirically and practically necessary and what is not so necessary. For instance, accepting 'consciousness' in the case of both ourselves and others is necessary from an empirical–practical point of view, but accepting a substance called mind or soul (*manas* or ātman) which has consciousness and exists independently of body is not necessary. Accepting the emergence of the present world from some causes is practically necessary but accepting God as the cause of this world is not necessary. Though accepting the empirical world is necessary, accepting a trans-empirical world which one reaches after death is not. Similarly the existence of living beings within their empirical lifespans is acceptable, but their existence before birth or after death is neither empirically nor practically necessary.

Some Implications

The proposed model has some important implications. It seems to be pragmatically more convincing than the earlier one, insofar as it avoids the two unintelligible and impracticable extremes, one consisting of scepticism and solipsism and the other consisting of transcendent metaphysics and blind ritualism. It does so by exposing the pragmatic contradictions and metaphysical incoherence that they may lead to. By avoiding solipsistic implications, it presents the picture of a human being as a rational being trying to lead a successful life in social framework. This is quite consistent with the Cārvāka approach to human goals[55] which emphasizes wealth and worldly pleasure as the substantial goals. This model also distinguishes the Cārvāka theory of pramāṇas from that of other systems of Indian philosophy like Buddhism and Vaiśeṣika, which also accept only two

55. For the discussion on the Cārvāka approach to human goals, see Chapter 6.

pramāṇas, namely perception and inference, but employ inference for justifying transcendental beliefs.

In fact the Cārvāka epistemology which adopts common-sense empiricism can be regarded as an answer to the typical objection which Naiyāyikas and others raise against the extreme empiricism of some Cārvākas. The non-Cārvāka systems generally criticize the sceptic and extreme-empiricist Cārvākas, saying that their denial of inference brings into question the common-sense beliefs and practices. Accordingly, the non-acceptance of inference invites pragmatic contradiction on the part of Cārvākas because when they try to communicate their non-acceptance of inference, this communicative act presupposes belief in the existence of other minds which cannot be defended without an inference. In this way non-Cārvākas pinpoint a weakness in the Cārvāka epistemology. Here we see that the mitigated-empiricist Cārvākas turn this weakness into a strength. They make 'avoidance of pragmatic contradiction' itself a criterion of acceptability of inferences and reject the transcendent inferences of non-Cārvākas which do not have pragmatic necessity. It may be noted here that 'pragmatic necessity' includes empirical and logical necessity. Hence these Cārvākas are suggesting here that we should not accept inferences unless they are based on logical, empirical, or pragmatic necessity. The inferences for God, soul, other worlds, and so on, do not possess any such necessity and hence they are not to be accepted. Inferences limited by a common-sense view of the world, such as the inferences about matter, other minds, and hedonistic values (inferences of space and time also can be included here), can be accepted in so far as they involve a kind of empirical-cum-pragmatic necessity.

***

Chapters 2–4 have dealt with three different epistemological positions of Cārvākas. The two chapters that follow will deal with their ontological and axiological positions respectively.

5

Aspects of Materialism in Cārvāka-darśana

The previous three chapters focused on the varieties of Cārvāka epistemology. They also hinted at, though cursorily, some ontological and axiological issues related to them. The present chapter[1] will deal with Cārvāka ontology and the next with Cārvāka axiology in a somewhat detailed way.

The previous chapters revealed the diversity in Cārvāka epistemology. Diversity is traceable in Cārvāka ontology as well. But there is no one-to-one correlation between the two diversities. While there are four different theories that Cārvākas have introduced in their epistemology (scepticism, extreme empiricism, positivist empiricism, and common-sense empiricism), they have apparently introduced only two theories in their ontology: ontological scepticism and materialism. The former is attributed to Jayarāśi, whereas the latter is generally attributed to all Cārvākas. (The forthcoming

1. This chapter is a revised version of the paper presented in the National Seminar on Celebrating the 50th Anniversary of the publication of Debiprasad Chattopadhyaya's *Lokayata*, Asiatic Society Library, Kolkata, on 24–25 November 2010. An earlier (partial) version of this chapter also forms a part of the article 'Materialism in Indian Philosophy: The Doctrine and Arguments', published in *Bloomsbury Research Handbook of Indian Epistemology and Metaphysics* (London: Bloomsbury Publishing Plc, 2015).

discussion will show that some amount of diversity can be found within Cārvāka materialism, but this is not an immediately relevant issue.) By materialism I mean the doctrine according to which consciousness is either reducible to matter or dependent on matter. It is the doctrine according to which consciousness cannot exist independently of matter. In this sense of the term, Cārvāka-darśana is the only system of Indian philosophy which advocates materialism. Chattopadhyaya uses the term in a wider sense to mean the doctrine which is 'characterized by the tendency to explain the constitution of the external world as being essentially material' and instead of preferring to call Sāṅkhya and Nyāya-Vaiśeṣika as realist (*bāhyārthavādin*), he treats them as materialistic.[2] Sāṅkhya accepts spirit (*puruṣa*) and matter (*prakṛti*) as two independent entities, but gives prominent role to matter in creation of the world. Nyāya-Vaiśeṣikas accept the conscious self (*ātman*) and the corporeal body as separable from each other but take consciousness in self to be generated by sense-object contact, and such like. But the classical Sāṅkhya and Nyāya-Vaiśeṣika cannot be called materialistic insofar as Sāṅkhya regards spirit as an independent entity having pure consciousness as its essence, and Nyāya-Vaiśeṣikas posit an independent entity called self as the substratum of consciousness. They do so in order to explain the phenomena such as life after death, rebirth, and the cycle of births and deaths. The case of early Buddhism, according to which mind and matter are said to be interdependent, can be discussed on similar lines. In fact the issue of materialism in Indian philosophy is connected with the issues of rebirth, bondage, and the liberation from cycle of births and deaths. Non-Cārvākas are non-materialists because they believe in these phenomena and Cārvākas are either materialists or sceptics because they do not. Hence the materialism of Cārvākas will be discussed here without mixing it in any way with the so-called materialism attributed by some scholars to systems such as Sāṅkhya, Nyāya-Vaiśeṣika, and Buddhism.

In this chapter, I will discuss three aspects of the materialism of Cārvākas.

1. The Nature of Cārvāka Materialism: I will discuss the extent and the sense in which the Cārvāka view concerning consciousness and self can be called materialistic.

2. Chattopadhyaya (1976: 293–4).

2. Epistemology of Cārvāka Materialism: I will discuss the cognitive apparatus and the arguments that would be most suitable for the knowledge and justification of Cārvāka materialism.
3. Social and Axiological Implications of Cārvāka Materialism: It is an interesting question whether the socio-economic form of materialism and the latter in its axiological sense would be implied by the kind of materialism which Cārvākas advocate.

The Nature of Cārvāka Materialism

The first question to be addressed here is: what is the materialist thesis of Cārvākas?

As has been stated, I am using the term materialism in the sense of the doctrine according to which consciousness is either reducible to matter or dependent on matter. One point of clarification would be in order. The word materialism is also used in an axiological sense according to which it is identified with sensualist hedonism. Whether Cārvākas were materialists in this sense also is an issue too, but this shall be discussed in the next chapter. This chapter will examine materialism as it is attributed to Cārvākas in its ontological sense. In the latter sense, materialism is a view about the nature of the world or the nature of a human being. Materialism about the nature of the world can be called cosmological materialism, whereas that about the nature of a human being can be called anthropological or psychological materialism. In each case, materialism can be either eliminative or non-eliminative. This is explained below.

At the cosmological level, materialism is an answer to questions such as: Is there consciousness over and above matter in the world? If there is consciousness, what is its status? How is it related to matter? A cosmological materialist will not accept the existence of consciousness or a conscious substance which exists independently of matter. But the answers from the viewpoint of eliminative materialism and non-eliminative materialism would be different. The answer from the former viewpoint would be that matter is the only reality and consciousness is not there at all; or whatever appears to be there as consciousness, is reducible to matter. The answer from the latter viewpoint would grant the reality of consciousness, but regard it as being dependent on matter.

At an anthropological or psychological level, the following questions are relevant to the issue of materialism: What is the nature of a human being? Is it just body (or brain or behaviour, or all these things together) or is there also consciousness? What is the self ('I') of a person? Is it identical with body or consciousness, or are both related to each other? If body and consciousness are related to each other, what is their relation? In response to these questions, a psychological/anthropological materialist would definitely deny the existence of a conscious self or mind which can exist independently of body. But again, the answers from the viewpoint of eliminative materialism and non-eliminative materialism would be different. An eliminative materialist would say that 'I' or 'self' is represented by the body alone (or the brain alone or behaviour alone)[3] and there is no role of consciousness in it, whereas a non-eliminative materialist would say that the body (or the brain or behaviour or all these things together) represent 'I' or the self only when they are qualified by consciousness.[4]

What is the Cārvāka approach to these two types of ontological questions? It seems evident that at the cosmological level the Cārvākas advocate non-eliminative materialism. That is because although they give primary importance to matter, that is, the four gross elements, and a secondary status to consciousness, they are not reducing consciousness to matter, but saying that consciousness arises from matter. At the psychological level, however, there does not seem to be unanimity in the answers that Cārvākas give. On the question, 'What is the self?', the preliminary answer is: 'The body is the self', or 'I am the body' (*dehātmavāda*). This would be an eliminative form of psychological materialism.[5] The ground for this type of materialism was that only the body can be perceived, the self, other than body,

3. The reductive theory in which 'I' is reduced to either brain or behaviour can be seen in some modern Western theories of the mind such as identity theory, eliminative physicalism (Horgan 1995), or behaviourism (Byrne 1995).

4. The view that the notion of 'I' should include bodily characteristics as well as consciousness is close to P. F. Strawson's theory that 'person' is the subject of both bodily and mental predicates. I will refer to this later in this chapter.

5. *sthūlo'haṁ taruṇo vṛddho yuvetyādiviśeṣaṇaiḥ/*
viśiṣṭadeha evātmā na tato'nyo vilakṣaṇaḥ// (*Sarvasiddhāntasaṅgraha* [*SSS*] 2.6)

[Self is nothing but body qualified by the descriptions such as 'I am fat', 'I am young', 'I am old', 'I am a teenager', and so on. It is not something different or excluded from it.]

cannot.[6] Against this, the possible objection was that if the body is to be identified with self, then even a dead body will have to be counted as self.[7] But this is impossible insofar as we mean by 'self' the self-identity of a person, or something representing the notion of 'I' of a person. So, Cārvākas, perhaps in response to such objections, presented a revised version which excludes dead bodies from the realm of self. According to this formulation, the self is body qualified by sentience (*caitanyaviśiṣṭa-kāya*[8]) or, to formulate it differently, 'I am the body qualified by consciousness.'[9] This gives us a non-eliminative psychological materialism.[10]

It should be noted here that the word 'ātman' in the term 'dehātmavāda' is used as a pronoun rather than as a noun. It means

6. *dehātirikte ātmani pramāṇābhāvāt. pratyakṣaikapramāṇavāditayā anumānāder-anaṅgīkāreṇa prāmāṇābhāvāt*' (*Sarvadarśanasaṅgraha* [*SDS*], Cārvāka-darśana)

[Because there is no authoritative means to the knowledge of self additional to the body. Because we accept only perception as the authoritative means to knowledge, the means such as inference have no authority, as they are not accepted by us.]

7. '*śarīrasya na caitanyaṁ mṛteṣu vyabhicārataḥ*' (*Kārikāvali* [*KA*], v. 48).

[Consciousness is not the property of body. Because (in that case it should belong to a dead body also, but) it does not belong to dead bodies.] This argument of Viśvanātha is aimed at showing that consciousness does not belong to body. But it can be easily applied to the question whether self-identity can be attributed to the body.

8. '*caitanyaviśiṣṭaḥ kāyaḥ puruṣaḥ*', included in many texts; see Bhattacharya (2012: 79).

9. In *Nyāyamañjarī* (*NM*), Jayanta sometimes considers and criticises the preliminary version of the Cārvāka view that body itself is the self. He criticizes the view by saying that desire, and such like, cannot have the body as their support because the body goes on changing whereas the mental characteristics such as desire presuppose continuity. (*NM*, part II, p. 10). At a later stage of discussion, he presents the sophisticated version by attributing it to learned Cārvākas, according to which the knower-element continues in body till death, but not after that.

yāvaccharīram avasthitam ekaṁ pramātṛtattvam anusandhānādivyavahārasamartham astu nāma; kastatra kalahāyate? śarīrādūrdhvaṁ tu tadastīti kimatra pramāṇaṁ? na ca pūrvaśarīram apahāya śarīrāntaraṁ saṁkrāmati pramātā (*NM*, part II, p. 39)

[Verily let there be a single knower-element, capable of performing the act of recollection and so on, which stays till the body exists. Who quarrels about that? But what is the evidence for its existence after the body dies? The knower does not transmigrate to another body by leaving the earlier body.]

10. This is the standard version of psychological materialism according to which the self is defined as 'body qualified by consciousness'. But in principle it is possible to formulate it as 'consciousness qualified by body (that is, consciousness which is essentially embodied)' or as 'the mind–body complex, where both are inseparable'. Particularly the second version ('essentially-embodied consciousness') seems to be attributed to 'learned Cārvākas' by Jayantabhaṭṭa. See note 9 in this chapter.

'I' or 'oneself' and not the metaphysical substance called ātman. Here the dehātmavāda (body-as-the-self doctrine) of the Cārvākas should be compared clearly with the doctrine of self (ātmavāda) of the spiritualists (*ātmavādins* such as Vedāntines, Naiyāyikas, and Vaiśeṣikas) and also with no-self doctrine (*anātmavāda*) of the Buddhists. The term 'self' in the doctrine of self refers to an eternal substance having consciousness as its quality or essence. Naturally, body-as-the-self doctrine is not a doctrine of self because the former does not regard self as an eternal substance. On the other hand, the no-self doctrine of the Buddhists which denies self does not deny it in its primary sense, namely 'I' or 'oneself', but denies it in the sense of eternal self-substance. Insofar as the body-as-the-self doctrine of the Cārvākas also denies the eternal self-substance, apparently it can be understood as a form of the no-self doctrine.

However, two points of difference between the no-self doctrine and the body-as-the-self doctrine will remain:

1. According to body-as-the-self doctrine, the corporeal body is non-eternal, but it has concrete/substantial existence, whereas consciousness is dependent on body, and has no substantial existence. According to the no-self doctrine, neither body nor consciousness (mind) is substantial; both are interdependent and none of them is existentially fundamental.
2. According to the body-as-the-self doctrine, the corporeal body being existentially fundamental, when the body disintegrates, consciousness ceases to exist. According to the no-self doctrine, consciousness does not cease when the body disintegrates. According to this, neither body nor consciousness has substantial continuity, they have serial continuity, which makes transmigration possible.

In this way the body-as-the-self doctrine is different from both the doctrines—that of 'self' and 'no-self'.

Knowledge and Justification of Cārvāka Materialism

The Cārvāka materialism, whether it is presented at a cosmological level or a psychological level, has to face an epistemological–logical challenge. The following questions become relevant at this juncture: Which means to knowledge are suitable for ascertainment of the materialist thesis of Cārvākas? Which are the arguments suitable for its justification? How can the Cārvāka materialism be defended against the opponents' arguments?

I have pointed out earlier that there is greater diversity in Cārvāka epistemology as compared to their ontology. All Cārvākas, except the sceptics, accept materialism, but try to support it by different forms of empiricist epistemology. It can be doubted, however, whether every variety of empiricism attributed to Cārvākas is equally capable of supporting their materialism. It is obvious that the popular Cārvāka epistemology of 'perception alone as the means to knowledge' is not suitable for the Cārvāka style materialism and that a certain type of inference will have to be accepted as a means to its knowledge and justification. Now the question arises as to what kind of inference is befitting for the justification of materialism. In the previous chapter, I have referred to the types of inference such as empirical inference (*utpanna-pratīti* inference), non-empirical inference (*utpādya-pratīti* inference), and commonsensical inference (*loka-prasiddha* inference). In terms of those inferences, I distinguished between two varieties of mitigated empiricism of Cārvākas, which I called positivist empiricism and common-sense-oriented empiricism respectively. Here I will discuss in some detail as to which form of empiricism is most fitting for the justification of Cārvāka materialism.

Cārvākas present their materialist argument mainly in the context of cosmological materialism that assumes the title *bhūta-caitanya-vāda*, which means that consciousness arises from the combination of four gross elements. Of course the argument also has an anthropological or biological aspect because according to this argument, the consciousness arises from that combination of matter which assumes the form of an organic body. The three aphorisms of Bṛhaspati seem to be relevant here:

1. Earth, water, fire, and air are the essential categories (*tattvas*).[11]

11. '*pṛthivyāpastejo vāyuriti tattvāni/*' (Bhattacharya 2012: 78).

2. Their combination gets designated as 'body', 'sense organ', and 'object'.[12]
3. Consciousness arises from them (the elements), which have assumed the form of body, like the power of intoxication arises from molasses and other things[13] [or, like the red colour that arises when betel leaf is chewed with other ingredients of 'paan'[14]].

The third aphorism mentioned is the core of the Cārvāka argument for cosmological materialism. But before considering its relevance for Cārvāka epistemology, it is necessary to make some points of clarification regarding the first two aphorisms, as they prepare the background for the third.

1. The first aphorism refers to the four elements as the essential categories. It is interesting to note that it does not refer to ether/space (*ākāśa*) as an element which is generally accepted in the orthodox systems. Curiously enough, it is a common tendency among the heterodox systems of Indian philosophy not to count ākāśa among physical elements. Here one has to distinguish between two concepts of ākāśa, as a positive material element (as a *bhūta* or *mahābhūta*) and as space (understood as a container or vacuum or place maker, and such like.). When heterodox systems accept ākāśa, they accept it in the second sense, but not in the first. Orthodox

12. *'tatsamudāye śarīrendriyaviṣayasaṁjñāḥ/'* (Bhattacharya 2012: 79).

13. *'tebhya eva dehākārapariṇatebhyaḥ kiṇvādibhyo madaśaktivaccaitanyamupajāy ate'* (*SDS*, Cārvāka-darśana). [From the same four elements which develop into the form of body, arises consciousness, like the power of intoxication which arises from molasses, and so on.]

14. *'jaḍabhūtavikāreṣu caitanyaṁ yattu dṛśyate/ tāmbūlapūgacūrṇānāṁ yogād rāga ivotthitam//'* (*SSS* II.7). [The consciousness, which is seen in the modified insentient elements, arises in them, like the red colour arises due to the combination of betel-leaf, betel-nut and (spice-)powder.] The metaphor refers to what is called *paan* in Indian regional languages and is termed as *tāmbūla* in Sanskrit. The *Monier Williams Dictionary* explains the term 'tāmbūla' as: 'Betel, especially its pungent and aromatic leaf chewed with the areca-nut catechu and sometimes caustic lime and spices as a carminative and antacid tonic.' The significant point here is that tāmbūla, which is mainly made of green leaf, when chewed, becomes red due to a biochemical reaction.

systems accept ākāśa primarily in the first sense and at times mix it up with that in the second sense. In both the senses, it is regarded as all-pervasive. Now I am suggesting that the Cārvāka policy of not including ākāśa in the list of essential categories is in agreement with the attitude of other heterodox systems. It is also theoretically more elegant to do so, because accepting ākāśa as an all-pervasive positive substance is problematic.[15]

2. In the second aphorism the Cārvāka author refers to the combinations of the four elements, but does not seem to be spelling out 'how' or 'why' such combinations take place. For other systems this question is very much relevant, because they accept some kind of divine order or Kārmic order behind whatever takes place. Atomist systems (like Nyāya-Vaiśeṣika, Jainism, and the realist schools of Buddhism) generally argue that body, senses, and external objects are all atomic combinations whereas Saṅkhya/Vedānta-oriented systems treat them as combinations of three strands of primordial matter or cosmic Illusion (*prakṛti* or *māyā*). All of them accept, over and above these phenomena as the natural causal factors, some 'unseen'(*adṛṣṭa*) causal factors rooted in the past karma and some of them would accept, in addition, God's will. Sāṅkhya system gives a general teleological explanation of these phenomena as taking place for the sake of the soul (puruṣa) but also refers to karmic sources, which form the subtle body. None of these is acceptable to Cārvākas. They would accept natural causal factors, but not the alleged factors such as karma, God's will, or the teleology of the soul. At that stage they would say that the occurrence of these

15. For example, it is hard to explain that an all-pervasive (and also part-less, indivisible) substance is a constituent of the mortal physical body, that it constitutes the auditory sense organ, and so on. Bhattacharya has pointed out that in Manimekalai, there are references to thinkers called *bhūtavādins* who accept five elements including ākāśa and that Guṇaratna refers to some sections of Cārvākas who consider space as the fifth element. See Bhattacharya (2012: 39–40). It is possible that some Cārvākas might have done so under the influence of Nyāya-Vaiśeṣikas or Saṅkhyas.

combinations is accidental (*yadṛcchā*) or rooted in the nature of things (*svabhāva*).[16]

Against this background, one can discuss the third aphorism which gives the core of the materialist doctrine of the Cārvākas. Historically, it may be noticed that except the school of the sceptic Cārvākas, such as that of Jayarāśi, all the epistemological schools of Cārvākas seem to accept this doctrine at the ontological level. Even the popular Cārvāka view found in the works like *Ṣaḍdarśanasamuccaya* and *Sarvadarśanasaṅgraha*, which denies inference as *pramāṇa*, is found to be presented along with cosmological materialism and also psychological materialism. This appears to be a discrepancy, because though the one who regards only perception as pramāṇa can claim to know the four gross elements and their sensible qualities by perception, and arguably, also one's own consciousness by internal perception, he or she cannot claim to know only on the basis of perception that consciousness arises from matter. Hence, the absolute empiricism of the popular Cārvāka school does not support its cosmological materialism. In order to know and then to justify that consciousness arises from matter, one needs an inference. But a question arises at this point: What kind of inference will serve the purpose?

To answer this question, one has to revive the two versions of the Cārvāka approach to inference from the previous chapter and apply them to the context of Cārvāka materialism.

16. This seems to resemble the views of Democritus for whom physical atoms combine and split on their own chance. We come across different cosmological theories in Greek philosophy for explaining the phenomenon of 'combination of atoms'. Empedocles, the pre-Socratic philosopher, says that earth, air, fire, and water are the basic stuff of the world. They are combined by love and separated by strife (Kirk and Raven 1977: 329–30). This comes close to the Cārvāka theory of *svabhāvavāda*. In Greek thought, the need to enter into the debate about cosmos was motivated by the need to get away from the religious worldviews of their times in the 5th century BC. Religious worldviews in ancient Greece explained change as the capricious ways of Gods and their using human beings as play things. Contrariwise, a more sophisticated scientific explanation was offered by the philosophers, namely Thales, Anaximander, and Anaximenes (Kirk and Raven 1977: 74–162). Non-Cārvāka thinkers in India seem to combine naturalist cosmological approach with a religious-teleological approach.

Positivist Empiricism (Acceptance of Empirical Inference)

One may recall here the positivist epistemology which Jayantabhaṭṭa attributes to those he calls the 'more learned' Cārvākas. Here we will ask the question whether this policy of the more learned Cārvākas would help them in establishing the materialist thesis. The materialist thesis of Cārvākas is brought out clearly by the third aphorism of Bṛhaspati, which states: 'Consciousness arises from the four gross elements, like the intoxicating power which arises from molasses.'[17]

What kind of inference is this? Is it an empirical inference or a non-empirical inference? That consciousness arises in four elements cannot be directly known either in our own person or in others. In the case of others we can see only body and not their consciousness. In the case of one's own self, one can be conscious of one's own consciousness only when one is conscious. One cannot be (directly) conscious of the stage in which one is not conscious (because that is logically impossible) and hence one cannot observe the transition of oneself from non-conscious stage to conscious stage. Hence empirical inference is not useful for establishing the materialist thesis.

Naturally, the Cārvāka argument for the material origin of consciousness is a non-empirical inference. I have tried to show in the previous chapter that common-sense-empiricist Cārvākas can accept an empirical inference as a source of knowledge as a rule and they are inclined to accept non-empirical inference only under the condition that it is lokaprasiddha, that is, acceptable within the framework of worldly way of life.

Common-sense Empiricism (Acceptance of Lokaprasiddha *Inference)*

In order to explore the possibility that the materialist argument of the Cārvākas be understood and explained as a lokaprasiddha inference, one has to concentrate on the version of the argument indicated by

17. Refer to note 13 in this chapter.

the third aphorism of Bṛhaspati and also its variant found in *Sarvasiddhāntasaṅgraha* (*SSS*) more carefully and systematically.

1. Bṛhaspati's version: 'Consciousness arises from the four gross elements, like the intoxicating power which arises from molasses.'
2. *SSS* version: 'The consciousness, which is seen in the modified insentient elements, arises in them, like the red colour arises due to the combination of betel-leaf, betel-nut and (spice-) powder.'[18]

Both the formulations have the form of an argument, though an incomplete one. The argument is incomplete because it contains statement of the thesis (*pratijñā*) and instance (*dṛṣṭānta*) but no reason (*hetu.*) So, an important question arises: What is the reason intended by Cārvākas?

In order to trace the reason, one needs to elaborate the contention of the Cārvākas. One thing that is certain is that here Cārvākas intend to express the idea of inseparability between body and consciousness.[19] Here one has to note the metaphors for consciousness used by the Cārvākas. Bṛhaspati's version uses the metaphor of intoxicating power. Intoxicating power presupposes intoxicating function. Accordingly, consciousness here is assimilated with a power (disposition) or a function. The *SSS* version uses the metaphor of red colour. Here consciousness is assimilated with a quality. The idea is that when consciousness arises in a combination of four elements, it arises like new quality or a new function or a new power. In all the three cases, the emergent quality or function or power is inseparable from the material combination which has it. Here, one is reminded of the notion of 'inseparably existent' (*ayutasiddha*) introduced by Nyāya-Vaiśeṣika thinkers. Nyāya-Vaiśeṣikas called the relation between the two inseparables as *samavāya* (inherence) and acknowledged five such pairs of inseparables: (*a*) quality and its bearer (*guṇa-guṇin*), (*b*) motion and its carrier (*kriyā-kriyāvān*), (*c*) universal and particular (*jāti-vyakti*),

18. See note 14 in this chapter.

19. We shall see in Chapter 7 that it is precisely this aspect of the so-called body–mind relation, that S. S. Barlingay emphasizes in his philosophical writings.

(*d*) whole and its parts (*avayavin-avayava*), and (*e*) uniqueness and eternal substance (*viśeṣa-nityadravya*).[20] Nyāya-Vaiśeṣikas did not acknowledge 'power and the powerful' as one such pair because they did not accept power (*śakti*) as an ontological category. But this is not the main point here. Whether one accepts inherence as an independent ontological category (*padārtha*) is a question, but this also is not the main point. The main point here is that Cārvākas try to understand consciousness on the model of a quality (*guṇa)* or function (kriyā) of a body, or disposition (śakti) of a body. If a quality or a function or a power arises in a substance, then the substance is called the material cause (*samavāyi-kāraṇa/upādāna-kāraṇa*) of that quality or function or power. In this sense, the body can be called the material cause of the consciousness, which arises in it. So at this stage, the Cārvākas are simply arguing that since consciousness is inseparable from the corporeal body, it must have the corporeal body as its material cause. So the reason which could be added to the above incomplete argument would be that,

> Because consciousness is inseparable from the combination of matter.
>
> By adding this reason the argument can be stated as follows:

1. Consciousness, which is a heterogeneous property of a body, must be arising from the body and not from a cause external to the body.
2. For it is inseparable from the body.
3. Any property found in a substance, has that substance itself as its material cause, like intoxicating power which arises in fermented molasses and red colour which arises in *paan*.[21]

20. '*yayordvayorekamavinaśyadaparāśritameva avatiṣṭhate tāvayutasiddhau.*' [The two are called 'inseparably existent' out of whom one resides in the other insofar as the former is not destroyed.] (See *Tarkasaṁgraha* [*TSa*], sec. 79.)

21. The argument, as I have formulated it, does not follow the so-called standard pattern of five-limbed inferential statement (*pañcāvayavi-vākya*) but of three limbs. I have suggested in Gokhale (1992: 95–8) that the formula of two premises ('vyāpti' and 'pakṣadharmatā') and the conclusion (either at the end of the argument or in the beginning in the form of the thesis to be proved) may be acceptable. In the present case, analogy (dṛṣṭānta) has a special role. Hence it has been included along with the statement of the general rule (vyāpti).

A question can be raised about the meaning of the word 'arising' in view of the two theories of causation well known in Indian philosophy: inherentism (*satkāryavāda*: 'the effect inherent in its cause') and non-inherentism (*asatkāryavāda*: 'the effect non-inherent in its cause'). This gives rise to two versions of the Cārvāka materialism. According to the inherentist version, consciousness is already inherent in the four material elements, it only becomes manifest when the elements are combined in a particular way. According to the non-inherentist version, consciousness is not already present in the matter; it emerges as something new. In some texts, both the options are kept open.[22] However, heterogeneity between consciousness and matter makes better sense if consciousness is regarded as non-inherent in the material elements.

The inference for Cārvāka materialism as formulated previously falls under the category of non-empirical inference. It is based on a very general type of generalization about material causation in general, and not about the law of origination of consciousness from material body which is a special case of material causation. Hence, it is the inference of an object seen in a general way (*sāmānyatodṛṣṭa* inference). It is also a kind of analogical inference, because intoxicating power, which is generated in molasses, is just a metaphor or analogy for consciousness and not an instance of it.[23] Now the question is: Would such a non-empirical, analogical inference be acceptable in the Cārvāka epistemological framework, and if so, under what conditions would it be acceptable?

Here I want to suggest that although the specified argument is a case of non-empirical inference, it can still be acceptable to

22. '*kecidabhivyjyate iti, ... anye tu prādurbhavatīti*' (*Nyāyakumudacandra* [*NKC*] (I), p. 342; *Tattva-Saṅgraha-Pañjikā* [*TSP*]: v. 1858–9). [According to some it ('arises') means 'becomes manifest'... according to some it means 'emerges'.]

23. Kar (2013: 31–4) argues that Cārvāka materialism is not metaphysical materialism in the sense that it is not based on any a priori presuppositions, but is derived on empirical grounds. Though I would largely agree with him, what I am arguing here is that Cārvāka materialism, insofar as their explanation of consciousness is concerned, adopts a methodology which cannot be completely dissociated from speculative reasoning. Still it is closer to science than to speculative metaphysics because, it is strongly supported by common sense and 'this-worldly framework'. The science tries to explain common sense and this-worldly existence, whereas speculative metaphysics has many times tried to explain them away.

mitigated-empiricist Cārvākas on the ground that it is lokaprasiddha, that is, commonly acceptable or acceptable within the framework of worldly way of life.

The argument for the material origin of consciousness will be a typical case of lokaprasiddha inference. The plausibility of such an argument is not based on 'logical necessity' or 'empirical necessity' but 'pragmatic necessity' or 'explanatory necessity'. One is claiming here that just as the power of intoxication in processed molasses cannot be explained without accepting their origin in the molasses themselves (it cannot be explained satisfactorily as a transcendent entity having an isolated existence or arising mysteriously as a miracle), similarly, consciousness that is found in body—and it is not found outside it—cannot be explained satisfactorily without accepting its origin in the material body itself.

Inference for the transmigrating soul as the substratum of consciousness is not acceptable because it transcends the limits of worldly life. But inference for matter as the cause of consciousness or the living body itself as the locus of consciousness is prima facie acceptable because it can be explained within the framework of worldly life.

Opponents' Objections and the Possible Cārvāka Responses

Cārvāka materialism, whether in cosmological form or psychological form is criticized and condemned by all the other systems of Indian philosophy because it goes against their deep-rooted belief in karma and rebirth.

The opponents of Cārvākas try to make two types of claims against the Cārvāka materialism. They try to show that consciousness cannot qualify the matter or body, but consciousness must belong to some locus other than body. Second, they try to show that the proper referent of the term 'I' cannot be body but some conscious being other than body.

Let us consider the main objections coming from the non-Cārvāka systems against materialism and the possible Cārvāka answers to them.

Argument from Heterogeneity

Cārvākas argue that consciousness must have the combination of material elements, that is, the corporeal body, as its material cause. The opponents of Cārvākas object precisely to this. They claim that since the body and consciousness are essentially different, consciousness cannot belong to the body.[24] They are thinking that in the case of material cause, there is homogeneity between cause and effect—the effect cannot be radically different from its material cause. For example if the threads are yellow, the cloth will also be yellow, if the earthen halves are red, the earthen pot will also be red. Here the opponents are distinguishing between efficient cause (*nimitta-kāraṇa*) and material cause (*upādāna-kāraṇa*). Efficient cause is externally related to the effect and can be heterogeneous to it. For example, a weaver is an efficient cause of the cloth. He is externally related to the cloth and can be heterogeneous with it. (For example, a weaver is sentient, whereas the cloth produced is insentient.) But threads are the material cause of the cloth; they are internally related to it and have to be homogeneous with it. So the opponents think that if consciousness has a material cause, it must be homogeneous with it. They think that the corporeal body being heterogeneous with consciousness cannot be its material cause. So they imagine a non-corporeal substance, a soul or a spirit, which they call ātman, puruṣa, jīva, and so on, as the cause or abode of consciousness. Buddhists do not believe in the substance called ātman, but they accept a continuum (*santāna*) of consciousness and regard 'immediately preceding consciousness' as the 'immediate cause' (*samanantara-pratyaya*) of the occurrence of consciousness at any given moment.[25]

24. This argument is implicit in almost all the systems of Indian philosophy which try to assert a sharp distinction between conscious and unconscious (*cetana* and *acetana*) and to put body, sense organs, and even 'manas' in the category of unconscious and ātman/puruṣa/jīva in the category of conscious. Buddhists placed *citta* (equivalent to manas) in the conscious category, because they denied ātman over and above citta. But they distinguished citta (that is, mind, along with cetasikas, that is, mental states) from *rūpa*, that is, matter.

25. *Samanantarapratyaya*, also called *anantarapratyaya*, is defined as '*samaśca asau anantaraśca asau avyavahitatvena, sa cāsau pratyayaśca hetutvāt samanantarapratyayaḥ*' (*Nāyabinduṭīkā* [*NBT*] on the definition of 'manovijñāna', p. 57). [Samantarapratyaya is the one which is similar to the effect, immediately preceding to the effect because of uninterruptedness, and is pratyaya, being a cause.]

The Cārvāka Response

Three-fold answer is possible from the Cārvāka side:

1. The Cārvākas use in their argument instances like intoxicating power generated in molasses and red colour generated in paan and thereby show that material cause and its effect can be heterogeneous in nature. The instances are modelled to show how a material cause can produce an effect, which is entirely new, different, and hence heterogeneous with it. Molasses, that is, the raw material used for producing liquor, does not initially have intoxicating function, but the intoxication arises in it anew through the process of fermentation. Also, the betel leaf and other ingredients of paan, do not initially have red colour, but it arises anew through the process of mixing and chewing the ingredients. Similarly, consciousness, which was not there before in the material elements, can arise in them if the elements combine in a peculiar way so as to form an organic body. Here the notions of 'processing', 'mixing and chewing', and 'peculiar combination' are significant, though Cārvākas have only suggested, and not used them explicitly. These may remind us of the distinction we are taught in school chemistry between a chemical compound and a mixture. In a mixture the ingredients which are mixed do not lose their own properties, but only add to each other's properties. For instance, lime juice mixed with sugar and salt has a taste that is sweet, sour, and salty. It does not have an entirely different taste, heterogeneous with the original taste, because it is just a mixture and not a chemical compound. But water (H_2O) is a chemical compound of hydrogen and oxygen, and has an entirely different property (useful for extinguishing fire) than the properties of its components—hydrogen, which is inflammable and oxygen, which helps burning. Similarly, Cārvākas are suggesting, corporeal body is not just four elements put together, but their biochemical compound which assumes an entirely different property, namely, sentience which was not there in the material elements.
2. The Cārvākas would point out that even those who regard the transcendent self as the locus of consciousness have to accept

the close relation between the body and consciousness. That is why, for instance, Naiyāyikas who accepted the self as all-pervasive, had to accept consciousness which was the quality of the self, as non-substance-pervading (*avyāpyavṛtti*) because it can arise only within the limits of body. Similarly the Jainas had to accept the soul as having the same size as the body.

Hence the inseparable connection between body and consciousness cannot be ruled out.

3. Jayarāśi's argument, which he gives in support of Bṛhaspati's alleged statement '*śarīrādeva*' ('consciousness arises from the body alone'), is relevant here. He addresses the argument to the Buddhists who accept causal inference (*kāryānumana*) as a kind of inference and inference of fire from smoke as its example. Jayarāśi presents the argument in the form of a dilemma in the following way.

Though fire is supposed to be the material cause of smoke, smoke and fire are heterogeneous in nature. Now if a material cause can be heterogeneous with its effect, then there should not be any harm in matter (rūpa) being the material cause of consciousness (vijñāna). If, on the other hand, the Buddhists hold that matter cannot be the material cause of consciousness because they are heterogeneous in nature, then fire cannot be the material cause of smoke. Hence, the causal inference accepted by the Buddhists will be problematic.[26]

26. Jayarāśi's argument runs as follows:

> The causal character of fire in relation to smoke is not tenable in the following way also. Does the fire produce smoke in the capacity of efficient cause or material cause? If former is the case, then the smoke-nature of smoke is not explicable without (a reference to its) material cause. If the latter, then we ask, how can a heterogeneous thing be a material cause? If we accept heterogeneous material cause, then consciousness can arise in the things like fetus from the complex of body and organs and hence there is no need to imagine consciousness belonging to another world.

Now if you say that consciousness cannot arise without the homogenous cause, namely (immediately preceding) consciousness, then how do you accept the generation of smoke from the heterogeneous cause, namely fire? If fire (according to you) is homogenous with smoke because both are material in nature, then the body too is homogenous with consciousness because both are 'unique particulars' (*svalaksana*) in nature. Keeping this in mind it has been said that '(consciousness arises) from body according to Bṛhaspati' (*Tattvopaplavasiṁha* [*TUS*]: p. 87, line 24 and p. 88, line 9; translation mine).

Jayarāśi presents the argument in the form of a dilemma because he, as a sceptic, does not want to commit himself to any side. He is making a case for materialism as a possibility, not as certainty.

Argument from Personal Identity

Non-Cārvākas argue that personal identity entails continuity of a conscious being independently of the changes in body. We recognize ourselves in old age as the same (continuous) persons as we were in childhood. Others also can recognize us in the same way. This personal identity becomes possible due to the faculty of memory (*smṛti*) and recognition (*pratyabhijñā*) which marks continuity in our conscious life. There is nothing common between the body of childhood and that of old age. If the body changes completely but consciousness is continuous, then it must belong to a locus different from the body.[27]

The Cārvāka Response

This argument was difficult to answer earlier because the role of the brain in memory was not known. Though the Cārvākas would accept that the body undergoes change, they do not say that everything is momentary. Although all the parts of the body, which consist of material elements, are subject to change and disintegration, some parts of the body change more rapidly than others. More specifically, the question of remembering in old age how one was in one's childhood is the question about long-term memory. Scientists claim that long-term memory is maintained by more stable and permanent changes in neural connections widely spread through the brain. Cārvākas today can appreciate this explanation and replace with it the doctrine of soul as a ground for long-term memory and recognition. The role of the self, which the traditional Cārvākas assigned to the body, the modern Cārvākas would assign to the brain. Jocularly it may

27. This is the argument from recognition used for proving the existence of permanent self: '*ahameva jñātavān ahameva vedmi ityādeḥ ekakartṛviṣayatayā pratyabhijñānasya bhāvataḥ sattvād ātmā prasiddhaḥ*' (*TSP*, v. 228). [The self is established from the real existence of the recognition such as 'I myself have known this (before) and I myself, am knowing (now)' which has a single subject as its object.] In Western philosophy, this argument refers to memory as the criterion of persistence of a person. See Olson (2010).

be said that the ancient doctrine of 'body-as-the-self (dehātmavāda) would be modified by the modern Cārvāka into the doctrine of brain-as-the-self (*brain-ātma-vāda*).

The learned Cārvākas referred to by Jayanta do not identify the self with body but they accept 'knower-principle' (*pramātṛ-tattva*), which is coterminous with the living body.[28] On account of this principle, the memory of the past events in this life becomes possible. But there is no question of recollecting events of the past life. As the learned Cārvāka of Jayanta says:

> The knower-principle does not leave the previous body and enter another body. If it would do so, then the person would recollect the things experienced in the past life like he recollects the things experienced in childhood, while being in the present body. If eternality of the knower and difference in the body is common in both the cases, we do not surmise any reason, why he should remember only what he has experienced in this life and not what he has experienced in another life. Hence the knower does not exist after the body dies. So leave the repeated story-telling about other worlds based on the doctrine of eternality of soul and stay happily.[29]

Argument from Karma and Rebirth

The main step the opponents take in this regard is to extend the continuity of consciousness beyond this life. This is done in two ways:

1. According to the doctrine of karma, everyone gets the fruit of each of their actions according to the moral/religious worth of the action. Since the operation of this rule is not fully observed

28. See note 9 in this chapter. It can be said that this knower-principle is more a disposition rooted in brain.

29. *na ca pūrvaśarīramapahāya śarīrāntaraṁ saṅkrāmati pramātā/ Yadi hyevaṁ bhavet tadiha śarīre śaiśavadaśānubhūta-padārtha-smaraṇavad atīta-janmānubhūta-padārtha-smaraṇamapi tasya bhavet/ nahi tasya nityatvāviśeṣe ca śarīrabhedāviśeṣe ca smaraṇa-viśeṣe kāraṇamutpaśyāmaḥ, yadiha-janmanyevānubhūtaṁ smarati nānya-janmānubhūtamiti/ tasmād ūrdhvaṁ dehān nāstyeva pramāteti nityātma-vādamūla-paraloka-kathā-kurukurvīm apāsya yathāsukhamāsyatām/* (NM, part II, p. 39)

within this life, one has to accept continuity of consciousness beyond this life.

2. Naiyāyikas believe that a newly born baby sucks her mother's nipple because it knows that it is a desirable act. This knowledge must be based on prior experience, which the child must have had in a previous birth.

The doctrine of karma is also aimed at explanation of the diversity in nature. Different animals have different physical features and capacities. They are born with those natures because of their past karma. Some persons are happy, some unhappy. This too cannot be explained without accepting past karma. Opponents generally accept God (*īśvara*) in addition to karma. God creates diversity in nature and distributes pleasures and pains to beings. But He does not do so from his will. In that case, God would be biased and partial. God creates diversity in accordance with the past karma of beings.

The Cārvāka Response

1. The Cārvākas do not accept the doctrine of karma because it is not supported by experience.
2. The Cārvākas would say that the tendency of the child to suck her mother's nipple is natural or instinctual. If it is due to the recollection of prior experiences, they argue, why don't they have explicit speech and recollection revived from previous birth?[30]

Cārvākas deny the opponents' claim that the diversity in nature is due to Īśvara or karma. Here, Cārvākas adhere to the doctrine of self-nature (*svabhāvavāda*) when they say:

> As for the pleasure and pain, the opponents should not imagine merit and demerit (as their causes). People become happy or unhappy by their own nature. There is no other cause.

30. *nāmābhyāsabalādeva yadi teṣāṁ pravartate/*
Tat kiṁ na visphuṭā vācaḥ smṛtirvā vāgmināmiva// (*Tattvasaṅgraha* [*TS*], v. 1945)

[If the said conceptual cognition of the newborn infants proceeds from the repeated cognition of names, how is it that they do not have the memory or the clear speech of the eloquent speakers? (Jha 1986: 928).]

Who makes peacocks colourful? Who makes cuckoos sing?
There is no cause other than self-nature in this case.[31]

Argument from Linguistic Usage

Opponents of the Cārvākas draw our attention to certain linguistic usages, which indicate that the first person singular pronoun 'I' refers to the self and not to the body. They are: 'I perceive the table', 'I am happy', and so on. Here one does not uphold propositions such as 'This body/visual sense organ perceives the table' or 'This body is happy'. Since the former are genuine and authentic usages, they clearly show that the one who is happy, the one who perceives, and so on, is not the body but someone other than the body.[32]

The Cārvāka Response

Here the Cārvākas draw our attention to other linguistic usages which are equally genuine and authentic, such as 'I am fat', 'I am young', 'I am old', and so on, where 'I' refers to body and not to the self (we don't say, 'my body is fat', 'my body is young', and so on).[33] In this controversy, both the parties regard certain usages as genuine and primary and certain others as non-genuine and secondary, when it seems that both are genuine and primary. Hence, both the ways—the eliminative way of reducing 'I' to body alone and the spiritualist's way of reducing 'I' to the self alone—become problematic. Here the non-eliminative psychological materialism which regards 'I' as 'body qualified by consciousness' fares better because then both physical and mental predicates can be attributed to 'I' without any difficulty. This does not mean, however, that 'I' refers sometimes to the body (alone) and sometimes to consciousness (alone). It would be more correct to

31. See note 25 in Chapter 3.

32. Kumārila, for instance, argues on these lines in *Ślokavārtikam* (*SV*, 'Ātmavāda', v. 110–38).

33. See note 5 in this chapter. Also, '*dehātmavāde ca "sthūlo'ham", "kṛśo'ham", "kṛṣṇo'ham" ityādisāmānādhikaraṇyopapattiḥ. Mama śarīramiti vyavahāro rāhoḥ śira ityādivad aupacārikaḥ*' (*SDS*, Cārvāka-darśana). [By holding the doctrine that the soul is identical with the body, the identity of reference (of subject and predicate) in the phrases such as 'I am fat', 'I am thin', and 'I am black' becomes intelligible. The expression, 'my body', is meaningful in secondary sense, like the expression, 'the head of Rāhu' (Rāhu being really all head)].

say that it refers to the complex of body and its sentience where the two are inseparable. Because regarding body and mind (or consciousness or sentience) as two different substances would be a category mistake for Cārvākas like it was for Gilbert Ryle.[34]

A Comparative Note

In the modern Western philosophical context, materialism (what is now a days called physicalism) developed as a response to Cartesian dualism and as an offshoot of development in neuroscience. In ancient India, materialism developed as a response to ātmavāda of the spiritualist schools (which believed in liberation of disembodied self as the ultimate goal). Śaṅkara, a leader of Indian spiritualism, anticipated the Cartesian cogito when he said that nobody can deny self because nobody can deny the existence of oneself.[35] The argument shares problematic nature with the Cartesian cogito, because though 'I' may be indubitable, this 'I' need not be the same as the 'self', the spiritual substance which can exist independently of body. As against the doctrine of self as a spiritual substance, one comes across two broad types of responses in India and the West:

1. No-self Doctrine: Accordingly there is no substance called self, the 'I' is just a mental construct (Buddhism) or a bundle of perceptions (Hume). Phenomenalism would belong to the same category
2. Materialism, Behaviourism, and so on: The 'I' does not stand for a spiritual substance, but for some essentially bodily/material

34. Ryle (2000), 'Descartes's Myth'.

35. *'sarvo hyātmāstitvaṁ pratyeti, na nāhamasmīti'* (*BSSB*). [Everybody experiences the existence of ātman (that is, oneself); nobody experiences, 'I am not'.] Another verse attributed to Śaṁkara closely resembles Cartesian argument from doubt:

> *asti svayamityasmin viṣaye kasyāsti saṁśayaḥ puṁsaḥ/*
> *Tatrāpi saṁśayaścet saṁśayitā yaḥ sa eva bhavasi tvam//* (*Svātmānandaprakāśikāryā*)

[Which person has doubt as regards the fact that he himself exists? If you have a doubt even about this, then whosoever is the doubter is the same as you.]

thing or process. Materialism/physicalism of reductive (eliminative) or non-reductive variety,[36] epiphenomenalism,[37] Searle's biological naturalism,[38] behaviourism,[39] functionalism,[40] cognitive science,[41] identity theory,[42] emergentism,[43] will all belong to this broad category. Even Strawson's theory of person, also called the double aspect theory, according to which person is the subject of both psychological and material predicates,[44] will fall in this category insofar as one does not conceive of the 'disembodied person'.

As I have suggested, Cārvākas generally do not go for a reductive form of materialism, according to which consciousness or mental states are reduced to bodily states or neurophysiological processes and such like. Their position will be closer to other physicalist or quasi-physicalist trends such as Strawson's theory of person, non-reductive physicalism, epiphenomenalism and Searle's biological naturalism. Let us briefly consider their similarity and differences with the Cārvāka materialism.

I have pointed out that according to the non-eliminative psychological materialism of Cārvākas, a person is identified as body qualified by consciousness. This idea comes close to Strawson's theory that 'person' is the subject of both bodily and mental predicates.[45] Of course Strawsonian version can be one version of this kind. Other versions could be (*a*) 'I' represents body characterized by consciousness, and (*b*) 'I' represents embodied consciousness. These three versions will differ linguistically but not substantially. The double aspect theory of Strawson can be called 'non-reductive materialist' insofar as we are not allowing the possibility of a disembodied person or a disembodied consciousness. If,

36. Stoljar (2009).
37. McLaughlin (1995).
38. Searle (1995: 545).
39. Byrne (1995).
40. Block (1995).
41. Thagart (2012).
42. Rosenthal (1995).
43. Stoljar (2009).
44. Snowdon (2009).
45. Snowdon (2009).

however, we are allowing such a possibility, then it will not be materialism. In that case it will be closer to Pudgalavāda of a Buddhist sect, which makes room for transmigration.

Non-reductive physicalism, being a form of physicalism, does not accept the existence of consciousness as independent of body. It claims that the mental supervenes upon the physical, though the mental is never over and above its supervening base. If you take away the physical base, you take away the mental too, since the mental is in some sense 'composed' out of or 'realized' by the physical.[46]

Scholars have claimed, however, that non-reductive physicalism, understood in this way is hardly distinguishable from epiphenomenalism.[47] The latter holds that mental phenomena are caused by physical phenomena, but they in their turn, cannot cause any thing. Mental phenomena are epiphenomena in this sense.

Though in Cārvāka theory of mind also, mental phenomena have been given a secondary status as compared to physical phenomena, it can be doubted whether the mental phenomena according to the Cārvākas are only effects and not causes of anything. They would, of course, say that the mental phenomena cannot be 'independent causes'; they can be causes only through or in association with bodily phenomena. Here the general causal model of Vaiśeṣikas can be applied according to which there is no non-inherent cause (*a-samavāyi-kāraṇa*) without an inherent cause (*samavāyi-kāraṇa*).[48] According to Vaiśeṣika theory of causation, for every event there has to be an inherent cause. The non-inherent cause, which is inseparably related to the inherent cause, always operates in association with the latter. The mental phenomena, if they have to function as causes, have to function as non-inherent causes. But what is the inherent cause with which mental phenomena are associated? Here, the difference between Lokāyata and Vaiśeṣika approaches becomes important. For Vaiśeṣikas mental events (such as cognition, desiring, trying, averting, being pleased,

46. See Horgan (1995).

47. See Crane (1995).

48. For the Vaiśeṣika classification of causes, see *TSa* (section 40). Athalye and Bodas translate samavāyi and a-samavāyi as intimate and non-intimate respectively (*TSa*, p. 206).

and being displeased) are the qualities of the substance called self, whereas this self exists independently of body. The self is regarded as the inherent cause of the mental phenomena, and the mental phenomena, are effects emerging in the self. However, the causal process does not come to an end there. The mental phenomena can further cause other mental phenomena or even bodily functions as non-inherent causes of the latter. They produce their effects by depending on the self which is their base. As against this, Cārvākas regard mental phenomena as the qualities or functions not of the independent substance called self, but of the body itself. All of these causal relationships will be available in Cārvāka-darśana by replacing the self by the body. Hence the mental events could cause further mental events or even bodily events with the body as their continuous base, that is, the inherent cause. This view might come somewhat close to what McLaughlin calls 'Type Epiphenomenalism', according to which, 'mental events may be causes in virtue of falling under physical types, but not in virtue of falling under mental types.'[49]

As I have suggested before, a modern Cārvāka might talk about brain instead of body as the causal base of mental phenomena and hence interpret the doctrine of body-as-self as that of brain-as-self. This brings it close to the biological naturalism of Searle, who defines his position as one where, (*a*) brains cause minds, and (*b*) minds are higher level features of brains.[50]

The controversies among the different positions described centre around the exact relationship between the physical and the mental. Unlike reductive or eliminative physicalism they do not try to eliminate the mental and reduce it to the physical. Hence, the mental is distinguishable, but inseparable from the physical. At the same time, these positions use the language of cause and effect which is generally used to refer to two 'distinct' events. All these features are seen in the Cārvāka conception of the mind–body relation. The point is that though we may not get an exact parallel of Cārvāka materialism in the Western philosophy of mind, we can identify a family of views of which Cārvāka can be a member.

49. See McLaughlin (1995).
50. Searle (1995: 545).

Social and Axiological Implications of Cārvāka Materialism

Thanks to Karl Marx, apart from cosmological and psychological levels, one can talk about materialism in socio-economic sense. It is a response to questions such as:

> How do social and cultural institutions come into existence? Are they determined by material conditions or by some divine or supernatural agencies or by some intermediate conditions—for instance by 'values' or by the human mind?

Marx's historical materialism is a possible materialist answer to the question raised earlier. His version of historical materialism can be stated in his words as:

> The mode of production of material life conditions the social, political and intellectual life process in general. It is not the consciousness of men that determines their being, but on the contrary it is their social being that determines their consciousness.[51]

Marx in his historical materialism understands by 'material conditions', economic conditions, namely the forces and relations of production. They are supposed to be at the basis of socio-cultural institutions. It can be noted here, however, that though Marx's materialism is continuous with cosmological and psychological materialism, it is neither identical with nor established by them. Hence a materialist at the cosmological or psychological level need not be a materialist at social level.[52] This is because one can maintain that although consciousness arises from material elements, once it arises, it starts dominating the scene. It is not only that matter controls mind but mind also controls material conditions. Such a view cannot be called social materialism or historical materialism in the strict sense of the term.

'Materialism' has also an axiological sense according to which it means a tendency to value material things such as bodily comfort and

51. Marx (1976: 3).

52. This is clearly seen in Ambedkar (1974: 185–6). In *The Buddha and his Dhamma*, where he interprets the Buddhist conceptions of body and mind (rūpa and nāma) as inseparable entities like magnetic field and electrical field. But he also says: 'Once consciousness arises, man becomes a sentient being. Consciousness is, therefore, the chief thing in man's life.'

wealth too much against spiritual and intellectual things. Insofar as the popular understanding of Cārvāka is concerned, Cārvāka accepts 'only pleasure (*kāma*)' or 'pleasure and wealth (*artha*)' as the goal or goals of life, and hence he is supposed to be a sensualistic and egoistic hedonist, that is, a materialist in axiological sense of the term. But the question is whether materialism in this sense necessarily follows from the materialism in ontological sense. This is in fact an example of the well-known is-ought-problem. Here I claim that though sensualistic and egoistic hedonism is consistent or compatible with the cosmological and psychological materialism of the Cārvākas, the former does not necessarily follow from the latter. It will be argued in the next chapter that though Cārvākas emphasize pleasure and wealth as the goals of life and deny obligations and liberation (dharma and *mokṣa*) as goals, they deny the latter goals as they are understood in the other-worldly or transcendentalist sense; but they could accept them consistently, if the latter are interpreted within this-worldly framework, for example, if the set of obligations is associated with social–moral virtues and obligations and liberation is understood as the free state of human beings-qua-human beings. I am suggesting that though a non-sceptic Cārvāka is generally an ontological materialist, he need not necessarily be a 'materialist' in axiological sense.

***

Certainly, the Cārvāka will not buy a religious axiology which attaches value to God, soul, or other worlds. He will also not develop a religion-centric approach to society. But apart from this, a modern Cārvāka could be open to different social and moral positions, provided that they are secular in nature. A Cārvākan exposed to modern Western philosophy could be a Marxist or a radical humanist, a phenomenologist or an atheistic existentialist, a positivist or a pragmatist. Similarly, in terms of a moral position, he could become a sensualist–hedonist or a utilitarian–liberal or a deontologist. I am suggesting that it is intelligible to consider Cārvāka-darśana not as a complete and closed system, but as an incomplete and open system, provided that the framework within which it opens itself is a secular framework. How this happens in Cārvāka theory of values will be discussed in the next chapter.

6

Cārvāka on Values

This chapter engages with the Cārvāka conception of values.[1] It is divided into four parts. The first part argues for the position that Cārvākas did possess a moral perspective, while the second deals with the diversity of their value-perspective. The third part turns to the nature of hedonism attributed to Cārvākas, and the last part deals with the theory of human goals (*puruṣārtha*s) that can be attributed to Cārvākas.

I

Cārvākas as Possessing a Moral Standpoint

Do Cārvākas have any moral standpoint at all? The opponents of Cārvākas are inclined to claim that they have none. Jayantabhaṭṭa is vocal on this point when he says:

> In Lokāyata doctrine no obligation is instructed. It is just a talk of baseless disputants (*vaitaṇḍika*). There is no scripture (that they accept).[2]

1. The chapter is a revised version of my paper 'The Value Perspectives of Cārvākas', published in Bhelke and Gokhale (2002).

2. *na hi lokāyate kiñcit kartavyamupadiśyate/vaitaṇḍikakathaivāsau, na punaḥ kaścidāgamaḥ//* (*Nyāyamañjarī* [*NM*], part I, p. 247)

The last sentence can also be translated as: It is not a scripture (which should be accepted).

Here Jayanta argues that Lokāyatikas do not (and cannot) prescribe any duties and obligations. The twofold reason he gives for this is that the Lokāyata doctrine is a perspective adopted by baseless disputants. Moreover, he also claims that they have no scriptural foundations. 'Vaitaṇḍika' in its technical sense means one who refutes another's position without having (or at least without presenting and defending) his or her own position. The sceptic Cārvākas can be said to be vaitaṇḍika because they have been refuting all epistemological and ontological theories without upholding any theory of their own. Yet Jayanta in this verse is not specifically referring to sceptic Cārvākas, but is charging all Cārvākas as vaitaṇḍika. He seems to be using the term 'vaitaṇḍika-kathā' not in the strict sense, but in an extended sense, namely 'arguing without any restriction'.[3] Here the restrictions that Jayanta appears to have in mind are the restrictions of a sacred text, such as Vedas. The very next statement Jayanta makes in the above verse, that there is no scripture that they accept, indicates this. In the original Sanskrit expression ('*na punaḥ kaścidāgamaḥ*') the word 'punaḥ' indicates that Jayanta here contrasts vaitaṇḍika-kathā with acceptance of a sacred text (*āgama*). This suggests the general attitude of the orthodox thinkers towards values. They believe that the values that we accept for regulating our conduct should be derived from sacred texts such as Vedas and Smṛtis. Reasoning has to work only within the confines of the sacred texts. It should be used for supporting, but never for contradicting them. Naturally, orthodox thinkers believed that the values of life can be derived only from sacred texts, whereby in the absence of the latter, one does not have values. Buddhists and Jainas too had their own sacred texts from which they derived their value-systems. Hence, Jayanta cannot be interpreted as accusing them of lacking a moral approach. He specifically targets the Lokāyatikas.

The presupposition that orthodox Brahmanical thinkers (and also Buddhists and Jainas who are not orthodox) seem to share is that

3. Lokāyata has been charged as *vitaṇḍā* elsewhere also. For example in Pali Buddhist literature, Lokāyata was described as *vitaṇḍasatthaṁ* or *vitaṇḍavādasattham* (Sanskrit: *vitaṇḍāśāstram* or *vitaṇḍāvādaśāstram*: see my discussion of this point in Chapter 1). I think it was this extended sense in which they were charged as that. This extended sense is applicable to all the schools of Lokāyata insofar as no school accepted the authority of any so-called sacred text.

free use of reasoning (which could be guided by experience but not by the so-called sacred texts) cannot give rise to a moral standpoint; it must result in what could be called moral scepticism or a-moralism or moral anarchy. As against this, it can be claimed that the use of reasoning not restricted by scriptures could at times lead to moral scepticism, but in its constructive application it can also lead to moral theorization which can regulate our conduct and way of living. In fact to accept only that which is supported by experience and reasoning and not to believe in the so-called sacred texts is itself a value having important moral implications. I would like to claim that Cārvākas, insofar as they were holding this epistemological view, had a definite moral stand.

Hence, Cārvākas' criticism of the Vedas, Vedic ritualism, priesthood, and asceticism represents their rational as well as moral standpoint. They were criticizing Vedas for the vulgar and violent practices promoted in them.[4] They criticized priesthood as a profession because it involved making one's livelihood by deceiving people.[5] They criticized *śrāddha* and such other rituals for their obvious irrational and

4. *trayo vedasya kartāraḥ bhaṇḍadhūrtaniśācarāḥ/*
jarpharīturpharītyādi paṇḍitānāṁ vacaḥ smṛtam//
aśvasyātra hi śiśnaṁ tu patnīgrāhyaṁ prakīrtitam/
bhaṇḍaistadvat paraṁ caiva grāhyajātaṁ prakīrtitam//
māṁsānāṁ khādanaṁ caiva niśācarasamīritam//
(*Sarvadarśanasaṅgraha* [*SDS*], Cārvākadarśanam)

[Vedas have three authors: buffoons, knaves, and demons. The meaningless utterances in them such as '*jarpharī turpharī*' are regarded as the talk of the learned persons. The obscene rites such as the queen holding the penis of the sacrificial horse are prescribed in them by buffoons. Various precious gifts to be accepted by the priests (are prescribed in them by knaves). Demons have prescribed in them eating different kinds of meat.]

5. *agnihotraṁ trayo vedāstridaṇḍaṁ bhasmaguṇṭhanam/*
buddhiparuṣahīnānāṁ jīviketi bṛhaspatiḥ// (*SDS*, Cārvākadarśanam)

[The *agnihotra* practice, (recitation of) three Vedas, holding ascetic's three staves, smearing oneself with ashes, all these are according to Bhartṛhari, the means of livelihood of those who lack intelligence and strength. (That is, they use such superstitious and deceptive means of livelihood because they lack enough power and intellect to use legitimate means.)]

tataśca jīvanopāyo brāhmaṇairvihitastviha/
mṛtānāṁ pretakāryāṇi na tvanyad vidyate kvacit// (*SDS*, Cārvākadarśanam)

[Moreover, all these ceremonies for the dead are the means to livelihood which the Brāhmaṇas have created for themselves. There is no other (fruit) obtained elsewhere.]

superstitious character.[6] They saw a lot of hypocrisy in Vedic sacrificial rituals because the latter often entailed the killing of animals in the guise of sending them to heaven.[7] They were also critical of asceticism because it involved making a livelihood by causing violence to oneself.[8] Cārvāka criticism of the Vedic value system had another important implication. The value system advocated by Vedas and Smṛtis viewed human beings as essentially governed by the hierarchical system of *varṇas* and castes and the unequal status of men and women governed by patriarchy. Obligations of humans were determined primarily by their caste status and gender status and only secondarily by their status as human beings. Vedic morality in this sense was non-egalitarian. Cārvākas were opposed to this caste-based value system.[9] They viewed a human being as free from this hierarchical framework imposed by this tradition.

All this can be read as an expression of the moral standpoint of Cārvākas which attached moral value to secular, rational life free from hypocrisy, superstitions, violence and hierarchical social order. All of

6. *mṛtānāmapi jantūnāṁ śrāddhaṁ cet tṛptikāraṇam/*
nirvāṇasya pradīpasya snehaḥ saṁvardhayet śikhām//
gacchatāmiha jantūnāṁ vyarthaṁ pātheyakalpanam/
gehasthakṛtaśrāddhena pathi tṛptiravāritā//
svargasthitā yadā tṛptiṁ gaccheyustatra dānataḥ/
prāsādasyoparisthānām atra kasmānna dīyate// (*SDS*, Cārvākadarśanam)

[If 'śrāddha' produces gratification to beings that are dead, then the oil added to the lamp will increase its flame even when the lamp is already extinguished. It is needless to give provisions to the travellers when they start. By performing śrāddha ritual for them at home, they will be gratified on their way. If beings in the heaven are gratified by our offering made in the śrāddha ritual here, then why not offer the food down here (on the ground floor) to those staying on the top of the mansion?]

7. *paśuścennihataḥ svargaṁ jyotiṣṭome gamiṣyati/*
svapitā yajamānena tatra kasmānna hanyate// (*SDS*, Cārvākadarśanam)

[If the beast slain in Jyotiṣṭoma rite will itself go to heaven, why does not then the sacrificer offer his own father there?]

8. *nagna śramaṇaka durbuddhe kāyakleśaparāyaṇa/*
jīvikārthe'pi cārambhe kena tvamasi śikṣitaḥ// (*Tattvopaplavasiṁha* [*TUS*], p. 79)

[Oh the muddle-headed naked ascetic! Oh the one engaged in torturing your own body! Who taught you this kind of activity aimed at your livelihood?]

9. *na svargo nāpavargo vā naivātmā pāralaukikaḥ/*
naiva varṇāśramādīnāṁ kriyāśca phaladāyikāḥ// (*SDS*, Cārvāka-darśana)

this poses a larger question as to how to understand the perspective or perspectives of Cārvākas on values in a more systematic way.

Moral Elements in the Cārvāka Perspective

I have suggested elsewhere[10] that a value perspective can be regarded as moral, only if it has a universalistic element. They have two-fold universality: agent-universality as well as object-universality.[11] A purely egoistic perspective cannot be regarded as a consistent moral perspective. So while discussing the perspective of the Yoga of Patañjali,[12] I have maintained that though the ultimate goal according to Yoga, namely isolated state of the soul (*kaivalya* of *puruṣa*), is purely individualistic and hence cannot be called moral, the Yoga of Patañjali can still be said to possess a moral perspective because practicing the universal values such as truthfulness and non-violence is a necessary step according to Pātañjali for achieving the individualistic goal.

While trying to identify the moral element in the Cārvāka perspective, we are faced with a similar but different problem. Here we cannot say that the ultimate goal of life according to Cārvākas is like the isolated state of the soul or seedless meditative trance (*nirbīja-samādhi*), which are both unsocial. Cārvākas, especially the common-sense-empiricist ones, who believe in commonsensical (*lokaprasiddha*) inference, can identify human beings not only as conscious configurations of matter but also as social beings who pursue pleasure

---

[There is no heaven, no liberation, no self which belongs to another world. The actions assigned to castes and stages of life too do not yield fruit.]

Also, '*tulyatve vapuṣāṁ mukhādyavayavair varṇakramaḥ kīdṛśaḥ*' (*Prabodhacandrodaya* [*PCU*] 2.44). [Meaning: When human bodies are equal in having limbs like mouth and so on, how meaningful is the order among varṇas?]

10. 'Re-understanding Indian Moral Thought', in Bhelke and Gokhale (2002).

11. By agent-universality I mean that a moral perspective should focus on the obligations to be assigned to all agents (*sādhāraṇa-dharmas*) rather than obligations specific to culture, status, role, and so on, of the agent (*viśeṣa-dharmas*). The latter should be influenced by the former and not the former by the latter. By object-universality I mean that a moral perspective should treat all objects (recipients/addressees) of actions equally without discrimination or partiality. (In terms of *Yogasūtra*, it should be like *yama*, which is *sārvabhauma*.). For my discussion see 'Re-understanding Indian Moral Thought,' in Bhelke and Gokhale (2002).

12. 'Is there a Moral Perspective in Patañjali's *Yoga-sūtra*?', in Bhelke and Gokhale (2002).

and wealth (*kāma* and *artha*) in a social set-up. Now the problem is different. Pleasure and wealth, though they are pursued in a social set-up, could be pursued in an egoistic way. But one cannot be moral in his pursuit of values without crossing the boundaries of egoism. So the relevant question here is whether there are indications of altruism or universalism in the Cārvāka perspective. Let us first take the note of such indications and bring out their implications.

1. In the Cārvāka-darśana of *Sarvadarśana-saṁgraha*, an appeal is made to the readers to adhere to the Cārvāka view for the benefit of many beings.[13] This implies that the Cārvākas' perspective is not meant for egoistic interests of some isolated individuals, but multiple beings. Here the Cārvākas do not construct any theory of altruism or universalism, but they at least express their altruistic intension.
2. Cārvākas' acceptance of polity and jurisprudence (*daṇḍanīti*) as a legitimate means to livelihood[14] indicates their preference for a system of justice and social order. Kauṭilya's inclusion of Lokāyata under Ānvikṣikī indicates that Lokāyata intends to regulate rationally the scopes of religion, economy, and polity.[15] This creates a scope for a moral–social approach based on reason.
3. Though there is no clear indication of the universal values such as truthfulness and non-violence being professed by Cārvākas, their critical attitude towards untruth, hypocrisy, and sacrificial violence is evident in Cārvāka literature, as noted earlier. Whereas Cārvākas advocate straight forward practical ways of livelihood such as agriculture, cattle-keeping, and commerce, they vehemently criticize dishonest and hypocritical ways exemplified in ritualistic practices. Cārvākas, thus, seem to be the lovers of straightforwardness, rationality, truthfulness, and non-injury.

13. '*bahūnāṁ prāṇinām anugrahārthaṁ cārvākamatam āśrayaṇīyam*' (*SDS*, Cārvākadarśanam).

14. '*kṛṣigorakṣavāṇijyadaṇḍanītyādibhirbudhaḥ/dṛṣṭaireva sadopāyairbhogānanu bhaved bhuvi//*' *Sarvasiddhāntasaṅgraha* (*SSS* 2.9–15). [A wise man should enjoy pleasures in this world only by observed (that is, empirically tested) means such as agriculture, cattle-keeping, commerce, and governance.] Here governance (*daṇḍanīti*) is concerned with maintenance of law and order through polity and jurisprudence.

15. See the section 'Lokāyata as *Ānvīkṣikī*' in Chapter 1.

II

Diversity in the Value-perspective of Cārvākas

Though, as indicated earlier, a case can be made for a universal moral standpoint in Cārvāka-darśana, I am not suggesting that all Cārvākas must have accepted such a standpoint unanimously. Like the diversity we have seen in the forgoing chapters, in the case of Cārvāka ontology and epistemology, diversity can be found in Cārvāka axiology. I have already made some suggestions to that effect in the first chapter. The point can be dealt with in more details on following lines.

Jayarāśi who denies all the means and objects of knowledge in his work *Tattvopaplavasiṁha*, does not discuss the problem of values. But his last remark is sufficiently suggestive about his general approach. He says, 'When in this way all essential categories are refuted, all the practices are all right insofar as they are beautiful for not being reflected upon [philosophically]'.[16]

Practices (*vyavahāra*) in this statement not only include linguistic practices (statements, utterances) but also behavioural practices. This statement of Jayarāśi is paradoxical in a sense because it implies that 'since nothing is all right, everything is all right'. The paradox can be removed if we take the first 'all right' in strong sense and second 'all right' in weak sense. The statement would then imply, 'Since nothing is compelling, everything is permissible'. By such a statement, Jayarāśi seems to allow a kind of anarchism in the realm of values.[17] He seems to suggest that we are not living in a world where values are readily established for us; nor can we establish them. So we are free to cherish any course of values according to our liking.[18] Jayarāśi's approach, however, has another aspect namely that of the denial of otherworldly belief systems, which is one of the marks of the legacy of Lokāyata he has accepted. That consciousness cannot be proved to exist apart from

16. '*Tadevam upaplutesu tattveṣu avicāita-ramaṇīyāḥ sarve* vyavahārāḥ *ghaṭante*' (*TUS*, p. 125).

17. Jayantabhaṭṭa in *NM* (Vol. I, p. 247) refers to this anarchism where he identifies Lokāyata with vaitaṇḍika-kathā; see note 2 in this chapter.

18. It is not necessary, however, that one who accepts scepticism in one's epistemology and ontology, should be sceptical or anarchical in his approach to values. Sometimes scepticism (suspension of judgments, negation of all dogmas) may itself be a value. 'Ataraxia' introduced by Sextus Empiricus is of a similar nature. See Popkin (1967: 449–61). I have discussed this possibility as 'concerned scepticism' in Chapter 2.

body and that neither another world nor after-life can be proved is an important part of Jayarāśi's sceptical argument.[19] Naturally his anarchism too has the framework of this-worldly way or ways of life. The difference between Jayarāśi and other Cārvākas seems to be that this-worldly beliefs or common-sense beliefs for the former is a matter of arbitrary assumption (accepted independently of pramāṇas) whereas it is a matter of rational justification for the latter.

When we pass from scepticism of Jayarāśi to the 'narrow empiricism' of some Cārvākas, we find that one is now in a position to recognize one's own sensuous pleasure, since it can be directly available, as value.[20] In this way a narrow-empiricist Cārvāka can accept narrow form of hedonism which is sensualist and egoist. But a broad-empiricist Cārvāka can go further by appreciating the value of many empirical objects which are not given directly but known indirectly. The latter is done through inference and probably confirmation by later experience. The difference between the moral attitudes of a narrow-empiricist and a broad-empiricist Cārvāka can be conceived as follows:

1. A narrow empiricist is likely to attach greater importance to enjoyment of pleasure (kāma) as a goal of life than to accumulation of means to pleasure (artha). That is because though the value of the enjoyment of pleasure can be grasped directly, the value of a means to pleasure can be understood only indirectly or inferentially. A broad empiricist on the other hand is likely to attach more or less equal importance to both the goals.
2. A narrow empiricist is likely to be concerned more with one's own pleasure as the goal of actions than with the pleasure of others. This is partly because one's own pleasure or pain is

19. *'Śarīrādeva iti bṛhaspatiḥ'*, *'paralokino'bhāvāt paralokābhāvaḥ'* (*TUS*, pp. 45 and 88).

20. One thing has to be made clear at this stage. Though the *pramāṇas* accepted by Cārvākas are basically meant for establishing facts or reality rather than values that ought to be pursued, they can draw the boundaries around the values which can be legitimately pursued. *Svarga* cannot be established, so it cannot be a legitimate value. Sensuous pleasure can be proved as an empirical fact so it can be legitimately pursued as a value. The connection between pramāṇas and values has to be understood in this light.

> directly cognizable by one whereas the experiences of other persons are always a matter of inference. A broad empiricist (especially a common-sense empiricist) can very well claim to understand and appreciate other persons' experiences. So a broad empiricist can consistently uphold an altruistic or universalistic form of hedonism.[21]

Thus, narrow empiricism seems to make a restricted axiological approach possible and a broad empiricism a broad one. Due to non-availability of sufficient historical data, it may not be possible to verify that there were such schools of Cārvākas or individual Cārvākas who held a narrow or broad approach consistently in epistemology, ontology, and axiology. But I suggest that it can at least be appreciated as a logical possibility if not as a historical fact.

In brief, it can be said that the value-perspective of Cārvākas is not unitary as it is generally supposed, but is diverse. The different value-perspectives which can be attributed to Cārvākas, however, have one element in common which unify them. It is the denial of otherworldly or transcendental values. We also see that the diverse value-perspectives of Cārvākas can be arranged in a logical order so that when we start with the sceptic Cārvāka and end up with the common-sense-empiricist Cārvāka, a growing degree of sophistication and maturity can be observed among the corresponding value perspectives.

Many a scholar of Indian philosophy has so far emphasized the narrow value perspective of the narrow-empiricist Cārvākas. This is partly because the historically available image of Cārvākas is created largely by their opponents who have presented them in their weak form. Philosophically, however, it is more important to present or even reconstruct Cārvāka position in its stronger form.

It is important, therefore, to present or reconstruct the value perspective which broad-empiricist Cārvākas must have developed or could have developed in past or at least can develop in future. I will

21. It is also possible to bring out a subtle difference between the value perspective based on perception + empirical inference and that on perception + commonsensical inference respectively. The concept of a person as a rational-social-historical being is easily available to the latter, as against the former. So the latter can develop into a secular humanist value-perspective which is not possible for the former. Here, however, I will not extend the point further.

attempt to take some steps towards this end in the remaining parts of this chapter.

III

The Hedonism of Cārvākas

Cārvākas' moral perspective has been described as 'hedonism, pure and simple'.[22] In recent times, Ramkrishna Bhattacharya has strongly opposed the charge that Cārvākas were hedonists. He has compared this charge with the similar one made in Western philosophy against Epicureans. Bhattacharya's view is acceptable on two counts:

1. Generally the term hedonism is used in a derogatory sense, in which the attainment of sensuous pleasures is the highest moral value. Bhattacharya rightly points out that Epicureans did not hold such a view. They were prescribing not the life of sensuous indulgence but moderation and self-control. Similarly, we do not find Indian materialists always prescribing sensuous hedonism. Ajita-keśakambalī, for example, was not.[23]
2. We have to distinguish between different senses in which the word materialism is used. For example, materialism in the ontological sense has to be distinguished from that in the axiological sense. Ontological materialism holds that matter is existentially primary and consciousness is secondary. Materialism in an axiological sense holds that material pleasure is the highest value of life. This latter type of materialism does not follow from the former type.[24] Cārvākas did criticize the so-called other-worldly pleasures and the divine bliss prescribed by the religious systems. But this does not mean that they regarded material pleasure as the highest value.

But there are other points Bhattacharya makes, which are debatable:

22. Hiriyanna (1973: 194).

23. Ajita's position described in the *Sāmaññaphalasutta* seems to imply moral scepticism on his part when he says, 'A good or bad action produces no result' (Bhattacharya 2012: 45).

Bhattacharya, however holds that Ajita had made a cult of asceticism rather than hedonism (Bhattacharya 2012: 30). For my comments see note 28 in this chapter.

24. See the last section of the Chapter 5. Also see Bhattacharya (2012: 29–32).

1. Though Bhattacharya succeeds in showing that hedonism as it is popularly understood (that is, sensualist hedonism), may not be the official position of Cārvākas, on the question as to what could be their official position, he does not seem to have any definite answer. He notices that there is great diversity in the value approaches attributed to Cārvākas, but does not consider this diversity and openness (within the framework of this-worldly approach) as the very characteristic of the Cārvāka approach to values. Here, Bhattacharya's stand is indeterministic,[25] not pluralistic. It is so probably because of his monistic belief that, 'Cārvāka doctrine was basically a this-worldly philosophy with its own systems of logic, epistemology, ontology and ethics'.[26]
2. He correctly points out that though Ajitakeśakambalī holds ontological materialism,[27] he does not advocate hedonism. But his claim that Ajita seems to advocate asceticism[28] is doubtful. Ajita not only denies other worlds and life after death, but also seems to deny moral life. He says, for instance, 'There is no such thing as alms, or sacrifice or offering. There is neither

25. 'What should we conclude from such contradictory reports: some Cārvākas were vegetarians and some were not; some were allied to Kāpālikas and some practiced total sexual abstinence. I think it will be wiser not to give credence to any of these. The opponents of Cārvākas jumbled up the positions of all anti- or non-Vedic schools and made it a nice mess of the *nāstika* views, imputing one's ideas to others' (Bhattacharya 2012: 127–8); and
'... nobody knows what exactly the Cārvākas thought of the ends of life (puruṣārtha)' (Bhattacharya 2012: 128).

26. Bhattacharya (2012: 129). The plural form 'systems' in the quotation does not refer to 'many systems of logic + many systems of epistemology etc.', but 'a system of logic + a system of epistemology etc. = many systems'.

27. 'Ajita Kesakambala: Nihilist or Materialist?' in Bhattacharya (2012: 45–53).

28. 'Ajita, it seems, had made a cult of asceticism, rather than of hedonism' (Bhattacharya 2012: 30). For refuting the claim that Ajita was a nihilist, Bhattacharya tries to give a novel interpretation of Ajita's statement that there is not this world as, 'There is no happiness in this world' (Bhattacharya 2012: 53), and tries to support his view that Ajita must have been an ascetic. I think that such a farfetched interpretation is not needed. When Ajita says, 'There is no this world and there is no other world,' he is really talking about the false pair which has been created by the believers, namely 'this world and another world'. Similarly when he is saying that there are no father and mother and there are no *opapātuka jīvas*, he is really referring to the false pair created by the believers that 'beings born from father and mother and those born without father or mother'. Ajita is really denying these false pairs or false classifications introduced by the believers. I think this solves the problem.

fruit nor result of good or evil deeds.'[29] (The second statement is more relevant in this context.) So Ajita's position seems to be that of a-moralism or moral scepticism.

3. While discussing the charge that Cārvākas were hedonists, Bhattacharya considers only one variety of hedonism, namely sensualist hedonism. Now suppose that Cārvākas were not sensualist–hedonists. Does it imply that they were not hedonists at all? Same question will arise about Epicureans. Bhattacharya could have said that Epicureans were not sensualist hedonists or vulgar hedonists, but enlightened hedonists. He could have added that a similar non-vulgar interpretation is possible even with respect to Cārvāka hedonism. Unfortunately Bhattacharya does not follow this route. He does not consider varieties of hedonism and locate Cārvākas in them.

I want to suggest here that though some modern scholars have labelled Cārvāka theory of values as hedonistic in the sense of sensualist hedonism, it is possible to take the label without such a prejudiced connotation and consider it in a more philosophical sense. For example, Andrew Moore (2004) describes motivational and normative hedonism in the following way: 'Motivational hedonism is the claim that only pleasure or pain motivates us. It is the most significant form of psychological hedonism. Normative hedonism is the claim that all and only pleasure is worth of value and all and only pain has disvalue. Jeremy Bentham endorsed both sorts of hedonism...'[30]

Understanding hedonism in this general sense, we can say that it is a dominant current in the ethical thought of the Cārvākas. So instead of simply denying the claim that Cārvākas were hedonists, one should try to specify as to what extent and in what sense they were hedonists.

Cārvākas have also been branded as egoistic hedonists. One can contrast egoism with altruism and universalism. This means that when Cārvākas regard happiness as the intrinsic value, they are talking about one's own happiness and not 'happiness of others' or 'happiness of all'. I think both these claims should be taken seriously as

29. Chattopadhyaya (1990: 48).

30. See Moore, Andrew (2004), 'Hedonism,' included in *Stanford Encyclopedia of Philosophy*.

philosophical claims. They are also relevant for placing Cārvākas on the conceptual map of Indian philosophy. Granting as a working hypothesis the claim that a dominant current in Cārvāka ethical thought is that it is egoistic hedonism, the question can be asked whether Cārvākas alone are egoistic hedonists. It seems that all the systems of Indian philosophy are hedonistic. They are also egoistic perhaps with the exception of Mahāyāna Buddhism. The notions of liberation (*mokṣa/kaivalya/nirvāṇa*), which refer to the *summum bonum* (the highest good) of liberation-oriented systems, are all hedonistic because they are defined in terms of happiness/pleasure/peace/bliss and absolute cessation of pain/suffering. It is also an egoistic ideal because it stands for the absolute pleasure or bliss which one attains for oneself or the absolute cessation of one's own suffering. Pūrva-Mīmāṁsakas who do not regard liberation as their ideal do talk about heaven (svarga) which too is a hedonistic and egoistic ideal.[31] The axiology centring on ritualistic obligations (dharma) that they advocate emphasizes such an egoistic–hedonistic other-worldly goal. So if Cārvāka advocates egoistic hedonism, he is not an exception to the general trend in Indian philosophy in that regard. The conflict between Cārvāka axiology and the axiological approaches of other Indian systems, therefore, is not the one between egoism and altruism or hedonism and anti-hedonism, but between different varieties of egoistic hedonism.

A hedonist is a consequentialist, who judges actions to be right or wrong, good or bad, better or worse by measuring pleasurable and painful consequences of the actions. Such a person wants to choose that course of action which is conducive to maximization of happiness and minimization of suffering. This implies measuring pleasures and pains caused by an action by applying some parameters or standards. The difference between the hedonism of other systems and that of Cārvākas can be understood in terms of the parameters or standards for measuring pleasures and pains applied by the respective systems.

31. In Pūrvamīmāmsā, 'svarga' is described as:

yanna duḥkhena sambhinnaṁ na ca grastamanantaraṁ/ abhilāṣopanītaṁ ca tatsukhaṁ svaḥpadāspadam//

[The pleasure which is not mixed with pain, nor is immediately followed by pain and which is available as per the desire, is called svarga.]

Here, I think, we can use Bentham's calculus of pleasure[32] as a useful device. Here I am not suggesting that we should accept Bentham's account of the dimensions of pleasure in the same way in which Bentham dealt with it, that is, as the constitutive feature of his own form of hedonism—but I am considering it as a methodological tool for comparing different forms of hedonism. Bentham may be wrong in his formulation of hedonism which implied that units of pleasure can be counted with exactitude and that different dimensions of pleasure are equally important and objectively so for all moral agents. But we can appreciate the minimal point in it that pleasure can be 'weighed' and valued in the light of its different dimensions, by different persons, from time to time. With this starting point, I would like to deviate from Bentham and say that different dimensions of pleasure are not and need not be equally important for all the moral agents under consideration. The same kind of pleasure with the same dimensions may be valued differently by different persons depending upon their own attitudes or choice—rational or emotional. This leads to the possibility of a variety of 'hedonisms' depending upon the relative importance given to different dimensions of pleasure by different advocates of hedonism.[33]

Now I want to suggest that the hedonism of Cārvākas and that of other Indian schools can be distinguished in terms of their differential approach to various dimensions of pleasure. Let us substantiate the point with reference to the six dimensions of pleasure mentioned by Bentham.

Intensity

We can distinguish different kinds of pleasures in terms of intensity:

1. Among the worldly pleasures, sensuous pleasure is supposed to be quite intense, and among sensuous pleasures, erotic pleasure is supposed to be the most intense one.

32. Bentham (1907).

33. I want to suggest here that 'the qualitative difference among pleasures' which J. S. Mill emphasized as a revision of Bentham's account can be explained or explained away in terms of our differential attitudes to quantitative dimensions themselves. As D. H. Monro suggests, 'higher pleasure' can be regarded as the one which has greater duration, fecundity, and purity. A lower pleasure may not possess these dimensions though it has intensity and propinquity (Monro 1967: 283).

2. Intellectual pleasure and aesthetic pleasure—they may have lesser intensity (though greater durability and fecundity).
3. Peace of mind (*śānti*), which involves cessation of craving (*tṛṣṇā–kṣaya*). This kind of pleasure could be said to be least intense but more durable and pure.

These three kinds of pleasures are in principle possible without otherworldly presuppositions. But there are at least two kinds of 'intense pleasures' accepted by the systems like Mīmāṁsā and Vedānta which are other-worldly or transcendent:

4. Heaven (svarga): Mīmāṁsakas and other metaphysicians including Buddhists and Jainas conceived of other worlds full of pleasure superior in terms of purity, intensity, and durability as compared to worldly pleasures.[34]
5. Spiritual pleasure (Brahmānanda): Vedāntins and some other spiritualists conceived of this kind of pleasure which had great intensity, purity, and infinite durability because it supposedly exhibited the very nature of the spiritual reality.[35]

The Cārvākas have serious doubts about the very possibility of the last two kinds of pleasure namely heavenly and spiritual pleasure. But there is no reason why Cārvākas would be opposed to the three kinds of worldly pleasure mentioned earlier in the list. Their statements about erotic pleasure give an impression that they preferred sensuous pleasures to other-worldly ones. There is no reason why broad-minded Cārvākas may not have preferred different kinds of worldly pleasures at different times or certain kinds of mental or intellectual pleasures consistently according to individual temperaments. Here the Cārvākas' statements about sensuous pleasure and pain can be explained differently. I offer the following explanation:

Statements: (*a*) The heaven is nothing but the pleasure arising by embracing a woman and so on. (*b*) The hell is nothing but the pain arising from thorns and other similar things.[36]

34. See the Pūrvamīmāṁsā definition of svarga given in note 31 in this chapter.
35. Upaniṣads define 'brahman' as 'the real, consciousness and bliss' (*sat-cit-ānanda*) and describe Brāhmic bliss (*brahmānanda*) as the greatest bliss.
36. '*aṅganāliṅganādijanyaṁ suhkameva svargaḥ, kaṇṭakādijanyaṁ duḥkhameva narakaḥ*' (*SDS*). *SSS* adds to 'sexual pleasure' the pleasure from eating delicious food, enjoying fine clothes, garlands, and perfumes. It illustrates the experience of hell by pains from enemy's weapons and diseases (*SSS* 2.9–10).

This can be explained as follows. Mīmāṁsakas and other metaphysicians imagine heaven as the paradigm of intense pleasure and hell as the paradigm of intense pain. But these are fictitious abodes. The paradigms of intense pleasure and pain are to be sought in our worldly experience itself in the form of erotic pleasure and intense sensuous pain.

I am suggesting here that there could be narrow-approached Cārvākas who insisted on sensuous pleasure as the paradigm. But the value perspective of Cārvāka-darśana as a whole should not be identified with sensualist hedonism. 'Learned' or 'more learned' Cārvākas who are able to think comprehensively about life in this world can understand and appreciate varieties of pleasures, both sensuous and non-sensuous.

Duration

This dimension of pleasure has been emphasized by other systems in the following way:

1. Worldly pleasures, especially sensuous pleasures have generally been condemned as temporary or even momentary.
2. Transcendent pleasures which may assume the form of heavenly pleasures or divine pleasures or bliss of emancipation have been praised as long-lasting or everlasting.

Cārvākas' account of duration of pleasures is not found in the extant literature. But the approach of the 'learned Cārvākas' on this issue can be formulated as explained further.

Cārvākas cannot accept the view that there are everlasting transcendent pleasures. Since living beings are mortal and there is no soul-like substance in them, the so-called everlasting pleasure cannot be proved.

So the durability of pleasure can be discussed fruitfully only within the limits of our life in this world.

But there are no direct references to durable pleasures of this life in the extant Cārvāka literature. And this is a gap in the hedonism of Cārvākas. The gap can be filled in by the following considerations.

1. Buddhists are known for their doctrine of momentariness. Though Cārvākas also believe in the impermanence of life, they do not seem to accept momentariness of all things. Hence, substantial durability, continuity, and stability make sense in Cārvāka philosophy of life.
2. Durability of pleasure in this life is possible if there is individual and social security and stability. So apart from the science of pleasure, some Cārvākas insist on the other *śāstras* such as economics (covering agriculture and commerce) and polity[37] (concerned with law and order), which in their turn give social security and stability for the pursuit of consistent and durable pleasures. Kauṭilya includes Lokāyata in 'logic-based philosophy' (ānvīkṣikī). It is concerned with the rational balancing of strengths and weaknesses of different sciences, which makes integrity of a human individual possible.[38] It 'benefits the people, keeps the thinking steady both in calamities and prosperities and also brings about expertise in knowledge, speech and actions'.[39]
3. Cārvākas are generally associated with the view that one may eat ghee even if one runs in debts. Whether this view was really held by Cārvākas is doubtful. But even if it is a Cārvāka view, it implies their concern for a long and healthy life, because here they ask one to consume more ghee (which is conductive to health and longevity according to Indian science of medicine).[40]

So it can be argued that there must have been at least some Cārvākas who were directly or indirectly concerned with duration as an important dimension of pleasure though it was to be sought within the boundaries of this life.

37. See note 14 in this chapter.
38. '*balābale caitāsāṁ hetubhiranvīkṣamāṇā ānvīkṣikī*' (*Arthaśastra* [*AK*] 1.2.11).
39. Chattopadhyaya (1990: 75).
40. See '*Ṛṇaṁ kṛtvā ghṛtaṁ pibet*: Who said this?' Bhattacharya (2012: 201–5). Bhattacharya points out in this paper that the earliest version of the verse occurs in *Viṣṇudharmottaramahāpurāṇa* as: '*yāvajjīvaṁ sukhaṁ jīvet, nāsti mṛtyoragocaram/ bhasmībhūtasya śāntasya punrāgamanaṁ kutaḥ//*' and that the distorted version in which the second quarter was replaced by the expression '*ṛṇaṁ kṛtvā ghṛtaṁ pibet*' was due to Sāyaṇa Mādhava, the author of *SDS*.

Certainty

Cārvākas were keen on the certainty principle as compared to the philosophers of other schools. Other schools believed in pleasure to be experienced in remote future or even in the next life if it was 'assured' by scriptures like Vedas, Smṛtis, and Āgamas. Cārvākas were sceptical about this assurance. One of the reasons why they denied dharma (the system of obligations involving otherworldly beliefs) was that it lacked certainty insofar as the fruits of dhārmic actions are concerned.[41] Scriptures which talk about trans-empirical matters cannot give one the certainty which can be obtained from perception and verifiable inference. The Cārvākas contended that the so-called non-empirical, otherworldly pleasures are more uncertain than the empirical, worldly pleasures, so that the latter are preferable to the former. And even with regard to empirical and worldly pleasures, one has to prefer the pleasures, which are more certain to those which are less.[42]

Propinquity

Propinquity, that is, nearness as a dimension of pleasure was again emphasized more by Cārvākas than others. Those, who believed in the doctrines like soul, rebirth, and life after death, could wait and hope indefinitely for pleasure (or 'absence of suffering'), which one is likely to enjoy in the next life or in another world or at the end of the cycle of births and deaths. The reasonability of such a hope was ruled out by Cārvākas. Naturally, one of the reasons for rejecting dharma was that the fruition of dhārmic actions is supposed to take place in the remote future.[43] Since this is the only life available to us and there is no complete security for the duration of this life, proximity of pleasure is to be valued even within this life. Proximate pleasure is to be preferred to remote pleasure. 'A pigeon today is preferable to a peacock tomorrow.'[44]

41. '*na dharmāṁścaret, eṣyatphalatvāt, sāṁśayikatvācca.*' (*Kāmasūtra* [*KS*] 1.2.25). [Religious obligations should not be practiced, because their fruit is to be obtained in future and because of doubtfulness.]

42. '*varaṁ sāṁśayikānniṣkād asāṁśayikaḥ kārṣāpaṇaḥ. iti laukāyatikāḥ.*' (*KS* 1.2.24). [A sure copper coin is better than a doubtful gold-coin. So say the Laukāyatikas.]

43. *KS* 1.2.25.

44. '*varam adyakapotaḥ śvomayūrāt.*' (*KS* 1.2.23).

This, of course, need not imply that according to Cārvākas one should be greedy and impatient about the pleasures to come. A morally conscious Cārvāka can very well understand the psychosomatic disadvantages of greed and impatience. The reference to Pañcaśikha from the *Mahābhārata*, which will be made in the concluding section of the chapter, implies that in spite of being a materialist one can opt for renunciation of worldly pleasures instead of running after them. Thus equanimity towards pleasure and pain could itself be a happy state which may be immediately available to a meditator independently of materialistic ontological commitments. Preferring this happy state of equanimity, which is immediately available, to other pleasures, which are more remote than that, is perfectly intelligible for a meditating Cārvāka.

Fecundity

The life abundant with pleasures where an action producing one kind of pleasure gives rise to a variety of other pleasures can consistently be a Cārvāka dream. The same cannot be said of those who want to regulate the life of wealth and pleasure by religious obligations and those who want to renounce such a life for ultimate liberation. Those who advocated religious obligations or liberation had a tendency to criticize enjoyments of worldly pleasures in different ways. They upheld, for instance, that a desire for worldly pleasure is not satiated by its enjoyment. Rather it goes on increasing like fire by fuel.[45] They said that it is desire; it is anger arising from instability (*rajas*), which is all-swallowing and most sinful. It has to be treated as an enemy.[46] Naturally, such advocates of religious obligations and liberation could not appreciate fecundity as a desirable dimension of pleasure. Religious obligations have tendency to regulate and restrict pleasures rather than to increase and diversify them. Liberation as a goal of life has tendency to encourage renunciation of worldly pleasures and even if liberated state itself is supposedly a kind of pleasure or bliss, as it is often described, it contains no diversity in it. It is a monotonous pleasure. Hence, a Cārvāka may not be generally interested in it.

45. *Manusmṛti* (*MS*) 2.94.
46. *Śrīmad-bhagavadgītā* (*BG*) 3.37.

Purity

One of the main defects of worldly pleasures according to non-Cārvākas is that they are mixed with pains and therefore, impure. They conceive at the same time of the otherworldly pleasure of heaven or the spiritual pleasure of liberation, which according to them is absolutely pure. The absolute cessation of suffering or absolute purity of pleasure is a state which is not found in this world. On the basis of this, they plead for the path of rituals leading to heaven or the path of austerity leading to liberation.

Cārvākas contend that this conception of absolutely pure pleasure is thoroughly mistaken because it cannot be established on the basis of any reliable evidences. So, criticizing and condemning worldly pleasures on the ground that they are impure will simply lead us nowhere. It is foolish to abandon worldly pleasures simply because they are mixed with suffering. The real skill lies in enjoying pleasure by removing or minimizing the pain associated with it.[47] To ask how absolutely pure pleasure is to be obtained is to ask the wrong question. Non-Cārvākas ask this question and try to answer it but by turning to the wrong direction.

This, however, does not mean that purity of pleasure is of no concern for Cārvākas, who will certainly prefer purer pleasures to less pure ones. They will also try to purify the objects of pleasure by removing painful elements from them.[48] But they will refuse to entertain the myth of absolutely pure pleasure or absolute cessation of pains and to reject the relatively impure pleasures tangible here and now.

In short, one can uphold that the dimensions of pleasure identified by Bentham can be used for comparing different types of

47. ... it is our wisdom to enjoy pure pleasure as far as we can, and to avoid the pain which inevitably accompanies it ...
The pleasure which arises to men from contact with sensible objects,
Is to be relinquished as accompanied by pain—such is the reasoning of fools
The berries of paddy, rich with finest white grains,
What man, seeking his true interest, would fling away, because these are covered with husk and dust? (Chattopadhyaya, 1990: 248–9; translation by E. B. Cowell)

48. Hence Hiriyanna is wrong in his observation: 'Nobody casts away the grain because of the husk. The Cārvāka is so impatient of obtaining pleasure that he does not even try to secure freedom from pain.' (Hiriyanna 1973: 194). Cārvāka is not prescribing consumption of husk along with the rice!

hedonism. Accordingly, we find that Cārvākas in their hedonism emphasize intensity, certainty, and propinquity more than non-Cārvākas do. Secondly, Cārvāka hedonism is more easily amenable to fecundity than those of others. Non-Cārvākas, on the other hand, seem to emphasize duration and purity more than Cārvākas do. But the non-Cārvākas extend the scope of purify and duration beyond the limits of this world and this life. Such an extension is not permissible according to Cārvākas. We can also say that though Cārvākas did not seem to emphasize purity and duration, this does not mean that they being Cārvākas cannot care for these dimensions. Purity and duration of pleasure within empirical practical limits was certainly a concern for at least some Cārvākas.

This is not to deny that there might have been Cārvākas who upheld sensualistic hedonism. This form of hedonism, however, cannot be regarded as the representative view of Cārvākas. As I have contended in the second part of this chapter, though rejection of otherworldly or transcendent pleasures was common to different schools of Cārvākas, their attitude towards worldly pleasures does not seem to be uniform or closed, but rather diverse and open.

IV
The Cārvāka Approach to Human Goals

Discussion on values in Indian tradition often takes the form of the conceptual framework of four human goals popularly called puruṣārthas. The four human goals are termed as kāma, artha, dharma, and mokṣa. 'Kāma' stands for worldly pleasure and the removal of pains. For the sake of brevity we will term this goal simply as pleasure. 'Artha', in the present context, literally means wealth, though its meaning is extended to anything which is instrumental to attaining pleasure and removing suffering. For the sake of brevity we will term this goal simply as wealth. 'Dharma' as a human goal is a complex notion which refers to (*a*) performance of rituals enjoined by scriptures which leads to otherworldly fruits, (*b*) fulfilment of religious obligations and duties, (*c*) fulfilment of social obligations and duties as prescribed in the sacred texts, and (*d*) pursuing a moral life. Different moral approaches emphasize different aspects of dharma and deemphasize others. So in my discussion, I will use the word 'dharma' without seeking its English parallel. 'Mokṣa' as a goal is generally considered as the ultimate goal of life. It has, as I will explain, two core aspects. It is supposed to be freedom from the cycle of births and deaths and it is also supposed to stand for the absolute cessation of sufferings. For the sake of brevity, I will term this goal as liberation. Sometimes these four goals are described as constituting a comprehensive theory of human goals. However, instead of saying that Indian philosophical or cultural tradition upheld a single theory of human goals, it is more elegant and realistic to say that in the Indian tradition, we come across different combinations and configurations of the human goals giving rise to different theories. For example, there is a tradition which emphasizes the first three goals and does not encourage the fourth, liberation. As against this, there are philosophical systems like Jainism, Buddhism, and Vedānta, which attach centrality to liberation.[49] The Cārvāka approach to human goals will be discussed on this background. I will argue that the Cārvāka-darśana can accommodate all the four human goals provided that the nature of dharma and liberation is radically reconstructed.

Traditionally Cārvākas are said to have accepted either pleasure as the only human goal or pleasure and wealth as the only two goals.[50] In any case, they do not seem to have accepted dharma and liberation as the goals as they were generally understood. Here while understanding Cārvāka approach to dharma and liberation I want to do two

49. For my discussion of this point, see 'Some Remarks on the Nature of Puruṣārthas and the Buddhist Approach to Them', in Bhelke and Gokhale (2002: 105–10).

50. See Bhattacharya's discussion of this point in Bhattacharya (2012: 93–4). One can understand his suggestion that the aphorisms prescribing only kāma or kāma along with artha as puruṣārtha probably were not original Bṛhaspati's aphorisms. But his conjecture that probably Cārvākas were not thinking in terms of puruṣārtha, because it is a typically Brahmanical concept, is dubitable. The notion of puruṣārtha as referring to a goal or value of human life was found useful by the thinkers of non-brahmanical schools as well. (For instance, the Buddhist Dharmakīrti begins his work *Nyāyabindu* by saying, 'Fulfilment of puruṣārthas is possible only through true cognition and hence it is being explained.' And the Jaina Amṛtacandrācārya writes a work called *Puruṣārthasiddhyupāya* ('Means to the Achievement of Puruṣārtha'). Using puruṣārtha categories is not the same as adopting a particular theory of puruṣārthas. One can very well use the puruṣārtha categories and present a non-brahmanical theory of human goals. And this is what Cārvākas seem to have done.

things. One, I want to understand the rationale behind the Cārvāka rejection of these two human goals. And two, I want to see whether the Cārvāka theory of human goals can be reconstructed in such a way that these two human goals in their re-interpreted form can be given some significant place in it.

Cārvāka Approach to Dharma

One of the reasons why the opponents of Cārvākas accuse them of not having a moral standpoint is that they oppose dharma. The opponents try to derive their own moral standpoint from the notion of dharma. Sometimes they even appear to equate dharma with morality which implies that to be *dhārmika* is to be moral and to be *adhārmika* is to be immoral. When Cārvākas oppose dharma, they are also opposing this equation. Their opposition to this equation seems to be based on two main reasons:

1. Dharma as understood in the Brahmanical tradition is supposed to be derived from the religious texts such as Vedas and Smṛtis. The actions enjoined by these religious texts are supposed to yield their fruits through the unseen power called *adṛṣṭa* or *apūrva* and many times the fruits claimed to be generated by these actions are also unseen and unverifiable; they are supposed to become ripe in the next birth or in some other world. Cārvākas are averse to this dogmatic faith in the religious texts and that in the unverifiable functions and fruits of actions.[51]

51. Different definitions and descriptions of 'dharma' indicate the strong association of the concept of dharma with ritualism and its derivation from Vedas and Smṛtis. For example:

1. '*yāgādireva dharmaḥ*' (*Ślokavārtikam* [*SV*], v. II.192, p. 77). [Sacrifices, and so on, alone are dharma.]
2. '*codanālakṣaṇo'rtho dharmaḥ*' (*SV*, p. 34). [The beneficial action enjoined by Vedic injunction, is dharma.]
3. '*alaukikatvād adṛṣṭārthatvād apravṛttānāṁ yajñādīnāṁ śāstrāt pravartanaṁ, laukikatvād dṛṣṭārthatvācca pravṛttebhyaśca māṁsabhakṣaṇādibhyaḥ śāstrādeva nivāraṇaṁ dharmaḥ*' (*KS* 1.2.7). [Dharma is inducing a person into the acts like sacrifices at the ruling of the sacred texts, as these acts are supra-mundane and giving supra-sensible results. Dharma is also preventing a person, again at the ruling of the sacred texts, from the acts like eating meat to which one is

2. The notion of dharma not only covers rites and rituals, but also social duties and obligations. In the case of the social obligations, an important distinction is made between specific and common obligations (viśeṣa-dharma and sādhāraṇa-dharma). The specific obligations are those determined by one's birth in a caste, family, gender, and so on. These presuppose and confirm social hierarchy in terms of caste and gender. Common obligations are supposed to be applicable to all human beings, irrespective of their caste or gender. They include the universal moral principles such as truthfulness, non-violence, and non-stealing. So really, the concept of morality could be traced to the realm of 'common obligations'. But there was a basic contradiction between specific obligations which were non-egalitarian and common obligations which were egalitarian. The Brahmanical system of dharma generally attached fundamental importance and a mandatory character to the framework of specific obligations and prescribed common obligations to be followed within this framework (without violating it). The hierarchical framework of the system of four varṇas imposed by *dharmaśāstra* was given by God and hence was not to be violated. The system was headed by the priest class which interpreted the system and guided the ruling class for its administration. As we have seen before, Cārvākas were opposed to varṇa system which was a prominent manifestation of dharma.[52]

This is all about the possible reason behind the Cārvāka rejection of dharma. But here arises a question. Is it not possible to formulate a conception of secular dharma which fits in the Cārvāka value perspective in general? Here I would like to suggest a way by which this can be done.

---

inclined because they are mundane and give sensible results.] This definition is important because dharma is defined here as a kind of puruṣārtha.

4. '*śrutistu vedo vijñeyo dharmaśāstraṁ tu vai smṛtiḥ/ te sarvārtheṣvamīmāṁsye tābhyāṁ dharmo hi nirbabhau//*' (*MS* II.10). [Veda is to be understood as *śruti* and the science of dharma is to be understood as *smṛti*. They are indisputable in all matters, because dharma has illumined from them.] The verses 6–13 in *MS* (chapter 2) elaborate this idea.

52. See note 9 in this chapter.

Accommodating Dharma in Cārvāka Perspective: A Formulation

As we have seen, Cārvākas are said to have accepted wealth and pleasure as the only human goals. I take this to mean that according to them wealth and pleasure are the only substantial goals which dharma and liberation are not. By substantial human goals, I mean those legitimate goals of life which are associated with specific objects which substantiate those goals. Pleasure as a goal is associated with various objects of pleasure and pain. Pursuit of pleasure as a human goal implies enjoying pleasant objects and avoiding painful ones. Wealth is pursued as a substantial goal of life because it essentially consists of various means to pleasure.

Now, what does dharma stand for? The upholders of dharma as a human goal associated dharma with some transcendent objects such as the other worlds (heaven and hell), the cycle of births and deaths, unseen power of rituals, soul, and so on. For them, the pursuit of dharma implied performing ritualistic activities for attaining remote fruits having unseen connection with the actions. Dharma in this sense was a substantial human goal for them. And it is exactly this sense in which Cārvākas were opposed to dharma.

Here I would like to introduce the concept of non-substantial or modal goal and apply it to dharma. By modal goal, I mean a goal which is not associated with specific or special kinds of objects, but stands for a mode or a configuration of the same objects which signify a substantial goal. I suggest that non-acceptance of dharma as a goal by Cārvākas can be taken to mean non-acceptance of it as a substantial goal. It goes well with accepting it as non-substantial, modal goal. Pursuing dharma according to this interpretation does not mean pursuing any special objects (that is, 'dhārmika' objects such as ritualistic objects or otherworldly objects) but it means pursuing the objects of wealth and pleasure in a special way (that is, in 'dhārmika' way). Hence we can distinguish between dhārmika and adhārmika ways of pursuing wealth and pleasure. What is this dhārmika way or mode of pursuing the two mundane goals? It simply means pursuing wealth and pleasure for oneself in such a way that others' pursuits of wealth and pleasure are recognized and honoured. Pursuing wealth and pleasure for oneself by hampering or harming others' pursuits of similar kinds, according to this view, would be the adhārmika way of pursuing them. The different modes of pursuing wealth and pleasure in this way constitute dharma and adharma.

Such a reconstruction of Cārvāka account of dharma, I think, takes a due note of the Cārvāka criticism of the traditional concept of dharma and fills up a gap, at the same time in their value-perspective.

Cārvāka Approach to Liberation

Just as Cārvākas opposed the traditional conception of dharma, they also opposed the traditional conception of liberation. While talking about such a traditional conception of liberation, I presuppose that though different philosophical systems in India understood liberation in different terms and with diverse metaphysical connotations, we can trace a common core of these various conceptions. That common core is something which is common among the concepts of 'Arhat'-hood (Theravāda Buddhism), 'Buddhahood' (Mahāyāna Buddhism), 'Nirvāṇa' (Buddhism in general), 'Kaivalya' (Sāṅkhya, Jainism) and 'Mokṣa' (Vedānta, Nyāya-Vaiśeṣika). Two aspects may be identified here as common:

1. Liberation is regarded as the stoppage of the cycle of births and deaths. The common presuppositions of all liberation-oriented systems was that we are caught up in the beginning-less cycle of transmigration (*saṁsāra*) and this cycle stops when one is liberated. Hence, if a person is liberated, then it is sure that he or she will not be reborn.
2. The notion of liberation has a strong hedonistic connotation. Minimally it is understood as complete and absolute cessation of suffering. Some systems include in liberation a positive experience of pleasure, which is variously described as happiness, joy, peace, or bliss, whereas some systems insist only on the negative aspect, namely the absence of pains.

I propose that these two aspects are the two most minimum aspects of liberation traditionally accepted by all liberation-oriented systems of Indian philosophy. Different systems explained this concept by using different metaphysical categories; but we need not be concerned with them here. One point, however, needs to be noted.

Along with the absolute concept of liberation, some systems also accept the notion of liberation as the ideal state of a person. Hence, they make a distinction between disembodied liberation (*videhamukti*) and embodied liberation (*sadehamukti* or *jīvanmukti*).[53] We also find that the absolute conditions of liberation get somewhat diluted in the descriptions of embodied liberation. For example, since the state of embodied liberation belongs to a human being, the liberated person in this state cannot be completely free from the pains of everyday life. Such a person has only mastered the technique of handling or managing these pains easily so that the pains are not transformed into 'sufferings'.

Against this background, we can ask the question as to what would be the Cārvāka approach to liberation. It is clear that out of the two common aspects of liberation stated above, the first aspect, namely cessation of the cycle of births and deaths, is not acceptable to Cārvākas. This is simply because they do not believe that such a cycle exists. Of course, independently of such a cycle, if liberation simply means non-rebirth of a living being after death, then according to Cārvākas this is going to be the case with every human being. In that sense everybody is guaranteed liberation. Similarly, if liberation means, 'absolute cessation of sufferings', then this too is guaranteed to everyone because this is going to be the case with everyone at the time of death. This is what Cārvākas mean when they say that death itself is liberation.[54] But liberation in this sense is not a state of 'Self'; it is not something one will 'experience' permanently. It is also not a state which one should aspire for. Liberation, as identified with death, is just a natural happening; it is not a human goal, which should legitimately be aspired for. So the Cārvāka statement that death itself is liberation should be taken as their criticism of the standard concept of liberation, and not as the expression of their conception of liberation as a goal. If we want to have a positive conception of liberation in Cārvāka-darśana, then we may have to search for it elsewhere.

53. The notions of *jīvanmukti* and *videhamukti* are found in Vedānta tradition. Similar distinctions are found in many other liberation-oriented systems. For instance, *sayogakevalī-ayogakevalī* (Jainism), *sopādiśeṣa-nirvāṇa—anupādiśeṣa-nirvāṇa* (Buddhism), *kevalajñāna-kaivalya* (Sāṅkhya), *nirbīja-samādhi—kaivalya* (Yoga), and *sthitaprajña-brahmanirvāṇa* (Gītā).

54. '*dehacchedo mokṣaḥ*' (*SDS*, Cārvāka-darśana). [The destruction of body is liberation.]

In fact there are two kinds of references to liberation in Cārvāka literature. On the one hand it is said that death itself is liberation. On the other hand, it is said that freedom (*svātantrya*) is liberation and dependence (*pāratantrya*) is bondage.[55] The first kind of statement, namely, death itself is liberation, as we have seen earlier, mainly serves to deny disembodied liberation than to present any positive concept of liberation. The second statement of Cārvākas, however, gives a positive conception of liberation. I interpret the statement as implying that one can overcome pains and suffering, within the framework of this-worldly human life, only by becoming independent or rather self-dependent,[56] physically as well as mentally. One can say that this is a notion of embodied liberation that Cārvākas are introducing. Of course there is a difference. When other liberation-oriented systems introduce a notion of embodied liberation, they introduce it as a stepping stone towards the so-called ultimate liberation, which is essentially disembodied. The former according to them has only an instrumental value whereas the latter has intrinsic value. As against this, in the Cārvāka scheme, the former would be accepted by denying the latter. The former is an intrinsic value whereas the latter is no value at all.

Here we can refer back to the distinction we made, while accommodating dharma in the Cārvāka scheme of human goals, between a substantial and modal goal. What I have said about dharma there can be said, mutatis mutandis, about liberation. Just as dharma would not be a substantial human goal according to Cārvākas, but only a modal one, so would liberation. Liberation according to liberation-oriented systems ultimately stands for transcendent state of the disembodied soul. (In Buddhism it would be understood as the mystical state of nirvāṇa or the metaphysical-mystical Buddha-hood.) Liberation in this sense would be a substantial goal explainable in terms of metaphysics which transcends material existence. For

55. *'pāratantryaṁ bandhaḥ, svātantryaṁ mokṣaḥ iti cārvākapakṣe'pi svātantryaṁ duḥkha-nivṛttiścet,avivādaḥ'* (*SDS*, Akṣapāda-darśana). [(Naiyāyika says:) If you say that self-dependence is understood as cessation of suffering in the Cārvāka position, as (it is said) 'Other-dependence is bondage. Self-dependence is liberation.' Then we have no dispute with this.]

56. The word svātantrya is an abstract noun derived from 'sva-tantra' which means governed by oneself (sva).

Cārvākas, no such transcendent metaphysics will be required for explaining liberation. Metaphysically this liberation would be a free state of a human person where the human person is understood as a configuration of four material substances having consciousness as its inseparable (though perishable) property. Of course even at this stage, Cārvākas would not accept liberation as the absolute cessation of pains or sufferings, because according to this conception, it is after all a human state having limitations. A liberated person in this sense may not be absolutely free from pains and sufferings, though he or she must have matured his or her personality in such a way that he or she can easily face and overcome pains and tensions of worldly life. Life according to Cārvākas consists of activities involving the pursuit of wealth and pleasure and the life of a liberated person is not an exception to this rule. Only this activity involving wealth and pleasure in the life of a liberated Cārvāka is considerably regulated and disciplined so that sufferings and tensions are eliminated to the largest possible extent. Liberation understood as 'self-dependence' is a modal goal in the sense that it refers to that modality of dealing with wealth and pleasure, which keeps the agent free from any kind of other-dependence.

That other-dependent life increases sufferings and a self-regulated life decreases them is not a view peculiar to Cārvākas. It was a matter of common acceptance in the orthodox tradition as well.[57] Svātantrya or freedom according to this understanding is not licentiousness, but self-regulation. This self-regulation, according to different schools, assumes different metaphysical forms and different practical details. But at minimal level it implies control over senses, regulation of desires, reduction of attachments, and emphasis on realization of one's true nature. This minimal practical aspect of self-regulation is not unavailable to Cārvākas who pursue liberation as a human goal.

The self-realization according to Cārvāka-darśana will definitely differ from that according to other liberation-oriented systems. It will involve the realization that, 'I am just a combination of material

57. Manu, for instance, says, '*sarvaṁ paravaśaṁ duḥkhaṁ sarvamātmavaśaṁ sukham*' (*MS* 4.160). [Everything controlled by others is painful. Everything in one's own control is pleasant.]

elements configured in a particular way with consciousness as their function. When this combination of matter disintegrates, the consciousness will simply cease to exist.' Such a materialistic self-realization need not necessarily support the life of attachment; it can very well boost the life of detachment. The Cārvāka seeking liberation may develop peace and tranquillity of mind based on deep realization of the possibilities and limitations of his or her own material existence. As a result, the minimal practical core of self-regulation which is commonly accepted by other liberation-oriented systems can also be accepted by Cārvākas. A liberated Cārvāka, like a liberated person of other schools, may withdraw from worldly pleasures, but the former's withdrawal will still be different because it will not imply any belief in otherworldly or transcendent pleasures. Such self-realization could still be 'materialistic' in the metaphysical sense of the term.

***

I would like to conclude the foregoing argument by summarizing what Pt. Laxmanshastri Joshi says on this issue:

In *Śāntiparva* of the *Mahābhārata* (chapters 218, 219, and 319) we come across two dialogues of Pañcaśikha with Janaka. In the first dialogue which occurs in chapters 218 and 219, Pañcaśikha expounds the doctrine of non-self, according to which there is no self independently of body. The teachings of Pañcaśikha in these chapters contain mainly three principles—(i) The whole world is impermanent and material (ii) There is no independent self; 'knower of the field' (*kṣetrajña*) or Self (*ātman*) is an idea of mind. (iii) Perception is the main source of knowledge, inference and verbal testimony may be accepted only if consistent with perception. Pañcaśikha concludes from these principles that there is no essence in life because life is inflicted by old age and death. So renunciation of everything is the highest thing.[58]

58. Summarized from his introduction (*Prastāvanā*) to Athavale (1997: 19–21) (translation mine).

After translating verses 23–28 from *Śāntiparva* chapter 219, Pandit Joshi makes a general point which is more important philosophically:

> Negation of other worlds (*Nāstikavāda*) can include both the paths—that of activity and that of detachment. One need not be surprised to see that the path of detachment based on materialistic naturalism was advocated by Pañcaśikha in *Mahābhārata*. Philosophical materialism does not necessarily lead to worldly hedonism. Nor does philosophical idealism necessarily lead to the path of detachment.[59]

59. Athavale (1997; translation mine). Hence although Bhattacharya's conjecture that Ajita Keśakambalī must have been an ascetic is doubtful (see note 28 in this chapter), the logical possibility suggested by Bhattacharya that a materialist can be an ascetic, can be well appreciated.

7

Revisiting Indian Philosophy through a Cārvāka Perspective

So far I have tried to present a picture of Cārvāka-darśana as a family of different trends in epistemology, ontology, and axiology. In spite of the diversity in all the three realms, Cārvāka-darśana has been opposed to the epistemology of scripture-based 'knowledge', the other-worldly, idealistic ontology, and ritualistic–religious axiology. These forms of opposition, though negative in nature, have given integrity to the Lokāyata-Cārvāka family. Because of these integrating factors, Cārvāka-darśana has been the object of criticism of all other systems. Many polemical works of other systems are available in which Cārvāka occurs as the first position to be refuted and discarded (*pūrvapakṣa*). Cārvāka occupies such a position probably because in its various forms, it happens to be the most noncommittal system. At a philosophical level, others believed that only the systems containing idealistic or otherworldly worldviews can develop a comprehensive and holistic perspective of life, whereas the Cārvāka perspective has to be incomprehensive, unwholesome, and thereby subject to refutation and rejection.

On the other hand, exceptionally few texts are available (such as Jayarāśi's *Tattvopaplavasiṁha*, which presents an extremely sceptical view) where other systems are presented as refutable positions and Cārvāka as the conclusive position (*siddhānta-pakṣa*). Generally non-Cārvāka systems, which emphasize otherworldly or transcendental beliefs, have dominated the scene of Indian philosophy. This image of Indian philosophy has rendered it as essentially idealistic or religious in its orientation.

The conditions under which philosophizing takes place in India have changed since the 19th and 20th centuries. Due to the growing importance of science, we find a tendency to 'secularize' religious philosophies. Modern religious thinkers have tried to shift the 'other worlds' from their positions and locate them in prosperous/sublime and degenerate conditions attainable in this world itself. They now emphasize the possibility of liberation in this world and this life itself. Moreover, they try to establish a greater dialogue between religion and science and reconstruct religious beliefs in a way that is apparently acceptable to science. We can roughly call this a secularist turn in religious philosophy. This turn can be located in the studies of Indian religious philosophies as well. Hence, we have some pro-scientific interpretations of Vedānta,[1] Buddhism,[2] Jainism,[3] and a materialistic interpretation of Sāṅkhya and Vaiśeṣika.[4] Elevation of the status of Cārvāka-darśana by some scholars of Indian Philosophy is a part of this process. In the earlier hierarchies of Indian philosophy, the spiritualist systems like Vedānta, Jainism, and Buddhism attained a high status. Each of these systems made a hierarchical rearrangement of all the systems, placed it at the top and other systems in their 'due' places. These systems in this way played the role of philosophies and also meta-philosophies. By playing the role of meta-philosophy, they talked about what

1. Vivekananda, the advocate of Neo-Vedanta said, 'I may make bold to say that the only religion which agrees with and even goes a little further than modern researchers, both on physical and moral lines is the Advaita and that is why it appeals to modern scientists so much' (Vivekananda 2011).

2. For example, the 14th Dalai Lama has often emphasized the rational approach of Buddhism and reliance on causality and empiricism as common philosophical principles shared between Buddhism and science.

3. Some Jaina scholars have compared Jaina atomism with scientific atomism, Jaina mathematics with modern mathematics, and Jaina theory of *ahiṁsā* with environmental awareness. See, for instance, Zaveri (1975); Jain (1973); Singh (1988); Shukla (2012).

4. This was done mainly by Debiprasad Chattopadhyaya in his works like *Lokāyata* and *What Is Living and What Is Dead in Indian Philosophy*.

philosophy is and developed a norm of what it should be, applied this norm to different philosophical systems, and then weighed the systems in the light of it.

In the 20th century, a new possibility could be envisaged according to which Cārvāka could play the role of meta-philosophy in this sense and regard itself as higher than other philosophical systems. The purpose behind this chapter is to revisit Cārvāka philosophy as performing this new role.

We will see in the first part of this chapter, how as a part of the inter-systemic dialectics, which took place in India, some philosophical systems behaved as meta-philosophies by developing comprehensive and critical approaches about Indian philosophy as a whole. Taking a cue from this, I will explore the possibility of Cārvāka-darśana playing such a role.

In the second part, I will consider the contributions of some scholars and thinkers, through which they have given central status to Cārvāka-darśana in some form in their understanding of Indian philosophy and by doing so, have created new possibilities of interpreting and examining other systems of Indian philosophy.

The Possibility of a Cārvāka Meta-philosophy

Inter-systemic Dialectics—Some Observations

It can be observed that initially the systems (*darśanas*) of Indian philosophy did not grow always as rival systems but many a time as disciplines (*śāstras*), which could be complementary to each other. (Here I presuppose a certain distinction between darśana and śāstra, which I will explain in due course.) Agniveśa in his medical work *Carakasaṁhitā* incorporates the then available accounts of Sāṅkhya, Nyāya, Vaiśeṣika, and even some Buddhist doctrines, without referring to the possibility of internal contradiction or conflict between them. Kauṭilya in 'Vidyāsamuddeśa' chapter of *Arthaśāstra* mentions *ānvikṣikī* (philosophy based on reasoning)[5] as a body of knowledge consisting of three systems: Sāṅkhya, Yoga (that is,

5. I have explored the possibility of identifying 'ānvīkṣikī' as philosophy elsewhere. See Gokhale (2012: 150–60).

Nyāya-Vaiśeṣika),[6] and Lokāyata. These three systems are not mentioned there as rival systems, but as alternative or collective ways of using reasoning for critically examining and balancing the other three bodies of knowledge namely religious tradition, economy, and polity. Similarly even after a few centuries we have Gauḍapāda who was a Vedāntin, but who in his *Āgamaśāstra* does not hesitate in praising the Buddha as the one who is untouched by the four modes of thinking.[7]

This is one side of the story because we also see that side by side rivalries among philosophical approaches were being introduced and maintained through the dichotomy of right view and wrong view (*samyak-dṛṣṭi* and *mithyā-dṛṣṭi* or *samyak-darśana* and *mithyā-darśana*). I venture to claim that the indiscriminate application of the word 'darśana' to various philosophical systematizations was a result of a happy compromise between these approaches, which looked at themselves as the right darśana and others as wrong darśana. (The word 'darśana' in this context simply means 'view'. It does not mean either 'perception' or 'insight'.) The systems at this stage develop rivalries against each other, presenting other systems as refutable positions (*pūrvapakṣa*) and themselves as conclusive positions (*uttarapakṣa* or *siddhānta-pakṣa*). But apart from developing rivalry, some systems also tried to develop an accommodative approach. This complex approach, which was critical as well as accommodative, amounted to imply—'Others are like us in some respect, but we are better than others in some important respects.'

Here I will try to explain what I mean by the distinction between śāstra and darśana. A śāstra, like a science, has a specific limited subject matter. It may deal with anything such as knowledge, the method of debate, the structure of the universe, human nature, human goals in general, or a specific human goal. The list is not exhaustive. Accordingly we can talk of the science of knowledge (*pramāṇaśāstra*), the science of debate (*vādaśāstra*), the science of the knowable (*prameyaśāstra*), the science of the sacred law (*dharmaśāstra*), the science of political economy (*arthaśāstra*), and so

6. I am following here Chattopadhyaya's interpretation of the term 'yoga'. See Chattopadhyaya (1976: 245–51).

7. *Gauḍapāda-kārikā* (*GK*) 4.1–2, 83–4.

on. Śāstras may overlap with each other, but they do not essentially clash with each other. Second, they do not generally claim to give comprehensive knowledge of all that is important. Darśanas, on the other hand, claim to be concerned with three major areas in their interrelatedness: knowledge, reality, and values. (The extent to which they have a deep or superficial concern in a particular area is a different matter). They also make claims for comprehensiveness and conclusiveness. Naturally they come in conflict with other systems which make different claims in a common area. At the same time, these systems while developing comprehensive approaches also try to interpret and accommodate other systems in their unique ways. This is how different philosophical systems are seen to develop meta-philosophies which consist of a critical yet accommodative approach towards other philosophical systems.

Three Meta-philosophical Approaches

A critical yet accommodative approach as described earlier is found in traditions of some Indian philosophical systems among which three are prominent: non-dualist Vedānta, Jainism, and Buddhism. Sāyaṇa-Mādhava, himself a non-dualist Vedāntin, in his 'Collection of all systems' (that is, *SDS*), arranged different philosophical systems in hierarchical order, so that systems closer to the non-dualistic 'ultimate truth' were placed higher and those which are remoter were lower. Cārvāka was considered to be the lowest system in this hierarchy. But there is another way in which the critical and accommodative approach of non-dualist Vedanta is available to us. This way is more fundamental because it is rooted in the non-dualist worldview itself. According to it, following Gauḍapāda, non-dualists claimed that dualists, who firmly adhere to their own systems, oppose each other, but they are not (rather, they cannot be) opposed to non-dualism.[8] The reason seems to be that non-dualists ultimately see no duality, which is a necessary presupposition of any opposition. In this way non-dualists seem to

8. *svasiddhāntavyavsthāsu dvaitino niścitā dhruvam/*
parasparaṁ virudhyante tairayaṁ na virudhyate// (*GK* 3.17)

[Dualists being firmly convinced about the establishment of their own doctrines, fight with each other; this (= non-dualism) does not fight with them.]

develop a meta-philosophical approach in terms of which they establish significant relationship with other philosophical systems.

The second system in which one finds a meta-philosophical approach, which is critical as well as accommodative about other systems, is Jainism. The meta-philosophical approach can be seen as inbuilt in the non-absolutism (*anekāntavāda*) of Jainas. Jainas hold that different philosophical systems are examples of different forms of absolutism (*ekāntavada*). For instance, Buddhism is the case of momentariness–absolutism (*kṣanikaikāntavāda*) whereas Advaitism is the case of permanence–absolutism (*nityaikāntavāda*). 'Reality is changing' and 'reality is permanent' are both partial truths about the reality. This is because reality in itself is both changing as well as permanent. Both can be appreciated as partial viewpoints. But Buddhists do not claim change as their partial viewpoint but as the complete truth. Similarly, Advaitins do not present permanence as their partial viewpoint about the reality but as the complete truth. To regard partial viewpoint as the complete truth is the fallacy of pseudo-viewpoint (*durnaya* or *nayābhāsa*) according to Jainas. Through their theory of pseudo-viewpoint, the Jainas try to show how different schools of philosophy, by taking an absolutist stand about the partial truths they have grasped, commit the fallacy of pseudo-viewpoint.[9] Jainas in this way appreciate all the other systems as representing partial truths about reality and try to enjoy the highest status by representing the comprehensive or the whole truth.

The third meta-philosophical system in this series is Buddhism. In its different phases, Buddhism presents itself as the true vision of reality and other philosophical schools as presenting extreme views (*antagrāha-dṛṣṭi*) or dogmatic views (*diṭṭhivāda*). In *Brahmajālasutta* of Dīghanikāya, the Buddha gives a long list of the dogmatic metaphysical views, which are mostly the wrong answers to the unanswerable questions (*avyākṛta-praśna*) which are unanswerable, because they are based on wrong presuppositions. The dogmatists of other schools generally commit the fallacies of eternalism (*śāśvatavāda*) or nihilism (*ucchedavāda*), whereas the truth is in the middle. Buddhism in this way presents itself as the philosophy of middle path and at the same type a meta-philosophical critique of dogmatic philosophies. The

9. Gokhale (1992: 201–13).

same spirit was carried forward in a new form by Nāgārjuna, who criticized different philosophical viewpoints as dogmatic views (dṛṣṭi), as based on essentialism (*svabhāvavāda*) of some form or the other and presented his own version of Buddhism upholding non-essential (*niḥsvabhāva* or *śūnya*) nature of all things.

The Possibility of a Meta-philosophical Approach of Cārvākas

On the background of the availability of such meta-philosophical approaches, I am suggesting that we can think of Cārvāka developing a meta-philosophical approach, which is both critical and accommodative. For this purpose, one has to think of Cārvāka-darśana as a strong and comprehensive philosophical system, rather than a weak and narrow one, as it is generally taken to be. It should be able to handle various epistemological, ontological, and also axiological problems efficiently and also evaluate and accommodate other schools of philosophy. In the foregoing chapters, while bringing out the diversity in Cārvāka-darśana, I have observed that common-sense-empiricist Cārvāka can be said to be the strongest and the most accommodative school of Cārvākas. We can recapitulate briefly the characteristic features and the points of strength of this school as follows:

1. Unlike the popular version of Cārvāka epistemology, common-sense-empiricist Cārvākas do not reject inference completely. Hence, they can escape the obvious charges arising from the complete denial of inference, for example, the charge that Cārvākas cannot even have communication with their opponents because communication presupposes the inferential knowledge of the meaning intended by the other person's statement.
2. At the same time, they can criticize the other-worldly and transcendent metaphysics of the other philosophical systems. Cārvākas with their wider epistemological apparatus can enjoy higher status in the order of philosophical systems and develop a different accommodative and critical relationship with them.
3. Cārvākas, except those who are sceptics, believe that the world consists of material elements, rather their living and non-living compositions. Earth, water, fire, and air are the gross

elements accepted in classical Cārvāka system. However, that these four elements are the only basic material elements is not essential to Cārvāka-darśana. The knowledge derived from physical sciences can be appropriated by learned Cārvākas, since it is also based on observation and inferences that are verifiable or falsifiable.

4. Materialist Cārvākas claim that consciousness cannot exist outside or independently of the physical body. Of course, consciousness is not reducible to the physical body. In this sense, epiphenomenalism or non-eliminative materialism and not strict behaviourism or materialism is accepted in the context of the mind–body relation. On this basis, Cārvākas can challenge the claim of their opponents that there is disembodied consciousness. At the same time, they can welcome the efforts of the thinkers of other schools to minimize otherworldly elements in their respective schools. Hence, in the new hierarchical arrangement of the Indian philosophical schools, those containing greater potential for materialistic reconstruction may be given a higher position whereas those which contain lowest potential of that kind may be given the lowest position. One might claim, for example, that Sāṅkhya can be reconstructed as a system without soul (*puruṣa*) as an independent category and Buddhism as a system accepting mind (*citta/nāma*) as inseparable from body (*rūpa*). The two systems then will have a higher status whereas non-dualist Vedānta or Yogācāra Budhism in which consciousness is essentially disembodied and independent will have a lower status.
5. Common-sense-empiricist Cārvākas claim that pleasure and wealth are the basic human goals. Dharma and liberation could be accepted, if they are re-defined as secular goals. The popular religious conceptions of dharma and liberation are rejected since they involve belief in disembodied soul and otherworldly existence. Emphasis on pleasure and wealth does not imply that only the pursuit of sensuous pleasures is prescribed. As argued in the previous chapter, control over senses can also be prescribed by Cārvākas, if it conduces to happiness within the boundaries of this world. Cārvākas in this sense can

> promote reconstruction of the world on secular–moral terms. The Cārvāka can even appreciate 'spirituality' if it is redefined as higher morality without reference to the transcendent metaphysical doctrines of spirit (Brahman, ātman, puruṣa, and so on) or other worlds.

I would like to suggest that Cārvāka-darśana, as outlined, can come to terms with other philosophical systems in a more confident and strong way. It can develop a critical and accommodative approach with respect to other systems. It can critically examine their epistemological, ontological, and axiological views in a more systematic way. It can set standards by which any philosophical system can be weighed. It can re-arrange all the systems in a new hierarchy. This latter could turn over the order standardized by Sāyaṇa–Mādhava in which Advaita–Vedānta is at the top and Cārvāka is at the bottom. The new ordering of Indian philosophical systems could also encourage or stimulate the reformulation or reconstruction of other systems such that they can establish a new and more meaningful relation with Cārvāka-darśana.

Now I want to suggest that we can identify some 20th-century scholars and thinkers who have revisited Indian philosophy in general or its specific philosophical systems from a 'materialist' or 'secular' point of view. I will indicate some such attempts in the next section.

Some Modern Pro-Lokāyata Approaches

Rajendra Prasad (1926–)

All the darśanas except Cārvāka, at least insofar as their popular versions are concerned, accept the doctrine of karma uncritically. Prasad[10] has played the role of a modern Cārvāka by criticizing the doctrine of karma systematically. In his seminal paper 'Karma,

10. An analytical philosopher of contemporary India, Prasad taught in Patna University and then in Indian Institute of Technology, Kanpur. He is the author of *Karma, Causation and Retributive Morality* (1989); *Varṇadharma, Niṣkāma-karma and Practical Morality* (2000); *Dharmakīrti's Theory of Inference* (2002); *A Conceptual Analytical Study of Indian Philosophy of Morals* (2008).

Causation and Retributive Morality,'[11] he critically analysed the doctrine by presenting a dilemma as to whether the doctrine is causal in nature or a moral one, and through that, questioned the moral force of the doctrine. He also questioned the doctrine of *karmayoga* (the doctrine of non-attachment in actions), which is sometimes presented almost as an offshoot of the doctrine of karma.

In another important paper,[12] Prasad has revaluated and reconstructed the theory of human goals (*puruṣārthas*). In addition to artha and kāma, which are mundane goals, this paper interprets dharma, without reference to its 'other-worldly' implications, as representing moral social obligations. Moreover, he does not accept liberation as an independent goal, but reduces it to kāma. Prasad's exercise can be understood as a secular reconstruction of the theory of human goals. The point relevant for our purpose is that through such a reconstruction, Prasad makes all the human goals (not just the first two) as available to Cārvākas. He says in the concluding part of his paper:

> As a *kāma*-goal *mokṣa* can be given a spiritual as well as non-spiritual interpretation, since theoretically speaking we can find personal peace in various kinds of acquisitions, spiritual and non-spiritual, religious and non-religious. Therefore even the Cārvāka theory of value can be said to be an exemplification of the theory proposed here. Dharma will have to be then given a non-theological, non-otherworldly interpretation and *mokṣa* will be pleasure, natural pleasure, and not any kind of heavenly, non-bodily, spiritual bliss.[13]

Debiprasad Chattopadhyaya (1918–1993)

Debiprasad Chattopadhyaya[14] is one of the few scholars of Indian philosophy who had highest regards for Lokāyata-darśana. This resulted

11. Prasad (1989, chapter 13: 210–74).
12. 'The Theory of Puruṣārthas: Revaluation and Reconstruction', as included in Prasad (1989).
13. Prasad (1989: 305), italics mine.
14. An eminent Marxist philosopher. The author of the books including *Lokayata* (1959), *Indian Philosophy* (1964), *Indian Atheism* (1969), *What is Living and What is Dead in Indian Philosophy* (1976), and *Science and Society in Ancient India* (1977).

in his rearrangement of the hierarchy of the traditional schools of Indian philosophy. Walter Ruben observes in his Foreword to Chattopadhyaya's popular Introduction to Indian Philosophy: 'If Mādhava began his *Sarva-darśana-saṁgraha* with the Lokāyata as the lowest school and ended with the Advaita-Vedānta as the highest school of Indian Philosophy, Chattopadhyaya, as a materialist, follows the opposite line.'[15]

But Chattopadhyaya's conception of Indian materialism was not restricted to the traditional Lokāyata. He took a bolder step than K. K. Mittal, who talks about 'materialistic elements' in different schools of Indian philosophy.[16] Chattopadhyay does not just talk of 'materialist elements' in non-Cārvāka systems, but claims that the systems, namely Nyāya-Vaiśeṣika and Sāṅkhya in their early forms, were in fact materialistic. In his famous work *Lokāyata: A Study in Ancient Indian Materialism*, he tries to show with an elaborate argument that the original Sāṅkhya must have been materialistic.[17] According to Sāṅkhya, the world originates from *prakṛti*, the insentient material cause of the world, and that is all insofar as the early Sāṅkhya is concerned. Classical Sāṅkhya showed that there existed the category of puruṣa, which was supposed to stand for pure consciousness that existed independently of prakṛti. This, according to Chattopadhyaya, was a later interpolation influenced by Vedantic idealism. In another work, *What is Living and What is Dead in Indian Philosophy*,[18] Chattopadhyaya presents his general position on Indian philosophy more systematically. According to him, the major philosophical conflict in India was between idealism and its antithesis, the most radical form of the latter being Lokāyata materialism.[19] Advaita-Vedānta and Yogācāra Buddhism were the major schools on the idealistic side whereas the antithesis of idealism consisted of Sāṅkhya, Yoga, and Lokāyata, that is, *ānvikṣikī* as Kauṭilya called it.[20] Other schools could be located between the two poles according to their affinity to idealism or materialism.

15. Chattopadhyaya (1964: xix).
16. Mittal (1974).
17. Chattopadhyaya (1978: 364–422).
18. Chattopadhyaya (1976).
19. Chattopadhyaya (1976: 213–15, 251).
20. *Arthaśastra* (*AK*) I.II.

According to Chattopadhyaya, Kauṭilya, by the term 'yoga' in this list of the three kinds of ānvīkṣikī, refers to Nyāya-Vaiśeṣika and not to the school of meditation as it is generally understood. He also claims that all the three disciplines clubbed together by Kauṭilya are materialistic in nature.[21] Here he uses the word materialism in a somewhat loose sense to cover some forms of dualism, where consciousness is accepted as existing independently of matter, but has a subordinate role to play. Hence, early Sāṅkhya and Nyāya-Vaiśeṣika are materialist in the sense that they regard matter as primary and consciousness as secondary.[22] Chattopadhyaya points out that Nyāya and Vaiśeṣika systems in their early forms were atheistic, though in the later development (or degeneration) they accepted God as the efficient cause of the world. Though early Nyāya-Vaiśeṣika accepts ātman as one of the substances, Chattopadhyaya argues that consciousness is not supposed to be an essential, but only an accidental characteristic of ātman. Consciousness arises due to the contact between object, sense organ, *manas*, and ātman. And because consciousness is accidental, ātman in liberated state according to Nyāya-Vaiśeṣika is devoid of pleasure, pain, desire, aversion, effort, and even consciousness. These are some of the indications of materialistic character of Nyāya-Vaiśeṣika system according to him.

It can be argued here that though Nyāya-Vaiśeṣikas regard consciousness as an accidental quality of ātman, they do regard ātman as the carrier of merit and demerit (dharma and adharma) due to which it is reborn again and again till it is liberated. Hence, the accidental character of consciousness does not affect the transmigration of soul. Similarly, it can be doubted whether Chattopadhyaya is right in his claim about Sāṁkhya as originally materialistic. Modern scholars claim that though these systems are realist, they are not materialist.

However, though Chattopadhyaya in this way does not succeed in showing that early Nyāya, Vaiśeṣika, and Sāṅkhya were materialistic, he succeeds in showing their close affinity to materialism. What is important is that he searches for 'Indian materialism' outside

21. Though Chattopadhyaya's identification of Yoga with Nyāya-Vaiśeṣika seems plausible, his claim that the three systems were clubbed together because of their materialist character seems to be unduly biased. Kauṭilya's approach in clubbing the three systems together, as we have seen in the first chapter, seems to be to underline their rational character rather than materialistic one.

22. Chattopadhyaya (1976: 288–95).

Cārvāka-darśana and widens the scope of materialistic thought in ancient India. Cārvāka-darśana now does not remain just one philosophical system to be singled out and criticized by other systems. Rather, it can now re-examine and hierarchically arrange other systems in terms of the relative status given to matter in their respective ontologies. It can do so also with reference to the status given to experience and scientific reasoning as against idealistic speculation in their respective epistemologies.

S. S. Barlingay (1919–1997)

S. S. Barlingay[23] assigns a central position to Cārvāka-darśana rather in an indirect way. He does this by way of making and applying the distinction between distinguishable-qua-distinguishables and separables in the context of philosophical problems in general and Indian philosophy in particular. Though this distinction of Barlingay is inspired by Nyāya-Vaiśeṣika distinction between conjunction (*saṁyoga*) and inherence (*samavāya*),[24] he dissociates it from this context and uses it freely to various problems of philosophy. While applying the distinction to mind–body problem in an article entitled 'Soul and Self', Barlingay claims that consciousness is distinguishable from material body, but not separable.[25] This is how he supports the Cārvāka theory of consciousness.

In the light of this distinction, Barlingay reinterprets and reconstructs other systems of Indian philosophy. His interpretation of Indian philosophy, however, differs from that of Chattopadhyaya. As we have seen before, Chattopadhyaya places Śaṁkara's Advaita-Vedānta in anti-materialistic idealist group. Barlingay disagrees with this understanding of Advaita-Vedānta. He expresses this disagreement as a comment on Com. S. G. Sardesai's monograph on Indian Philosophy[26] and also as a comment on Chattopadhyaya,

23. A recent Indian philosopher, and the author of the works like *A Modern Introduction to Indian Logic* (1965); *Beliefs, Reasons and Reflections* (1983); *Re-understanding Indian Philosophy* (1998); *A Modern Introduction to Indian Aesthetic Theory* (2007).

24. Barlingay (1983: 5).

25. Barlingay (1983: 82–4).

26. Sardesai (2006). Sardesai in this book has followed the same line as Chattopadhyaya in *What Is Living and What Is Dead in Indian Philosophy* (1976).

the author of Lokāyata.[27] Barlingay's interpretation of Advaita Vedanta brings it close to Lokāyata, when, for instance, he says 'Advaita ... could allow spatio-temporality and even matter occupying space and time in their thesis. The matter can be charged with consciousness.'[28]

Now the question is, if Śaṁkara's Advaita, as interpreted by Barlingay, is close to Cārvāka, who is on the opposite side? Here, Barlingay's writings provide a different dichotomization of Indian philosophy. The school which advocates the doctrines such as soul, karma, rebirth, other worlds, ritualism, and hierarchical social order based on *varṇa* and caste, according to Barlingay, is Pūrvamīmāmsā. The other systems such as Sāṅkhya, Advaita-Vedānta, Buddhism, and Jainism raise a banner of revolt against Pūrvamīmāmsā.[29] Accordingly Barlingay reinterprets Sāṅkhya, Vedanta, and Jainism whereby the secular, pro-materialistic, and anti-ritualistic aspects of these systems get highlighted.

In this spirit, while interpreting Jainism Barlingay highlights the spatio-temporality of *jīva*[30] and interprets the division between jīva and *ajīva* as the one between animate and inanimate matter.[31] Through his interpretation Barlingay tries to show that Jaina theory of jīva and ajīva is close to common sense, as he says, 'While interpreting Jaina theory it is the common sense which we have to depend upon. The common sense tells us that matter is to be divided in to living and non-living and is not to be abstracted into matter and non-matter'.[32]

Similarly while interpreting Sāṅkhya, Barlingay upholds that '*puruṣa* or consciousness in metaphysics will not have to be treated as separate from prakṛti, though in expression they would appear to be different and separate.'[33] Similarly, 'When we talk of *puruṣa*'s *kaivalya*

27. Barlingay (1998: 307–13).

28. Barlingay (1998: 31, 226).

29. Barlingay (1998: 29–30).

30. 'For the Jainas the *jīva* and *deha* can be distinguished but not separated. They assert that jīva has extension' Barlingay (1998: 93).

31. 'If we look at experience at macroscopic level, it will be clear that world consists of jīva or the animate and things different from jīva or the inanimate' Barlingay (1998: 143).

32. Barlingay (1998: 150).

33. Barlingay (1998: 40).

or *artha* ... we will have to talk of *puruṣa* as a concrete living object. He will be an embodied *puruṣa*. He will have to be a person.'[34]

Hence, the central focus of Barlingay's philosophical attention is a this-worldly common-sense approach, which can be called a Lokāyatika approach in its essence. He juxtaposes this approach with the Pūrva-Mīmāṁsā approach, which is essentially ritualistic and otherworldly, and understands different philosophical systems as primarily rooted in common sense, but falling prey at times to Pūrva-Mīmāṁsā type of thinking in their further development or, rather, degeneration. Here again, Barlingay develops a common-sense meta-philosophy of Indian philosophy, which is essentially Lokāyatika in character.

B. R. Ambedkar (1891–1956)

Finally in this series, I would like to refer to B. R. Ambedkar,[35] a revolutionary social and religious thinker of 20th-century India, who established the close affinity of Buddhism to Lokāyata through his magnum opus *The Buddha and His Dhamma*. Unlike the thinkers we have discussed earlier, Ambedkar was not a professional philosopher.[36] But he can be called a social and religious philosopher for the reason that he, through his rigorous intellectual exercise, created powerful conceptual tools to be used by the Indian intelligentsia as well as the society at large, for a social and religious reform. Through the critique of anti-egalitarian caste system in particular and Hindu religion in general he came to the conclusion that the so called Hindu śāstras such as *Manusmṛti* need to be abandoned and replaced by the texts which advocate liberty, equality, and fraternity. Disappointed by the passivity and antipathy of the religious Hindu leaders in taking radical

34. Barlingay (1998: 26).

35. The principal architect of the Indian Constitution; the author of many works such as: *Castes in India: Their Mechanism, Genesis and Development*; *Annihilation of Caste*; *Who Were the Shudras*; *Philosophy of Hinduism*; *Riddles in Hinduism*; and *What Congress and Gandhi Have Done to the Untouchables*. His books and articles are included in different volumes of *Dr. Babasaheb Ambedkar: Writings and Speeches*, published by Education Department of the Government of Maharashtra, Mumbai.

36. In his post-graduate studies at Columbia University, Ambedkar had economics as his major subject and philosophy as his minor. He had John Dewey, the American pragmatist philosopher as one of his teachers, whose influence is visible in his writings.

steps towards annihilation of untouchability and caste, he decided to convert to another religion. He found Buddhism to be the most progressive religion. But as a rational and scientific thinker, he was unhappy with certain aspects of traditional Buddhism, such as its pessimism and other-worldly beliefs. On the basis of his rigorous and comprehensive study of Buddhism, he gave his rational reinterpretation of Buddhism in *The Buddha and His Dhamma*. In what follows we will consider those features of his reinterpretation of Buddhism, which mark the secularization of Buddhism, or what is relevant for our purpose, the approximation of Buddhism to Lokāyata.

B. R. Ambedkar attached central importance to the Buddha's doctrine of no-soul (*anattā*). But the Buddha is also said to have accepted the karma doctrine and rebirth, which presuppose continuous existence of the soul-like principle. Dr Ambedkar discerns this to be inconsistent, and asks:

> If there is no soul, how can there be karma? If there is no soul, how can there be rebirth? These are baffling questions. In what sense did the Buddha use the words karma and rebirth? Did he use them in a different sense than the sense in which they were used by the Brahmins of his day? If so, in what sense?[37]

In order to remove this inconsistency, Ambedkar rejects the karma-doctrine and rebirth in their traditional form and re-interprets them in such a way that they do not imply 'life after death' (in its traditional sense) or other worlds.

He explains the relation between consciousness and body, that is, nāma and rūpa as the relation between electrical field and magnetic field such that one cannot exist without the other in a living being. He argues:

> To give an analogy from science, there is an electric field and wherever there is an electric field, it is always accompanied by a magnetic field. No one knows how the magnetic field is created or how it arises. But it always exists along with the electric field. Why should not the same relationship be said to exist between body and consciousness? The magnetic field

37. Ambedkar (1974: xlii).

> in relation to the electric field is called an induced field. Why cannot consciousness be called an induced field in relation to *Rūpa-Kāya*[?][38]

In response to the problem of rebirth, Ambedkar distinguished between two questions: 'Rebirth of what?' and 'rebirth of whom?' As the answer to the second question, he claimed that rebirth is nothing but the production of consciousness from the same gross elements—however, it is not to be accepted in the sense of rebirth of the same person (or 'soul' or 'self').[39] As the answer to the first question he gave a materialistic interpretation of rebirth. The four elements namely earth, water, fire, and air constitute human body. When the human body dies, the elements are not destroyed, but they join the mass of similar elements floating in space. When the four elements in the floating mass join together and constitute a new living body, a new birth takes place. The elements in the new body are not necessarily from the same dead body, but they may be drawn from different dead bodies. This is the kind of rebirth according to Ambedkar, which the Buddha accepted.[40]

Ambedkar gave a different interpretation of the doctrine of karma as well. According to the traditional doctrine, every action one performs does produce a result which he or she has to experience. Conversely, every experience of pleasure or pain must be rooted in past action of the same person. Thus, it is supposed that there is a pre-established moral order in the universe. As against this, Ambedkar considers universal moral order not as a fact (as it is supposed to be by the upholders of karma-doctrine) but as a value. It is not a natural or a pre-established moral order, but it is something that man creates and contributes to or upsets.[41]

38. Ambedkar (1974: 185), diacritical marks added.

39. 'He (the Buddha) believed in the regeneration of matter and not in the rebirth of the soul' Ambedkar (1974: 238). 'Does the same dead person take a new birth? Did the Buddha believe in this thesis? The answer is, "Most improbable"' (Ambedkar (1974: 238).

40. Ambedkar (1974: 236).

41. 'But according to the Buddha the moral order rests on man and on nobody else.'

> 'The theory of the law of *Kamma* does not necessarily involve the conception that the effect of the *Kamma* recoils on the doer of it and there is nothing more to be thought about it. This is an error. Sometimes the action of one affects another instead of the doer. All the same it is the working of the law of *Kamma* because it either upholds or upsets the moral order' (Ambedkar 1974: 1972).

This had an implication to the ideal of Buddhist way of life, namely *nibbāna*—emancipation. Nibbāna, according to Ambedkar, is not to be understood as a transcendent, eternal state but a way of life to be lived, which involves control over passions and cassation of craving.[42]

Ambedkar's interpretation of Buddhism brings it very close to materialism. In his reconstruction of Buddhism, Ambedkar describes the phenomenon of birth and death almost in the way the materialist Ajita-Keśakambalī would describe it. But Ajita in the Buddhist literature was described as 'annihilationist' (*ucchedavādin*) not just because he did not believe in rebirth, but mainly because from his materialist ontology he derived a-moralist conclusion. The Buddha of Ambedkar, although he accepts materialist ontology, escapes the charge of being annihilationist mainly because of his strong adherence to morality.

***

We have seen how different systems of Indian philosophy have been reinterpreted and reconstructed by some eminent scholars and thinkers of the last century in such a way that some of these systems, which were traditionally regarded as opponents of Cārvāka, become more compatible with the common-sense-empiricist school of Cārvākas. One point needs to be noted here. Most of these scholars and thinkers who are reconstructing Indian philosophical systems are making historical claims. They uphold that these systems must have been originally materialistic or pro-materialistic, but due to external influences they have lost their pro-materialistic nature. The external influence for some is that of idealism, for some that of Pūrvamīmāmsā or Brahmanism. To what extent these claims as historical claims are tenable is a different debatable issue. But apart from making a historical claim, these scholars and thinkers are also

42. Ambedkar devotes one section (III.III.3) of *The Buddha and His Dhamma* to the concept of nibbāṇa. In this section he acknowledges three ideas underlying the Buddha's conception of nibbāṇa: (*a*) Happiness of a sentient being as against 'salvation of the soul'; (*b*) Happiness of a sentient being in '*saṁsāra*', that is, when he is alive; and (*c*) Nibbāṇa as the exercise of control over the flames of passion. See Ambedkar (1974: 164).

making, implicitly or explicitly, another type of claim, namely the intelligibility-claim. Chattopadhyaya claims that Nyāya-Vaiśeṣika and Sāṅkhya will be more intelligible and consistent if they are understood as materialistic. Barlingay suggests that 'puruṣa' of Sāṅkhya and 'jīva' of Jainism are intelligible only if they refer to an embodied sentient being, otherwise they will be mere abstractions. His reconstruction of Advaita–Vedānta suggests that the Brahman of Advaita will be intelligible if it is taken to be the first order reality which is very much material and spatio-temporal having consciousness as its essential character; the notion of Brahman according to him is not intelligible as abstract, pure, disembodied consciousness. Similarly, Ambedkar's reconstruction of the Buddha's *dhamma* implies that the latter will be intelligible only if the logical consequences of the doctrines of impermanence and no-soul are pursued by abandoning traditional karma-rebirth framework and by understanding nibbāna as a secular human ideal.

All these claims together carry the message that if we want to study Indian philosophy today as a relevant and meaningful subject, then we should highlight its secular and rational aspects, rather than its other-worldly and religious aspects. Our inquiry in Indian philosophy should not be based on scriptural authority, but it should be based on experience and reason. The importance of Indian philosophy should not be highlighted any more by guaranteeing eternal disembodied liberation as the fruit of the philosophical inquiry, but the relevance of Indian philosophy for a happy and meaningful life in this world itself should be sought for and emphasized. Studies in Indian philosophy should become more relevant to common sense and science and should establish a critical dialogue with them. In this sense a Lokāyatic turn in Indian philosophy is very much necessary.

Glossaries

Sanskrit–English

[The Romanized Sanskrit (or Pali) words are ordered according to English alphabetical order irrespective of diacritical marks. The meanings given here are those in which the Sanskrit/Pali words are used in the text. The possibility of the words having other additional meanings is not excluded.]

adharma	(1) demerit (Vaiśeṣika) (2) non-pursuit of *dharma* as a human goal, immorality
adhārmika	(1) irreligious (2) immoral
adṛṣṭa	(1) a kind of *anumāna* which is non-verifiable (2) unseen effect of an action: merit or demerit (Vaiśeṣika)
ajīva	non-soul, (Jainism)
ākāśa	(1) space (2) ether (a substance which has sound as its quality)
anattā	non-soul, the doctrine of *anattā*: the view that there is no soul (Buddhism)
anumāna	inference
anupādiśeṣa-nirvāṇa	liberation without residual of aggregates (Buddhism)

anvaya-vyatireki anumāna	positive–negative inference, inference based on both agreement and difference
ānvīkṣikī	name of the discipline of which reasoning is the core, philosophy (as a reason-oriented inquiry)
apūrva	unseen power supposed to be generated by a sacrifice (Pūrvamīmāṁsā)
arhat-hood	ideal state of human being according to Theravāda Buddhism
artha	(1) wealth as a value of life (2) purpose, goal
arthāpatti	explanatory implication, reasoning based on non-explicability of something without another thing
asura	(1) demon (2) a non-āryan clan
ātman	(1) soul, self (2) oneself
ātmavāda	the view that self/soul exists independently of body
avyabhicāri	non-deviating, (cognition) not deviating (from the object)
bārhaspatya	one belonging to or established by Bṛhaspati
Bārhaspatya-darśana	the school of philosophy founded by Bṛhaspati
Bṛhaspati	the (mythological or historical) founder of the Lokāyata school
Cārvāka	(1) a heterodox school of Indian philosophy which questions the dogmas such as other worlds, life after death, soul, and God (2) a thinker belonging to the Cārvāka school (3) name of a character in the *Mahābhārata*
Cārvāka-dhūrta	a sub-school of Cārvāka described by Jayantabhaṭṭa as that of knave Cārvākas
darśana	school of Indian philosophy
dehātmavāda	the doctrine that body (or body qualified by consciousness) itself is the soul
dhamma	moral–religious teaching of the Buddha
dharma	(1) merit (2) the ritualistic practices such as sacrifice prescribed by the Vedas (3) the rules of conduct prescribed by Vedas and Smṛtis (4) moral obligation or duty
dharmaśāstra	(1) a religious law-book of Hindus such as the *Manusmṛti* (2) the science of right conduct
dhūrta	knave (an alleged category of Cārvākas)
dṛṣṭa	a kind of inference, the object of which has been experienced before (empirical inference)

hetu	*probans*, mark, reason, reason-property
iṣṭavighātakṛt	the (fallacious) reason which destroys (contradicts) the intended target-property
jīva	soul (Jainism)
jñāna	cognition
kaivalya	liberation (according to Sāṅkhya, Yoga, and Jainism)
kāma	(1) fulfilment of desires (mainly sensuous and aesthetic desires) as a value of life (2) desire
karmayoga	performing actions without attachment (or without desire for fruit) as a way to liberation
kāya	body
kevalānvayi anumāna	purely positive inference, inference based only on agreement, not on difference
kevalavyatireki-anumāna	purely negative inference, inference based only on difference, not on agreement
loka	(1) world (2) this world (3) perception
lokaprasiddha-anumāna	inference acceptable within the framework of this-worldly way of life; commonsensical inference
lokasaṁvṛti-satya	conventional truth
lokavyavahāra	worldly practices
Lokāyata	a school of Indian philosophy which accepts only this world.
lokāyatika	(1) a follower of Lokāyata (2) belonging to Lokāyata
manas	internal sense organ (Nyāya)
mokṣa	liberation as a value of life
nāma	mind (Buddhism)
naiyāyika	follower of the Nyāya school
nāstika	a non-believer, non-believer in the authenticity of the Vedas
naya	a partial stand-point (Jainism)
nayābhāsa	a fallacy of judgement, a fallacious stand-point (Jainism)
nibbāṇa (Pali)	liberation, cessation of cravings and sufferings (Buddhism)
nirvāṇa	liberation, cessation of cravings and sufferings (Buddhism)
Nyāya	a realist orthodox school of Indian philosophy primarily devoted to epistemology, logic, and the theory of debate
paan	(a word current in Indian languages) betel leaves combined with beetle nuts and spices; *tāmbūla* (Sanskrit)

pariśeṣānumāna	inferring the residual by excluding all other alternatives
prakṛti	primordial nature, nature, matter (Sāṅkhya)
pramāṇa	(1) means to knowledge (2) authoritative means to knowledge, authority
prameya	knowable, object of knowledge, ontological category
prameyaśāstra	the science concerning objects of knowledge
prasaṅga	*reductio ad absurdum*
pratyakṣa	perception
pratyakṣa-pramāṇa	perception as an authoritative means to knowledge
pudgala	person, person-principle
pudgalavāda	the view of some Buddhists that there is a person principle in a person over and above the five aggregates
puruṣa	soul (Sāṅkhya)
puruṣārtha	human value, goal of life
pūrvavat	a kind of inference (Nyāya, Sāṅkhya)
rūpa	matter (Buddhism)
sādhya	probandum, target-property, the object of inference
sāmānya	universal, common
sāmānyato-dṛṣṭa	a kind of inference, the object of which has been experienced in a general form
śāstra	science, a systematic body of knowledge
śeṣavat	a kind of inference (Nyāya and Sāṅkhya)
śiṁśapā	species of a tree ('Dalbergia Sissoo'—Monier Williams (1976))
smṛti	(1) memory, recollection (2) *Dharmaśāstra* text
śrāddha	the ritual performed for satisfying the departed ancestors
śruti	Vedas
suśikṣita	learned (Jayantabhaṭṭa's nomenclature of a school of Cārvākas)
suśikṣitatara	more learned (Jayantabhaṭṭa's nomenclature of a school of Cārvākas)
sūtra	aphorism
sūtra-bhāṣya tradition	an intellectual tradition which starts with an aphorismic work and develops through its commentaries and sub-commentaries

svabhāvavāda	essentialism, naturalism, the view that things are how they are because of their own nature
svātantrya	self-dependence
tarka	(1) reasoning (2) hypothetical reasoning, *reductio ad absurdum* type of reasoning (3) inductive generalization (Jainism)
tattva	essentially existing thing, important thing, ultimate truth, principle
utpādya-pratīti	(the inference) the object of which is yet to be experienced (the inference), the object of which is non-empirical; non-empirical (inference)
utpanna-pratīti	(the inference,) the object of which is experienced before, empirical (inference)
vaitaṇḍika	one who debates with an opponent without committing to any position as one's own
vaitaṇḍika-kathā	a kind of debate conducted by a *vaitaṇḍika*
vārtā	the body of knowledge dealing with agriculture, cattle-keeping and commerce, in a broader sense, economics
varṇa	a class (out of four) determined by one's birth and determining one's social role and status in the traditional Hindu society
Vedānta	an orthodox school of Indian philosophy, which claims to be based on Upaniṣads; the school is further divided into sub-schools such as absolute non-dualism (*Kevlādvaita*), qualified non-dualism (*Viśiṣṭādvaita*) and dualism (*Dvaita*)
viśeṣa	particular, exclusive, uncommon
vitaṇḍā	a type of debate in which one of the parties refutes the position of the other party without committing to any position as one's own
vitaṇḍā-śāstra	a discipline which conducts debates of *vitaṇḍā* type
vitaṇḍa-sattha (Pali)	*viataṇḍā-śāstra* (Sanskrit): a discipline which conducts debates of *vitaṇḍā* type
vyabhicāra-adarśana	non-observation of *hetu*'s existence without *sādhya*
Vyākaraṇa	the Grammar school of Indian Philosophy
vyatireki anumāna	argument based on difference, negative inference

vyavasāyāt-maka	determinate
Yoga	(1) an orthodox school of Indian philosophy founded by Patañjali (2) the school of philosophy mentioned by Kauṭilya, claimed by some scholars to be identical with early Nyāya-Vaiśeṣika
yuktipramāṇa	causal reasoning as a means to knowledge (*Carakasaṁhitā*)

English–Sanskrit

[The English analogues used for Sanskrit technical terms are arranged in alphabetical order. The contexts in which the analogues are used are sometimes mentioned in brackets.]

absolutism (Jainism)	*ekāntavāda*
accidentalism	*yadṛcchāvāda*
annihilationist	*ucchedavādin*
body-as-the-self doctrine	*dehātmavāda*
causal efficacy	*arthakriyā*
commonsensical inference	*lokaprasiddha-anumāna*
demerit (Vaiśeṣika)	*adharma*
efficient cause	*nimitta-kāraṇa*
economics (Kautilya's *Arthaśāstra*)	*vārtā*
embodied liberation	*jīvanmukti, sadehamukti*
empirical (inference)	*dṛṣṭa (anumāna), utpannapratīti (anumāna)*
essence-less	*niḥsvabhāva, śūnya*
essentialism	*svabhāvavāda* (Buddhism)
eternalism	*śāśvatavāda*
ether	*ākāśa* (a *dravya* accepted by Vaiśeṣikas)
explanatory implication	*arthāpatti*
extrinsic (authenticity/truth)	*parataḥ prāmāṇya*
gross element	*mahābhūta*
heaven	*svarga*
hell	*naraka*
human goal	*puruṣārtha*
inapplicable definition	*asambhava* as *lakṣaṇa-doṣa*
inference	*anumāna*

inherence	*samavāya*
inherent cause	*samavāyi-kāraṇa* (Vaiśeṣika)
intrinsic (authenticity/truth)	*svataḥ prāmāṇya*
knave Cārvāka	Cārvāka-dhūrta
learned Cārvāka	Suśikṣita-Cārvāka
liberation (as a human goal)	*mokṣa*(*-puruṣārtha*)
means to knowledge	*pramāṇa*
mental perception	*mānasa–pratyakṣa*
more learned (Cārvāka)	Suśikṣitatara(-Cārvāka)
naturalism	*svabhāvavāda* (Lokāyata)
negative debate	*vitaṇḍā*
nihilism (Budhism)	*ucchedavāda*
non-absolutism (Jainism)	*anekāntavāda*
non-empirical (a kind of inference)	*adṛṣṭa* (*-anumāna*); *utpādypratīti* (*-anumāna*)
non-inherent cause	*asamavāyi-kāraṇa*
non-inherentism (causation)	*asatkāryavāda*
non-judgmental perception	*nirvikalpaka–pratyakṣa*
no-soul doctrine	*anattā* (Pali), *anātmavāda* (Sanskrit), (Buddhism)
non-substance-pervading quality	*avyāpyavṛtti-guṇa*
perception (as a means to knowledge)	*pratyakṣa*(*-pramāṇa*)
philosophy (Kautilya's *Arthaśāstra*)	Ānvīkṣikī
pleasure (as a human goal)	*kāma*(*-puruṣārtha*)
polity (Kautilya's *Arthaśāstra*)	*daṇḍanīti*
positive concomitance	*anvaya, anvayavyāpti*
primordial matter	*prakṛti* (Sāṅkhya)
primordial nature	*prakṛti* (Sāṅkhya)
purely negative inference	*kevalavyatireki-anumāna*
purely positive inference	*kevalānvayi-anumāna*
quality (Vaiśeṣika)	*guṇa*
reason-property	*hetu, hetu-dharma*
recognition	*pratyabhijñā*
soul	*ātman* (Nyāya-Vaiśeṣika, Buddhism), *puruṣa* (Sāṅkhya), *jīva* (Jainism)
system (Indian philosophy)	*darśana*

target-property	*sādhya, sādhya-dharma*
too narrow a definition	*avyāpti*
too wide a definition	*ativyāpti*
undeterminable (Śrīharṣa)	*anirvacanīya*
unique particular	*svalakṣaṇa*
universal (Nyāyavaiśeṣika)	*jāti, sāmānya*
universal concomitance	*vyāpti, avinābhāva*
verbal testimony	*āgama, śabda-pramāṇa*
void-ness	*śūnyatā*
wealth (as a human goal)	*artha(-puruṣāthra)*

Bibliography with Abbreviations

Sanskrit and Pali Works with Abbreviations

AK: *Arthaśastra of Kauṭilya*, edited by Gaṇapatishastri, translated by V. P. Unni. Delhi: New Bharatiya Book Corporation, 2006.

AVD: *Anyayogavyavacchedadvātriṁśikā*, as included in *Syādvādamañjarī of Malliṣeṇa*, edited by A. B. Dhruva. Poona: Bhandarkar Oriental Research Institute, 1933.

BG: *Śrīmad-bhagavadgītā* (The Vedānta Text), edited by J. L. Bansal. Jaipur: JPH, 2013.

BSSB: *Brahmasūtraśāṅkarabhāṣyam*. Madras: Shri Kamakotikoshasthanam, 1954.

BSV: *Bṛhatsaṁhitā-vṛtti by Bhaṭṭotpala, the Commentary on Bṛhatsaṁhitā by Varāhamihira*, edited by A. Tripathi. Varanasi: Sampurnananda Sanskrit Vishvavidyalaya, 1968.

CS: *Carakasaṁhitā of Agniveśa*, Kashi Sanskrit Series 194, part I. Varanasi: Chauchambha Sanskrit Sansthan, 1994 (Fourth Edition).

CU: *Chāndogya Upaniṣad* passage (Translation), as included in *Cārvāka/Lokāyata*, edited by Debiprasad Chattopadhyaya in collaboration with Mrinal Kanti Gangopadhyay. New Delhi: ICPR Publications, 1990.

GK: *Gauḍapāda-kārikā*, edited by R.D. Karmarkar. Poona: Bhandarkar Oriental Research Institute, 1953.

KA: *Kārikāvali of Viśvanātha Nyāyapañcānana Bhaṭṭācārya with the Commentaries Siddhāntamuktāvali, Dinakarī, Rāmarudrī (Upamāna and Śabda section)*, edited by John Vattanky. Delhi: Sri Satguru Publication, 1997.

KKK (1970): *Khaṇḍanakhaṇḍakhādyam*. Varanasi: Choukhamba Sanskrit Series, 1970.

KKK (1979): *Khaṇḍanakhaṇḍakhādyam (Śrīharṣapraṇītam)*. Varanasi: Ṣaṭdarśana Prakāśana Pratiṣṭhānam, 1979.

KS: *Kāmasūtra of Vātsyāyana*, edited and translated by Radhavallabha Tripathi. Delhi: Pratibha Prakashan, 2005.

MS: *Manusmṛti, with Manvarthamuktāvali, the Commentary by Kullūkabhaṭṭa*, Bombay: Nirnay Sagar Press, 1915.

MSN: *Madhyamakaśāstra of Nāgārjuna*, edited by P. L. Vaidya. Darbhanga: Mithila Institute, 1960.

NB: *Nyāyabindu of Dharmakīrti* as in *NBT*.

NBh: *Nyāyabhāṣya of Vātsyāyana* as in *ND*.

NBT: *Nāyabinduṭīkā by Ācāryadharmottara*, edited by Shrinivasashastri. Merath: Sahitya Bhandar, 1975.

NBu: *Nyāyabhūṣaṇam of Bhāsarvajña*. Varanasi: Saddarshana Prakashan Pratishthan, 1968.

ND: *Nyāyadarśanaṁ with Vātsyāyana's Bhāṣya, Uddyotakara's Vārttika, Vācaspatimiśra's Tātparyaṭīkā and Viśvanātha's Vṛtti*, Vol. I. Calcutta: Metropolitan Printing and Publishing House Ltd, 1936.

NK: *Nyāyakusumāñjali of Udayanācārya with the Sanskrit Commentary of Śrī Haridāsa Bhaṭṭācārya*. Varanasi: Chowkhamba Vidya Bhawan, 1962.

NKC: *Nyāyakumudacandra of Prabhācandrasūri*, edited by Mahendrakumar Nyayashastri. Mumbai: Pandit Nathu Ram Premi, Manik Chandra Digambar Jain Series, 1938.

NM: *Nyāyamañjarī of Jayantabhaṭṭa*. Varanasi: Chaukhamba Sanskrit Series, 1971 (Second Edition).

NMGB: *Nyāyamañjarīgranthibhaṅga of Cakradhara*, edited by Nagin J. Shah. Ahmedabad: L.D. Institute of Indology, 1972.

NS: *Nyāyasūtra of Gautama*, as included in *ND*.

NSMn: *Nyāyasiddhāntamañjari by Jānakīnāthabhaṭṭācārya*, edited and translated by Baliram Shukla. Delhi: Eastern Book Linkers, 1995.

NVTT: *Nyāyavārtikatātparyaṭīkā of Vācaspatimiśra* as in *ND*.

PCU: *Prabodhacandrodaya by Kṛṣṇamiśra*, edited and translated by S.K. Nambiar. Delhi: Motilal Banarsidass, 1926.

PV: *Pramāṇavārtikam of Ācārya-Dharmakīrti*, edited by Ram Chandra Pandeya. New Delhi: Motilal Banarsidass, 1989.

SDS: *Sarvadarśanasaṅgraha of Mādhavācārya*, edited by Vasudevshastri Abhyankar. Poona: BORI, 1978 (Reprint).

SDSam: *Ṣaḍdarśanasamuccaya of Haribhadrasūri*, edited by Mahendra Kumar Jain. New Delhi: Bharatiya Jnanpith Publication, 1989.

SK: *Sāṁkhyakārikā of Īśvarakṛṣṇa*, as in *STK*.

SK(G): *Sāṅkhyakārikā of Īśvarakṛṣṇa with Gauḍapādabhāṣya and Other Two Commentaries*. Varanasi: Chaukhamba Surabharati Prakashan, 2009.

SMV: *Sumaṅgalavilāsinī*, part I, edited by M. Tiwari. Nalanda: Nava Nalanda Mahavihara, 1974.

SSS: *Sarvasiddhāntasaṅgraha of Śaṅkarācātya*, edited and translated by M. Rangacharya. Delhi: Eastern Book Linkers, 2006.

STK: *Sāṁkhyatattvakaumudī of Śrī Vācaspatimiśra*, edited and translated by G. S. Musalgaonkar. Varanasi: Chaukhambha Sanskrit Sansthan, 1979.

SV: *Ślokavārtikam*, edited by Dvārikādāsa Śāstrī. Varanasi: Tara Publications, 1978.

TB: *Tarkabhāṣā (Śrīkeśavamiśra-praṇītā)*. Merath: Sahitya Bhandar, 1979.

TS: *Tattvasaṅgraha of Śāntarakṣita, with Commentary of Kamalaśīla*. Baroda: Oriental Institute, 1984.

TSa: *Tarkasaṁgraha of Annambhaṭṭa*, edited and translated by Athalye and Bodas. Pune: Bhandarkar Oriental Research Institute, 1963.

TSP: *Tattvasaṅgrahapañjikā of Kamalaśīla* as in *TS*.

TUS: *Tattvopaplavasiṁha of Shri Jayarāśibhaṭṭa*, edited by Sanghavi Sukhlalji and Rasiklal Parikh. Varanasi: Bauddha Bharati, 1987.

TV: *Tantravārtika* as included in *Mīmāṁsādarśana of Jaimini* (1.2 to 2.1), edited by Vasudevshastri Abhyankar and Ganeshshastri Joshi. Pune: Anandashram, 1970.

VP: *Vākyapadīya by Bhartṛhari (Brahmakāṇḍa)*. Varanasi: Chaukhambha Sanskrit Sansthan, 1975 (Third Edition).

VS: *Vaiśeṣikasūtra of Kaṇāda*, edited by Muni Jambuvijayaji. Baroda: Gaekwad's Oriental Series No. 137, 1961.

VV: *Vigrahavyāvartanī*, included as Appendix 5 in *MSN*.

Secondary and Other Works

Ambedkar, B. R. *The Buddha and His Dhamma*. Bombay: Siddhartha Prakashan, 1974 (Second Edition).

Antarkar, S. S., Pradeep P. Gokhale, and Meenal Katarnikar. *Recollection, Recognition and Reasoning: A Study in the Jaina Theory of Parokṣa Pramāṇa*. Delhi: Sri Sadguru Publications, 2011.

Athavale, Sadashiv. *Cārvāka, Itihāsa Āṇi Tattvajñāna* (Marathi). Wai: Prājña Ṛāthshāla Mandal, 1997 (First Edition 1958).

Ayer, A. J., ed. *Logical Positivism*. New York: The Free Press, 1959.

Barker, Stephen F. *The Elements of Logic*. New York: McGraw-Hill Book Company, 1974 (Second Edition).

Barlingay, S. S. *A Modern Introduction to Indian Logic*. New Delhi: National Publishing House, 1976 (Second Edition).

———. *Beliefs, Reasons and Reflections*. Pune: IPQ Publication, 1983.

———. *Re-understanding Indian Philosophy: Some Glimpses*. New Delhi: D. K. Printworld, 1998.

Bentham, Jeremy. *An Introduction to the Principles of Morals and Legislation*. Oxford: Clarendon Press, (1789), 1907.

Bhattacharya, Ramkrishna. *Studies on the Cārvāka/Lokāyata*. Delhi: Anthem Press India, 2012.

Bhelke, S. E. and Pradeep P. Gokhale, eds. *Studies in Indian Moral Philosophy: Problems, Concepts and Perspectives*. Pune: IPQ Publication, 2002.

Block, Ned. 'Functionalism (2)'. In *A Companion to the Philosophy of Mind*, edited by Guttenplan, 323–32. Oxford: Blackwell, 1995.

Byrne, Alex. 'Behaviorism'. In *A Companion to the Philosophy of Mind*, edited by Guttenplan, 132–40. Oxford: Blackwell, 1995.

Chatterjee, S. C. *Nyāya Theory of Knowledge*. Delhi: Bharatiya Kala Prakashan, 2008.

Chattopadhyaya, Debiprasad. *Indian Philosophy: A Popular Introduction*. New Delhi: People's Publishing House, 1964.

———. *What Is Living and What Is Dead in Indian Philosophy*. New Delhi: People's Publishing House, 1976.

———. *Lokayata: A Study in Ancient Materialism*. New Delhi: People's Publishing House, 1978 (Fourth Edition).

———. *In Defence of Materialism in Ancient India*. New Delhi: People's Publishing House, 1989.

Chattopadhyaya, Debiprasad (in collaboration with Mrinal Kanti Gangopadhyay), ed. *Cārvāka/Lokāyata*. New Delhi: ICPR Publications, 1990.

Chattopadhyay, Madhumita. *Walking Along the Paths of Buddhist Epistemology*. New Delhi: D. K. Printworld (P) Ltd., 2007.

Cohen, Morris R and Ernest Nagel. *An Introduction to Logic and Scientific Method*. New Delhi: Allied Publishers Ltd. (Third Indian Reprint), 1976.

Crane, Tim. 'Physicalism (2): Against Physicalism'. In *A Companion to the Philosophy of Mind*, edited by Guttenplan, 479–84. Oxford: Blackwell, 1995.

De Pierris, Graciela and Michael Friedman. 'Kant and Hume on Causality'. In *Stanford Encyclopedia of Philosophy*, edited by Edward N. Zalta. Stanford: Stanford University, 2008.

Franco, Eli. *Perception, Knowledge and Disbelief (A Study of Jayarāśi's Scepticism)*. Delhi: Motilal Banarsidass, 1987.

Ganeri, Jonardon, ed. *Indian Logic: A Reader*. London: Curzon Press, 2001.

Gokhale, Pradeep P. *Inference and Fallacies Discussed in Ancient Indian Logic (with Special Reference to Nyāya and Buddhism)*. Delhi: Sri Satguru Publications, Indian Books Centre, 1992.

Gokhale, Pradeep P. 'Cārvāka Theory of *Pramānas*: A Re-statement'. *Philosophy East and West* 43, no. 4 (1993): 675–82.

———. 'Nāgārjuna's Scepticism vis-à-vis Those of Jayarāśi and Śriharṣa'. *The Philosophical Quarterly* 5, nos 1–2 (1999): 1–12.

———. 'The Value Perspectives of Cārvākas'. In *Studies in Indian Moral Philosophy, Problems, Concepts and Perspectives*, edited by S. E. Bhelke and Pradeep P. Gokhale, 185–205. Pune: IPQ Publication, 2002.

———. 'Three Necessities in Dharmakīrti's Theory of Inference'. In *Purisuttamanussati–Pavacana–Sangaho (P. V. Bapat Memorial Lectures)*, edited by Kalpakam Sankarnarayan, 67–84. Mumbai: Somaiyya Publications, 2006.

———. 'Nāgārjuna's Ways of Argumentation: Some Logical Issues'. In *Buddhist Culture in Asia: Unity in Diversity*, Vol. II, edited by Supriya Rai, 189–200. Mumbai: Somaiya Publications Private Limited, 2010.

———. 'Identifying Philosophy in Indian Tradition'. In *Dimensions of Philosophy*, edited by R. C. Sinha, Jatashankar and A. D. Sharma, 151–60. New Delhi: New Bharatiya Book Corporation, 2012.

Guttenplan, Samuel, ed. *A Companion to the Philosophy of Mind*. Oxford: Blackwell, 1995.

Hamblin, C. L. *Fallacies*. London: Methuen and Co. Ltd., 1970.

Hempel, Carl. 'The Empiricist Criterion of Meaning'. In *Logical Positivism*, edited by A. J. Ayer, 108–29. New York: The Free Press, 1959.

Hiriyanna, M. *Outlines of Indian Philosophy*. Bombay: George Allen & Unwin Ltd., 1973.

Horgan, Terence E. 'Physicalism (1)'. In *A Companion to the Philosophy of Mind*, edited by Samuel Guttenplan, 471–9. Oxford: Blackwell, 1995.

Hume, David. *An Enquiry Concerning Human Understanding*. New York: Oxford University Press, 2007.

Jain, L. C. 'Set Theory in the Jaina School of Mathematics'. *Indian Journal of History of Science* 8, nos 1–2 (1973): 1–24.

Jha, Acharya Ananda. *Cārvāka Darśana* (Hindi). Lucknow: Hindi Samiti, 1969.

Jha, Ganganath, trans. *The Tattvasaṅgraha of Śāntarakṣita, with the Commentary of Kamalaśīla*, Vols I and II. Delhi: Motilal Banarsidas, 1986 (Reprint).

———, trans. *Tantravārtika by Kumārilabhaṭṭa*, Vol. I. Delhi: Pilgrims Book Private Ltd. 1998 (Reprint).

Kar, Bijayananda. *The Philosophy of Lokāyata: A Review and Reconstruction*. Delhi: Motilal Banarsidass, 2013.

Kirk G. S. and J. E. Raven. *The Pre-Socratic Philosophers*. London: Cambridge University Press, 1957 (1977 Reprint).

Malcolm, Norman. 'Two Types of Knowledge'. In *Theory of Knowledge: Classical and Contemporary Readings*, edited by Louis P. Pojman. Belmont: Wadsworth Publishing Company, 1999.

Marx, Karl. 'Preface'. In *Preface and Introduction to a Contribution to the Critique of Political Economy*. Peking: Foreign Language Press, First Edition, 1976 (available at www.marx2mao.com/M&E/PI.html, last accessed June 2015).

Matilal, Bimal Krishna. *Perception: An Essay on Classical Indian Theories of Knowledge*. Oxford: Clarendon Press, 1986.

McLaughlin, Brian P. 'Epiphenomenalism'. In *A Companion to the Philosophy of Mind*, edited by Samuel Guttenplan, 277–87. Oxford: Blackwell, 1995.

Mittal, K. K. *Materialism in Indian Thought*. New Delhi: Munshilal Manoharlal, 1974.

Mohanta, D. K. 'The Concept of *Pramāṇa* and the Sceptical Arguments of Nāgārjuna'. *Indian Philosophical Quarterly* XXIV, no. 1 (1997): 53–72.

Monier-Williams, Sir Monier. *Sanskrit-English Dictionary*. New Delhi: Munshiram Manoharlal, 1976.

Monro, D. H. 'Bentham, Jeremy'. In *The Encyclopedia of Philosophy*, Vol. I, edited by Paul Edwards. New York: Macmillan, 1967.

Moon, Vasant, ed. *Dr. Babasaheb Ambedkar: Writings and Speeches*. Mumbai: Education Department, Government of Maharashtra, 1979–1995.

Moore, Andrew. 'Hedonism', *Stanford Encyclopedia of Philosophy*, edited by Edward N. Zalta. Stanford: Stanford University, 2004.

Moore, G. E. 'A Defence of Common Sense'. In G. E. Moore, *Philosophical Papers* (London: George Allen and Unwin Ltd., 1959).

Morris, William Edward. 'David Hume'. In *Stanford Encyclopedia of Philosophy*, edited by Edward N. Zalta. Stanford: Stanford University, 2013.

Olson, Eric T. 'Personal Identity'. In *Stanford Encyclopedia of Philosophy*, edited by Edward N. Zalta. Stanford: Stanford University, 2010.

Pathak, Sarvananda. *Cārvāka Darśana kī Śāstrīya Samīkṣā* (Hindi). Varanasi: Chaukhamba Vidyabhavan, 1965.

Popkin, Richard. 'Skepticism'. In *Encyclopedia of Philosophy*, Vol. 7, edited by Paul Edwards, 449–61. New York: MacMillan Company and Free Press, 1967.

Prasad, Rajendra. *Karma, Causation and Retributive Morality, Conceptual Essays in Ethics and Meta-ethics*. New Delhi: ICPR Publication, 1989.

———. *Varṇadharma, Niṣkāma-karma and Practical Morality: A Critical Essay on Applied Ethics*. New Delhi: D. K. Printworld, 1999.

———. *Dharmakīrti's Theory of Inference: Revaluation and Reconstruction*. New Delhi: Oxford University Press, 2002.

———. *A Conceptual Analytical Study of Indian Philosophy of Morals*. New Delhi: Concept Publishing Company, 2008.

Radhakrishnan, S., ed. *History of Philosophy, Eastern and Western*, Vol. I. London: George Allen and Unwin, 1952.

———. *Indian Philosophy*, Vol. I. New Delhi: Oxford University Press, 1996.

Randle, H. N. 'A Note on Indian Syllogism'. *Mind* 33, no. 132 (1924): 398–414, as reprinted in Jonardon Ganeri, ed., *Indian Logic: A Reader* (London: Curzon Press, 2001).

Rosenthal, David, 'Identity Theories'. In *A Companion to the Philosophy of Mind*, edited by Samuel Guttenplan, 348–55. Oxford: Blackwell, 1995.

Ryle, Gilbert. *The Concept of Mind*. London: Penguin Books, 2000.

Sardesai, S. G. *Bhāratīya Tattvajñāna, Vaicārika āṇi Sāmāgika Saṅgharṣa* (Marathi). Mumbai: Lokavanmaya Griha, 2006.

Searle, John. 'Searle, John'. In *A Companion to the Philosophy of Mind*, edited by Samuel Guttenplan, 544–9. Oxford: Blackwell, 1995.

Sharma, Chandradhar. *A Critical Survey of Indian Philosophy*. Delhi: Motilal Banarsidass, 1973.

Shastri, D. R. 'A Short History of Indian Materialism, Sensationalism and Hedonism'. In *Cārvāka/Lokāyata*, edited by Debiprasad Chattopadhyaya (in collaboration with Mrinal Kanti Gangopadhyay). New Delhi: ICPR Publications, 1990.

Shukla, S. K. 'Ecological Perspectives of Jainism'. In *Environmental Ethics: Indian Perspectives*, edited by Devendra Nath Tiwari and Ananda Mishra, 93–102. Varanasi: Banaras Hindu University, 2012.

Singh, Navjyoti. 'Jaina Theory of Actual Infinity and Transfinite Numbers'. *Journal of Asiatic Society* XXX, nos 1–4 (1988): 77–111.

Sinha, Jadunath. *Indian Philosophy*, Vol. I. Delhi: Motilal Banarsidass, 1999 (Reprint).

Snowdon, Paul. 'Peter Frederick Strawson'. In *The Stanford Encyclopedia of Philosophy*, edited by Edward N. Zalta. Stanford: Stanford University, 2009.

Stoljar, Daniel. 'Physicalism'. In *The Stanford Encyclopedia of Philosophy*, edited by Edwarn N. Zalta. Stanford: Stanford University, 2009.

Thagart, Paul. 'Cognitive Science'. In *The Stanford Encyclopedia of Philosophy*, edited by Edward N. Zalta. Stanford, Stanford University, 2012.

Vivekananda. 'Jñānayoga'. In *The Complete Works of Swami Vivekananda*, Vol. II. Advaita Ashrama, Kolkata: Mayavati Memorial Edition, 2011.

Warder, A. K. *Outline of Indian Philosophy*. Delhi: Motilal Banarsidass, 1971.

Wittgenstein, Ludwig. *Tractatus Logico-Philosophicus*, translated by D. F. Pears and B. F. McGuinness. London: Routledge and Kegan Paul Ltd., 1971 (Reprint).

Zaveri, J. S. *Theory of Atoms in the Jaina Philosophy: A Critical Study of the Jaina Theory of Paramāṇu-Pudgala in the Light of Modern Scientific Theory*. Ladnun: Agama & Sahitya Prakashan, Jaina Vishva Bharati, 1975.

Index

About the Author

Pradeep P. Gokhale is Dr B. R. Ambedkar Research Professor, Central University of Tibetan Studies, Sarnath, India. He is also former Professor, Department of Philosophy, Savitribai Phule Pune University, India. His previous publications include *Hetubindu of Dharmakīrti: A Point on Probans* (1997) and *Inference and Fallacies Discussed in Ancient Indian Logic with Special Reference to Nyāya and Buddhism* (1992).